RETURN TO POLAND

Denis Hills

THE BODLEY HEAD
LONDON

British Library Cataloguing
in Publication Data
Hills, Denis
Return to Poland.
1. Poland ——History——20th century
I. Title
943.8 DK4400
ISBN 0 370 31154 X

Printed in Great Britain for
The Bodley Head Ltd
32 Bedford Square, London WC1B 3EL
by The Alden Press Ltd,
Oxford
First published 1988

ACKNOWLEDGMENTS

I am grateful to Edward Lowbury for letting me use his unpublished poem "The Hejnal".

Permission to use the following extracts is gratefully acknowledged: extract from *A Warsaw Diary* by Kazimierz Brandys published by Chatto & Windus; extract from *Dora by Jean Michel published by Weidenfeld & Nicholson Ltd; extract from Native Realm* by Czeslaw Milosz published by Carcanet Press Ltd.

While every effort has been made to trace the correct owners of all copyright material reproduced in this book, the publishers regret any errors of omission that may have unwittingly occured and will be happy to make suitable acknowledgment in any future editions.

CONTENTS

For Roy and Christine Lewis

PREFACE

.

I spent my first two nights in Poland in a Gdynia police cell. I had not long come down from Oxford (1935) and after four months of rough travel – using country buses, local trains and walking – among the German-speaking minority peoples who lived in the border lands surrounding Hitler's Reich and Austria, I was returning through the Polish Corridor from Danzig to Berlin when I decided to break my journey for a few hours in Gdynia. Late that evening I was picked up by the Polish police as a "suspicious foreign vagrant" – it seemed they were on the look-out for straying seamen – and taken to a crowded basement gaol. It was pitch dark. Every now and then there were bumps when new arrivals were dragged down the stairs. In the morning a Danzig seaman rolled me a cigarette, the cell was emptied and I was left alone till the following night when fresh guests were pushed inside. Next day I was released and told I could stay in Poland for another week if I wished. I spent the time in Bydgoszcz before going on to Berlin. I didn't mind the experience and had no hard feelings. Experience, after all, was what I was looking for.

It was indeed this first glimpse of Poland that aroused my curiosity to find out more about the Poles. The Germans looked down on *Polacken*. *"Polnische Wirtschaft"* was the derisive German term for a broken-down economy. Poland was the underdog – a "lost cause". But this, to a young Oxford graduate, made her doubly attractive. There was also the bizarre and romantic side of Poland. Her history of gallant victories in defeat, of uprisings, of music and poetry: the horse-drawn cabs, the mazurka, the cavalry tradition, the strange-looking language with few vowels, the cobble-stoned villages and painted way-side shrines. Back in England I bought a Polish grammar and dictionary in the Charing Cross Road and after a further visit to Germany – now teeming with armed men – answered an advertisement in *The Times*. The Baltic Institute of Gdynia was looking for an English editor of its cultural publications. I was accepted and sailed from Hay's Wharf just before Christmas 1936 in the Polish cargo boat *Lech*.

By this time I had grown out of my calf-love for the Germans. The Nazis had destroyed it. The appalling vulgarity of Hitler, the bullying and arrogance of the Nazis, their insulting rhetoric, the crudity of their propaganda machine and their sinister and growing hold over the crowd and the common people had turned me against them. I was convinced, through my many contacts with Germans, that the next war would start with a German *revanche* attack on Poland. I wanted to be on the spot.

At Gdynia a cab-driver drove me through snow-covered streets and an icy wind to my new employers. I was given an office, warned never to open the window, and Dr Borowik the director handed me a stack of manuscripts to prepare for the next issue of the Institute's quarterly magazine *Baltic and Scandinavian Countries*.

The Institute was subsidised by the Polish government. Its editorial policy was to assert Poland's voice as a key member of the Baltic and Scandinavian bloc and to promote economic, political and cultural ties with them. It stressed Poland's rights to Upper Silesia and the Polish Corridor including Danzig Free City, and hammered away at Poland's "historical claims" in Old Prussia (overrun centuries ago by the Teutonic Knights) and in other territories stretching as far as the Elbe and into Czechoslovakia. Our contributors were mainly Polish academics and professors from Sweden, Finland, Estonia, Latvia and Lithuania. The London School of Slavonic Studies contributed to the magazine. Most manuscripts were written in poor English and I had to prepare and sub-edit them. Some had been excellently translated by two brilliant linguists – Professor Massie, a wounded war veteran who was honorary consul in Poznan, and Truszkowski, who lived among a jumble of papers in a dark flat in Warsaw.

The magazine was printed by a small Polish firm in a working class district of Danzig about an hour's journey by train and tram from Gdynia. Young Nazis sometimes waylaid us when we left work. By keeping together we generally avoided trouble, though more than once I returned home with blood on my shirt. Danzig had a large German population, the Nazis had the city firmly under control, and towards the end of my stay we had for security reasons to print in Bydgoszcz. Even here the German minority was causing trouble, and there were affrays in bars and villages.

The Poles were justifiably proud of the brand new port of Gdynia. It had been built during the twenties and thirties with the help of French capital on the site of a poor Kashubian fishing village. It was linked by rail to the Silesian heavy industry area and handled Polish coal exports, Swedish steel products, Polish shipping lines and emigration. Hundreds of Jews used to assemble on the quaysides for a passage to America in Polish liners, young men with gleaming side-curls and flashy new suits, bearded elders, women and children guarding baggage, an exodus that was sad and ominous as well as fortunate for it was to prove their passport to survival. As a new city Gdynia was uncouth and uncultured. It had attracted bankrupts and adventurers, widows, shipping businesses and a new class of Polish seaman (there was a navy school and a beautiful cadet sailing ship *Dar Pomorza*). There were few Jews, no theatre and no music. At the Anglo-Polish club a veteran Everest climber (Ruttledge) talked to us about Everest, and Robert Byron, who looked surprisingly sallow and flabby for an explorer, described his Near East journeys. I sometimes escorted my landlady, an attractive Polish woman from Lwow with a sharp temper, to the Maskot, the only decent night club. The hostesses at Maskot were crafty and professional and sent you home in the small hours with empty pockets. Merchant seamen roamed the port area – silent Chinese, lascars, ponderous Swedes, a few English. The bars they frequented were dangerous. Once, during a "trial of strength" which started as a joke and suddenly turned nasty, an English seaman and I were beaten on the head with bottles. I was held down and remember counting the blows – six! which meant a visit to the infirmary for head shaving and sticking plaster and a tactful lie to Dr Borowik.

I missed rugby and cricket, but could swim off the sand dunes or from the Hel peninsula. Summer tourists went to nearby Zoppot, which had a casino and a famous inn papered with worthless bank notes from the German inflation period of the early twenties. In winter the sea was frozen for hundreds of yards. A bitter wind blew from the north and east, and to keep warm I ran to and from the office – I was living a mile away at the top of a wooded hill (ul. Lesna). On the way to the industrial area the gutters were strewn with empty vodka bottles (*malpki*, small monkeys): a thump to loosen the cork, a quick swig, was what the worker needed to start the day with on a cold, dark wintry morning.

Towards the end of 1938 it was clear that Hitler's Reich had irrevocably stirred up the Germans living in the Corridor and in Danzig and was preparing for violent action. Polish friends warned me that if I wanted to see more of Poland I must go to Warsaw before it was too late. Pat Howarth arrived from London to take over my job, and I moved to Warsaw to teach at the Anglo-Polish school on Mokotowska.

Barking back at Hitler's propaganda machine (the Germans had opened a rival institute to ours in Königsberg), irritating them with Polish nationalist claims (Copernicus, though born in Thorn, was a Pole!), had been enjoyable and positive work. I do not know what happened to my colleagues Borowik, Sidow, Zakrzewski and Pani Meznicka. But Pat Howarth escaped from Gdynia in the last ship to Copenhagen.[1]

I had arrived in Warsaw just in time. Chamberlain's announcement of a unilateral guarantee of Poland's frontiers (on 31 March 1939) led to a brief Anglo-Polish honeymoon, and learning English became the fashion. Classes expanded at the Anglo-Polish school, Noel Coward came to visit us, and as an Englishman (there were not many in Warsaw) I was fussed over by housewives and given favoured treatment by droshky drivers and waiters. Chamberlain's guarantee was designed both as a deterrent and a challenge to Hitler. But the Poles knew there would be war. The prospect excited but did not alarm or depress them. There were black-out exercises, reserve officers

---

[1] See *Undercover*, London 1980, for his later Polish experiences as an S.O.E. officer. His biography of Cavendish-Bentick, former Ambassador to Poland, was published in 1986 by The Bodley Head, entitled *Intelligence Chief Extraordinary*.

were recalled to their units, and a colourful May Day parade of
Silesian coal miners, Polish armoured vehicles, artillery and
cavalry. In July people noticed that Mars was glowing more
brightly than usual – another omen – and it was predicted that
the Germans would attack as soon as the harvest had been
gathered. In August (the holiday month) I took Wanda on a
walking tour in Galicia. Her family welcomed the idea, saying
that if war broke out she would be in a part of Poland near to
friendly neighbours. I had a presentiment that Wanda's family
didn't expect to see her again for a long time. Then on
1 September, a few days after the Hitler–Stalin pact, the
Wehrmacht struck.

On 3 September, near Kolomyja, a Jewish shopkeeper saw
me in the street and beckoned me over to his store where a
group of peasants was bending over a radio. Faraway I could
hear the voice of Chamberlain. "Britain," he announced, "is at
war with Germany." In that moment my status miraculously
changed. The peasants shook my hand, people came into the
shop to greet me. I was no longer an onlooker but a participant
in Poland's drama.

There was no way of getting back to Warsaw. As the days
passed village squares filled up with peasants in smocks
and mocassins who had been mobilised but had no movement
orders or transport. It was rumoured that the British fleet had
sailed into the Baltic and that the RAF was flying to Poland's
help. The weather stayed cloudless, the countryside ominously
quiet. Day after day the peasants looked up at the blue sky and
saw no vapour trails. Then refugees began to arrive by car from
Warsaw – lawyers, artists and writers, people who had the
resources and initiative to save themselves, and they brought
the first signs of panic. Shortly before the Russians marched in
I was tipped off by an official at the *voivodstvo* that the Red
Army was being deployed near the border and it would be
unsafe for me to stay ("if the Russians catch you, you'll disappear"). I took Wanda and a fibre suitcase into Roumania. We
caught a country bus to Czernowitz and from there went in a
train packed with Poles to Bucharest.

In Bucharest I found friends and decided to stay and see how
the "phoney" war developed in the West. The Anglo-Roumanian
Institute, run by the British Council, took me on as lecturer at

the Commercial Academy and I began a bizarre, even absurd life. Cafés were full of Roumanian officers eating sweet Turkish cakes. There were gypsy night clubs with astonishing violinists, melodies and cymbalon players: hot *suika* (plum brandy) with sugar lumps; watchmen sitting round braziers in the snow outside the King's palace; Jewish street markets and Polish refugees. German "experts" were starting to infiltrate Roumania, and cinemas showed news-reels of the Luftwaffe bombing British merchant ships. Yet the British Council carried on as though nothing had happened. It lectured on Bernard Shaw, held debates ("Woman's Place is in the Home"), and Reggie Smith ("Guy" of Olivia Manning's *Balkan Trilogy*) produced *Othello* at the National Theatre with the British Military Attaché Major Davidson-Houston as Iago. Every Sunday I played rugby football in the national league – Roumanians had a flair for the game and their best teams had players of international standard.

By the time the war flared up with Germany's attack on Holland and the Channel ports I was impatient to leave. I had joined the officers' emergency reserve, and on instructions from the military Attaché went to Constanza with Wanda to await transport to Egypt. Some days later another forty passengers arrived, shepherded by the major. They were mostly British oil engineers from Ploesti. Their assignment, which was to sabotage the oil fields and refineries in the event of German attack, had been cancelled when King Carol's government lost its nerve (there had been some amateurish attempts to sink barges loaded with cement in parts of the Danube). Denis Wright, who was on his way to Trebizond as consul (he later became ambassador to Ethiopia) had attached himself to the group. We were an odd collection of Scotsmen, saboteurs and wives and our ship was a joke: a Jewish hulk owned and manned by members of the Aaronstein family. They wore cloth caps and baggy suits and had hidden their treasure in the lifebelts. As we chugged away at snail's pace for the open sea the German consul at Constanza impudently waved goodbye from the quayside. He had put on his white motoring helmet. Only the day before I had been slogging a cricket ball into his flower beds. We were in retreat, a shipload of failures.

In Egypt my aim was to resume my old connection with the Poles. I learned that the Carpathian Brigade had been forced to

leave Syria as a result of Vichy's surrender and was manning a
sector of concrete bunkers at Dikheila near Mex (Alexandria) as
part of the harbour defences. The Poles had salvaged some
French equipment – Citröen trucks and machine guns – and
collected a few horses in Palestine, and were getting used to the
life of a British colonial force that wore shorts. On completing
the infantry course in Moascar I stayed for a month with the
brigade. But my first posting was to an English regular battalion
in the Western desert. Wanda was living in Gezira.

We lived in holes in the sand protected by mine fields.
Wavell's desert offensive just before Christmas swamped us
with Italian prisoners. When the battalion was relieved we took
over guard duties at the Citadel in Cairo. I had to wait to the
end of 1941 before I was able to resume my association with the
Poles. The Carpathian Brigade had been sent in the meantime
to reinforce Tobruk garrison and I was posted as training officer
to a Polish unit of reserve officers (*Legia Polska*) encamped
west of Alexandria. The prospect of vegetating among these
delightful veterans was a gloomy one. Then came the dramatic
news in early 1942 that Stalin was releasing 70,000 Poles from
Soviet internment. They were to be evacuated to the Middle
East and come under British command. This huge reinforce-
ment, which arrived in two waves and eventually numbered
over 100,000 Poles including dependants, entirely changed the
scale of Poland's contribution to the war.

I was sent with a British military mission (later changed into
a liaison unit) to Irak to organise desert reception camps, first at
Habbaniya and later Khanaqin, for the new Polish drafts, who
were ferried in tankers to Pahlevi and completed their journey
in open trucks. After their hardships in Russia many were in
poor condition, suffering from malaria and the after-effects of
typhus. Among those who arrived at Khanaqin was General
Okulicki.[1] He had a lady with him and was rather ashamed of
his ill-fitting khaki shorts, wrinkled socks and white legs. But he
had a sense of humour and I issued him with a new Indian tent
and Australian blankets, which pleased him. The Poles had

---

[1] General Okulicki was sent back to Poland as last commander of the
Home Army. He and other Polish Resistance leaders were sentenced to
death in Moscow in June 1945 as "saboteurs and subversionist bandits".

brought their camp followers with them – ballet dancers, cabaret artists and musicians. Zofia Terne, the well-known Warsaw cabaret star, small and jolly, was one. Begin, the future Zionist terrorist leader and prime minister of Israel, was among the anonymous other ranks shuffling about in baggy khaki.[1]

The first task was to weed out the dependants and the unfit, who were evacuated to Palestine, East Africa, Cape Town and India. Reorganising the able-bodied into a corps of two infantry divisions (two brigades each) and an armoured brigade with supporting arms and services on British war establishment lines, training and equipping and preparing them for battle, were completed in Kirkuk, Mosul, Syria and Palestine towards the end of 1943. It had meant a long period of re-education, sweat and toil in desert camps from the Little Zab to the sand dunes of Askalon: 20,000 drivers had to be trained from scratch before the corps could become mobile. I was attached to 5 Kresowa Division under General Sulik, a composed, fatherly man with a bushy moustache. Our divisional sign was a brown bison (the Carpathian Division had a fir tree, Corps troops the Warsaw siren). My batman was an illiterate peasant from Grodno. I gave him a watch but he declined to use it. He fetched me Spartan breakfasts from the cookhouse: two slices of bread spread with a mixture of tinned margarine, cheese and jam and a glass of tea without milk. We had Canadian beer. In Khanaqin and Kirkuk our neighbours were Kurdish villagers. Because of drunkenness, brawls and enteritis – the soldiers had a passion for water melons and drinking spirits in the morning – their villages were put out of bounds. Our artillery shoots sometimes set fire to their crops.

At the end of the year (1943) Polish Corps with 50,000 men was ready for battle with the Tedeschi and we embarked at Port Said for Taranto.[2] The Poles' role as the sword-bearers of an

---

[1] See Appendix 1 (A and B).

[2] During embarkation it was discovered that hundreds of Polish Jewish soldiers were missing (it was later confirmed that some 3,000 of Anders's original Jewish contingent of 4,000 men had deserted in the Middle East). Their loss was serious. They had been trained in special skills – in ordnance and signals, as sappers, artificers and clerical staff – and they had vanished. It was rumoured that they had gone to ground in Palestine in the kibbutzim. Later it was understood that they had deserted because for

occupied country was now to be put to a vital test of honour and courage. The new adventure began in the wintry snow of the Appenines. In early April we moved to Cassino to prepare for our part in the final assault on this bitterly defended obstacle that blocked the road to Rome.

I was attached to the Lwowska Brigade which took over the forward positions of the 78th (Battle Axe) Division, relieving, in the sector I was sent to, the Inniskillings. The Germans were so close that bodies had lain unburied for weeks. Patrolling was not possible. Movement and supplies took place at night. In the daytime the valley behind us was obscured by smoke. We were under constant harassing fire.

The Kresowa Division had been given a difficult job. Its first task was to cross open stony ground under heavy machine-gun and mortar fire and take Phantom Ridge (the Carpathian Division, operating on its left, was to capture Point 593). Then to push forward against the German strong points, outflank the monastery, attack and penetrate the fortified Adolf Hitler Line on the reverse side of Cassino hill. The assault started on 11 May at 23.00 hours with a massive artillery barrage of 1,600 Allied guns. It failed. Both Polish divisions regrouped and tried again. On 18 May Polish soldiers occupied the monastery, where they stuck a makeshift Polish flag on a pole and Corporal Czech sounded the Cracow *Hejnal* on the bugle. Aerial bombing had crushed the historic abbey into a jumble of ruins from which the last Germans had escaped, leaving only a few wounded behind. The monastery was indeed a useless trophy. The Adolf Hitler Line with its dug-in Tiger tanks and wrecked church tower was then pierced at Piedimonte and the road to Rome was open. In a fortnight the Poles had lost 281 officers and 3,503 other ranks, of whom one third were killed and only

them the enemy had changed. They were under orders from their own leaders to lie low until the time came for them to turn their weapons on the British. It was Britain, the Mandatory power in Palestine, who had become the Zionists' prime enemy now that Hitler was seen to be losing the war. Nevertheless other Jewish soldiers (some of whom I knew) stayed with the Polish army to the end; many were awarded decorations for gallantry. See Appendix 1 (A).

102 missing. The memorial in their war cemetery at Point 593
bears this inscription:

> We Polish soldiers
> For our freedom and yours
> Have given our souls to God
> Our bodies to the soil of Italy
> And our hearts to Poland

From Cassino the Poles were sent to the Adriatic coast for the
long summer advance through fortified river-crossings and over
rolling hills and farmland to Ancona and Rimini. There were
days of elation when we "liberated" villages and swallowed vino
and raw eggs, followed by days of sharp fighting – the Todt
organisation had built the German defences well – and of dis-
appointment when the retreating Germans blew up the bridges
under our noses. The "Bolonis" with their eagle cap-badges
became familiar figures to the Italians. They went to the village
churches, swopped their rations for wine, and distilled their
own strong spirits from grapes. There were dips in the sea –
though few Poles could swim – forays for geese, chickens, eggs
and scraps of furniture for the canteens. There was some mild
looting; mattresses and bicycles were favoured but were too
unwieldy and had to be abandoned. Cavalry officers – now in
armoured reconnaissance regiments – sought out the few rural
contessas who had stayed behind in their silent, echoing
manors. Behind the lines the Poles enjoyed their own self-
contained social and cultural life. They organised clubs and
concerts, leave centres in Naples and Rome, they had their own
newspaper, nurses, choirs and restaurants.

As winter set in the advance halted in the hills south of
Bologna. It was there that I spent my last Christmas with the
Poles. They were living in farms and sleeping in big peasant
beds under strings of onions. Only the guns were keeping up
the ritual of war, firing into the leafless trees and frozen ditches.
One of my last memories is of sharing an OP as our gunners
smashed, one after the other, some little white buildings on a
ridge where German infantry, stinking of sweat and leather,
were concealed. Soon after my ties with the Poles were abruptly
cut. By what seemed to my Polish friends an act of apostasy I

was given a new posting that was to involve me with the arch-
enemy – the Russians. The recent capture of an entire Turkoman division near Ravenna was causing problems for politicians
and embarrassing Stalin. I was to help handle these reluctant
Soviet citizens and deal with Moscow's military mission.

In retrospect this may have been the right moment for me to
leave the Poles. They had been through several crises and
suffered some bitter blows: the discovery of the Katyn massacre; the loss of Sikorski in a flying accident; the defeat of the
Warsaw rising in the summer of 1944 and the destruction of
their capital; the occupation of Poland by the Red Army. The
Yalta agreement of February 1945 delivered a final and desperate blow to their morale. It broke the soldiers' hearts. Men who
had fought in the hope of returning to their homes in eastern
Poland – and many in the Kresowa division came from those
areas – woke up one day to find they had nothing to go back to.
I was told that for a short time there was a serious danger of the
soldiers refusing to go on fighting. They went on, however, to
take Bologna and the war was over. Alas, with the Russians
firmly in control of their country, Bologna for the Poles seemed
but another useless victory.

I was to meet the Poles again under changed circumstances
in the summer of 1946. A repatriation camp for the relatively
small number of Poles who had opted to return to Poland rather
than settle down in Britain or the Commonwealth and build a
new life in exile, had been opened at Cervinara near Naples. A
Polish Military Mission from Warsaw under an elegant colonel
who wore a magnificent peaked cap was responsible for the
Polish side of the evacuation. He was making difficulties and
AFHQ Caserta sent me to help sort them out. I found the
atmosphere in the camp unpleasant. The soldiers had been
politicised. They were suspicious, morose and confused by
divided loyalties. The Warsaw colonel thought that the British
were impeding the operation. I noticed Colonel Jakovliev of the
Soviet Military Mission in Rome prowling about the camp (he
was sent away).

It was a sad moment when I stood at the quayside in Naples
watching the last draft of repatriated soldiers climb up the
gangway of the American Liberty ship that was to take them to
Gdynia. They had left their friends behind. They were going

back to an uncertain and perhaps dangerous future in a country
whose government suspected their integrity. Russian refugees
used to carry a sack of potatoes as their iron rations for emergency. The Poles were weighed down with spare boots and
blankets strapped to their packs. Some of the men, it is true,
were not "real" Poles, but Silesians of mixed Polish and
German stock who had been conscripted into the Wehrmacht,
captured or surrendered, and then recruited by Anders to make
up his battle losses. Yet there were other Poles in the repatriation drafts who had outstanding military records: men whose
sense of duty towards their country was paramount however
dubious the reception that awaited them.

The repatriation operation, however, didn't go without a
hitch. At the medical examination, just before the final draft
left, the MO found fifteen cases of syphilis. They were not
allowed to embark, and were put in an army truck to be driven
to hospital. They didn't arrive and I never heard of them again.

The dismembering and Communisation of Poland, and the
disbanding of 2 Polish Corps, brought total disillusionment to
the Polish cause and severed my emotional ties with the Poles:
for my loyalties had been with the soldiers. The great majority
of them chose exile, and there could of course be no place for
me in a Communist country after I had compromised myself
with the Russians by hindering their forcible repatriation plans
(1945–47) for Soviet – or alleged Soviet – citizens. I lost touch
with the Poles and after returning to civilian life in 1950 I went
to Germany to work as a university teacher. This was not a
question of fraternising with former Nazis. The Germans were
still culturally isolated and young people were hungry to resume
relations with the West. What better way could there be of
identifying with the new generation than to become a teacher?

In subsequent years I met few Poles: a Makerere librarian in
Kampala, a female doctor at a leper hospital near Jinja, a
solicitor in Johannesburg. Then (1978) in Churchill Avenue,
Umtali (Rhodesia), a slight grey-haired man tapped my arm. I
had not seen Rotmistrz Emil Mentel for over thirty-five years. I
remembered him as a handsome lieutenant recovering from a
head wound in the Western Desert. "*Czolem!*" he said. "Come
and stay at my farm."

It was like coming home. A big Polish eagle (crowned) hung

inside the entrance to his homestead. Looking through his wartime photograph albums I recognised many of my old Polish
acquaintances. Emil put on a cracked record of Polish cavalry
marches. Two Polish neighbours, Princess Lubecki (née
Sapieha) and her daughter Maria, were staying with him: their
farm, a few hundred yards away, had been attacked by terrorists with bullets, rockets and a mortar (the two ladies fired back
with a Beretta shot-gun and a long-barrelled Spanish pistol) and
they had come to Emil for shelter with their dogs and two old
riding horses.

I was to stay with Emil several times. He kept a small
armoury and I was happy to keep him company, to look after
the farm and labour force when he was away and to share the
night watches – his farm, at the foot of Christmas Pass, was two
miles from the Mozambique border and the district was overrun by Mugabe's terrorist bands, who mined and ambushed
vehicles, attacked farmsteads and killed cattle and labourers. It
was this shared adventure – and the election of a Pole as Pope,
which I saw as a mighty blow for freedom – that stirred up the
past and made me decide to revisit Poland. It would be a
gesture of loyalty to a memory: an intellectual test after the
simple years of outdoor life in Africa: an experiment in self-
assessment among the ravages of change in a once familiar
European environment. It would also be my opportunity to find
out – it might entail some risk – if I was still on some faded
Moscow black list as a "Fascist Major".

Two of Emil's remarks which stay in my memory could only
have been made by a Pole. "If I cannot fight Communism in
Poland," he said, "I can fight it here." He greeted Mugabe's
victory at the polls with anger. "First Churchill betrayed us,
and now Mrs Thatcher!"

D.C.H
Oxford – Twickenham
June 1987

I
RETURN
TO
POLAND (1)

I
RETURN TO WARSAW

Going back to Poland after a gap of forty-five years with a store of romantic but rusty memories was bound to be an emotional experience. That first sight of cobblestones, tumbledown villages and plodding farm carts across the Oder. The endless beetfields. Flaking churches, flower-strewn graveyards, unpronounceable names. Like Rip Van Winkle I would find much that was barely recognisable: rebuilt city centres, new ideologies and war memorials. I might be disappointed – one should never, it is said, go back to a place that one has once loved. Prepared for Iron Curtain shortages I had taken care to stock up in the supermarkets of Brunswick with provisions and small camping accessories.

At the East German border crossing at Marienborn I was given a twenty-four-hour transit visa (costing 5 DM) that at my usual bumbling progress of forty to forty-five miles an hour would get me to Frankfurt-an-der-Oder, 170 miles to the east, well before dusk. I am a slow traveller. I stop when I feel like it, brew tea, chat to people or go into a bar. It was a fine, clear morning and the engine droned steadily, as though enjoying the outing. But I had not yet learned to trust the van. It was old and scarred – a 1967 Bedford camper – and it was a miracle that the former owner, a carpet fitter who had left the vehicle lying out for months in a field, had managed to get it through the MOT test; perhaps the garage mechanic in Henley-in-Arden was his friend. I feared that sooner or later something vital might break loose and I would be stuck in some lonely place in a country without spares.

However, the swish and roar of the motorway traffic – West

German cars streaking along the grey concrete like rockets, clapped-out Trabants, huge pantechnicons and East German army trucks – didn't perturb me, though the big lorries hooted when I refused to swerve off on to the hard shoulder. By my own standards I was well equipped. I had a spare wheel, a jack and foot pump, reserve petrol, sausages and black *Vollkorn* bread. All my lights – and even the stuttering horn – were working. My papers were in order, and unless disaster struck I had enough money to pay for a frugal journey of some months.

The first landmark was Magdeburg. Its Socialist-style high-rise blocks stuck out hideously a mile or two away over the flat arable plain. A single church spire showed through the industrial murk like an old tooth. Towards Brandenburg the autobahn ran through stands of pine and birch that stood motionless and erect like soldiers on parade. It was these dense regiments that had impressed me when, as an Oxford undergraduate in 1933, I had first walked through the countryside outside Berlin: the dry, toasted smell of fallen needles, the stillness and shadowy light, the rows of tall trunks still as guardsmen. Ever since those days I have associated them with *Pickelhauben* and marching men and tow-haired schoolchildren searching for mushrooms. After I had left the Berlin Ring, where most traffic turns off to the capital, I had a clear run as far as the Polish border.

At Frankfurt-an-der-Oder I looked for petrol and got lost in a towering maze of tenement blocks. Morose people were walking about with shopping bags and briefcases. There were green articulated trams and a long deserted street where two soldiers were guarding a great building with hundreds of closed windows. Feeling conspicuous – for this was enemy country where the bayonets pointed westward – I turned back. It was dusk when I bowled down a slope to the frontier barrier which seals off the Oder bridge.

The narrow space between the customs sheds was congested with vehicles. Their drivers, hardened to the system, were chain-smoking or listening to their radios. I joined a line of twenty vehicles and unwrapped my bread and sausage.

Travellers reporting their imbroglios with frontier officials tend to echo a pattern. Their officials are caricatures – obdurate and corrupt or oily and vain. One knows that the intrepid wayfarer will outwit them all with his *sang froid* (Kinglake's description in *Eothen* of his entry into the Sultan's dominions at Belgrade in 1834 where the plague was raging – "and now my eyes would see the Splendour and Havoc of The East" – is on a different level, and is literature). Here at the door of Poland I was facing unsmiling bureaucrats in peaked caps. The Iron Curtain atmosphere was chilling. Every traveller was suspect. The rules would be different.

We were allowed to move forward a few feet at a time. East German officials walked round the vehicles peering through the windows at the contents and marking them for search or not. One youngish man with a hard face seemed especially interested in my van and the boxes of food and books. I scented trouble.

After an hour – it was dark by now – the official told me to drive into a cubicle with an inspection pit, trestle tables and bright lights. He closed the door and said, "Take everything out and put it on the tables." This took time. Being a self-sufficient traveller – what the Germans call an *Einzelgänger* – I had a lot of books, old letters and a miscellany of surplus clothes which, if I was broke, I intended to swop for meals.

The official tapped and opened everything: my spectacle case, food tins and tea bags, shaving cream and hold-all. He emptied my tobacco pouch, sifted the sugar, unscrewed the engine cover (which made his hands oily), poked at the ad-hesive tape bindings on the steering column, looked under the floor mats and stuck his fingers through holes in the seats.

When he turned to my books I explained that I was a teacher of history, retired (*emeritus*) – hence my library. "I didn't ask you who you were," he replied coldly. He put a dozen books on one side, passed some German newspaper cuttings on Solidarity and General Jaruzelski, scrutinised my old supplementary benefit receipts from Leamington, and then climbed down into the inspection pit to look under the chassis. Ever since I had bought the old wreck it had shed specks of rust like soot whenever I backed or jerked the wheel. I felt alarmed for the official's green uniform. When he thumped the side of my van a little shower of rust fell on his clothes.

By now the cold river air was making me shiver and I gave him an unfriendly look which was meant to say, "I'm seventy-one, man, a Senior Citizen, and I don't want to stand on your bloody draughty bridge all night."

To my relief he returned my books and began to dust his hands. "You can put everything back in your van," he said. Then he went without another word, leaving me to confront the Poles.

The Polish official was a small terrier-like man. He seemed out of his mind or drunk. "Where is the *mleko* (milk)?" he insisted, "how many kilos and what brand?"

"I have no *mleko*," I said. "Just enough for my tea."

"The *mleko*," he repeated, and gave me a form to fill in.

He disappeared for half an hour. "You haven't declared the *mleko*," he said when he came back. "How many kilos?"

Was he really interested in powdered milk? Or did *"mleko"* have some special meaning? Was it smugglers' cant for brandy, cocaine, women's tights? How was I to appease this humorist?

"Psiakrew!" I said. "I don't like milk."

He smiled at this, stamped my customs form and passed me on to the frontier cashier. She was a tired, pale-faced girl sitting on an uncomfortable stool behind a window. There was no trouble here. She exchanged my sterling vouchers for Polish currency at the official rate of £8 a day for the proposed length of my stay in Poland, paying me in 10,000 zloty notes. When I objected that it would be difficult to change such large denominations on the road she said "We have no *drobne*," and closed the shutter.

It was well after midnight when I drove slowly into the welcoming darkness of the Polish night. The lights of the old German fortress town faded away in river mist and I was alone among the shadowy trees.

ROAD TO WARSAW

The road was not lit, the moon shone on frozen puddles. I had difficulty making out the sign posts to Swiebodzin where I was to join the highway to Poznan. After a dozen miles I found a gap in the forest and pulled into a clearing. I was too weary to clear a space for my stretcher-bed among the chaos left behind by the customs search, and it was bitterly cold. I spent the night crouched among my boxes like a drunken cabby.

I was scraping the rime from my windows in the early morning when I saw two young men on a motorcycle coming towards me from the road. They offered me an American cigarette and asked if I had dollars.

"No," I said.

"Sterling? We will give you five times the official rate in zlotys."

I was already loaded with zlotys. The pound notes were my lifeline. The longer they lasted the longer I could spin out my journey. And I had a suspect vehicle that might need costly repairs.

"I'm not interested," I replied. We swopped cigarettes and the young men rode away on their little motorcycle. I would at any rate have no trouble finding black market dealers if I needed them.

About thirty miles on I stopped at a small restaurant in a cobbled street. The parlour was filled with men, some noisily drunk, others eating soup with tin spoons on dirty table cloths. I ordered my first Polish meal. It was a rissole with gravy and red cabbage, stewed plums, and *herbatka* served in the Polish manner: a glass of boiling water with a tea bag and lumps of sugar in the saucer.

An elderly man in an overcoat, wearing a beret, must have seen me enter for he immediately came over. He introduced himself as the local photographer – he had a studio opposite – and said he had relatives in England. We spoke in Polish. He seemed anxious for English news.

He told me he had served as a soldier under General Macek. I knew about the general. He had commanded Polish armoured units in the Allied advance across Holland. But when I pressed him to tell me more about the campaign he had nothing to add and I thought he was boasting.

He then gave me a searching look. "Why did Churchill and Roosevelt sell Poland to Stalin?" I gave him my stock answer. "The Western Allies were war weary. The Germans had been defeated. Our soldiers wanted to go home. And Churchill," I added, "lost patience with the bickerings of Polish politicians over a peace settlement. But the real cause of the betrayal was that the Red Army was already encamped in Poland and only force could have driven them out."

"You admit then," said the photographer, "that you left the war unfinished and abandoned central and eastern Europe to the Red Army. You and the Americans are still paying for this crime."

I could not argue with this brutal truth. As the Poles have never tired of reminding us, the Western Allies didn't finish the job. General Anders's Polish soldiers in Italy, I recall, were almost broken-hearted when hostilities came to an end on 9 May 1945. "The whistle has blown," they said, "but only for half-time." My own memories of British army attitudes in Italy and Austria at that time were painful. For months sergeants of the newly formed Army Education Corps had been preaching half-baked Socialist ideas to the troops, while the men themselves had but a single desire: to hurry home for football and fish and chips and to "poke their bints"; and they were grateful to Russia. Smokey Joe's Red Army, far from being considered a menace, had saved thousands of their own comrades' lives by killing Germans on the eastern front.

"Why is Britain against the bomb?" asked the photographer. "What about the Greenham Common women?"

"They are mostly freaks," I said. "Neurotics. Wild people (*dzikie ludzie*)."

"Why are you fighting the Irish?"

"The Irish war is a vested interest for some, a sport for others," I said. "The priests and pastors are much to blame."

This was my first long conversation in Polish, a test of my ability to recall the language that I had known so fluently forty years before. Alas, my memory had rusted. I knew the words but I had to grope for them, and they sometimes got mixed up with the Russian – and indeed Swahili – equivalents. The photographer, however, was delighted to have an answer to his questions and complimented me on my Polish. "You and I can discuss serious things seriously," he said. "I see you can rough it too (*pan jest zahartowany*)," he added, looking rather doubtfully at my decrepit van parked outside on the cobblestones. He gave me a packet of Carmen cigarettes ("the best"). They tasted like the strong home-grown Rothandl brand that German workmen used to smoke before Virginia blends took over the market.

Before I left the photographer took me to see his studio. It was a small mean room. There was a battered rocking-horse for children to pose on, some bits of painted cardboard as a backdrop, a chair and a tripod. It was as poor as anything I had seen in an Asian or African alley shop. The photographer gave me tea then made it clear that I was to go. Neighbours would be gossiping and the police would be suspicious. I understood.

My next stop would be Poznan, and as I bowled through the country landscape I sorted out my first impressions. They were bound to be over-coloured or only half true. That woman in a thick skirt and head scarf bending over a field was surely like any other peasant woman in the world. Toil and no glamour. Yet she was different. She kissed the crucifix hanging at the wayside. She paid homage at graves and left flowers. She prayed in Polish. Her myths were Polish. Her husband and sons got drunk like Hottentots on vodka. She was always there, with her thick knees and workaday clothes, grumbling, cooking, carrying, never far from the byre and the well.

Spring was late. The flat green fields were lined with leafless poplars and naked birches with skeletal white limbs. Pylons wandered untidily across the skyline. The cows had not yet been let out. A few peasants, some working in pairs, were scattering seed on the ground by hand from a basket or satchel. Near villages I passed shrines with candles and wreaths of fresh flowers. Women were queueing outside stores with shopping bags. The churches were weatherworn and solid. New brick cottages stood among old wooden buildings with crooked wooden frames. There was little traffic on the highway: small Polish Fiats and Ladas, tractors and carts, muddy country buses and Polish and Hungarian-made lorries. The fast moving vehicles had German number plates or were imported cars with Polish stickers.

I turned on my transistor radio and listened to a church service with a priest's homily and fine singing. The weather bulletin forecast snow and cold winds from Scandinavia. Late in the afternoon I pulled into a space behind a warehouse and waited for the night. I had one visitor, a small friendly boy with a bicycle. He was rather rude about my van. "It's very old," he said, looking at the rust that hung below the chassis like twisted brown icicles. But he admired my water-tap. I didn't tell him that the basin waste-pipe was rusted up and could not be used.

I reached Poznan on Sunday morning and followed the trams

to the Centrum, where I bought petrol coupons from the cashier
at the Merkury hotel. Petrol is rationed in Poland, and foreign
motorists have to buy their coupons in hard currency. I bought
sixty litres for 112 DM. This regulation, and the daily fee
charged for a visa, plus hotel charges in hard currency, are the
Polish government's way of soaking foreign visitors. But as the
black market value of the zloty is abysmally low, the authorities
would be foolish to let foreigners ("who are rich") pay their bills
in cheap local money.

Poznan has been heavily industrialised and is under rapid
development. It took me some time to find my way through the
new factory suburbs and building sites. The mammoth painted
factory stacks, the big cube-shaped tenement blocks for workers,
the mud and uncompleted roads, stretched like a nightmare
over the dying fields. In the afternoon I called at a restaurant
near Konin. It was crowded with young Poles in their Sunday
clothes: jeans, rough sweaters (no ties), thick-soled shoes.
The waitress brought me half a chicken and a plate of carrots
mashed with apple juice. There was a thick fug. Poles – men
and women – smoke compulsively in and out of doors as though
they had never read of cancer warnings ("life is short anyway").
Most people were drinking beer. The few staggering drunks
were being handled with good humour. Over the bar hung the
printed words "Alcoholism brings unwelcome diseases, and
tragedy to your family". But it was still early. The vodka
drinking, drunken speeches and thuds had not yet started.

Next to the restaurant there was a row of new shops selling
furniture and rugs, agricultural tools and prams. The goods
were roughly finished and dusty and no attempt had been made
to arrange an attractive window display. The goods had been
produced in some Socialist enterprise, they had been put on
sale, and they would be bought: customers had no other choice.

I found a damp garden to sleep in, in a forest clearing outside
a motel. A party of middle-aged Italians with a Polish priest in
charge had just arrived by bus. They looked pinched with cold
and hurried to the toilets as though after a day on the road they
had bladder trouble. While I was brewing tea on my buthane
gas cooker a taxi drove up and a smart girl got out. She hurried
towards me.

"*Przepraszam pana*, what time is it?"

"My watch," I said, "doesn't go."

"Are you a Hollander? Where is your woman? Have you dollars?"

I looked at her more closely. She was made up, thin-faced, aggressive.

"No, I've had enough of women, and I don't carry dollars."

"Have you nothing to sell? Tobacco, coffee, brandy, spare clothes?"

"I'm sorry," I said, "I travel light."

Disappointed, she left abruptly, a taxi-driver's bait for foreigners. "Where is your woman?" This is what black people used to ask me when I was travelling rough in Africa. They saw a white man cooking or washing his shirt in a bucket or sitting alone on a folding chair, and the women would approach softly and shyly and ask *"Wapi bibi, bwana? Bibi hapana?"* as though without a female mate a man was odd, unnatural, perhaps sick. Why indeed should he do his own laundry and cook his meals himself? For simple Africans a traveller with a motor car is rich. A black woman's services are cheap, and her velvet body is expected to provide warmth during the long hours of night.

Another bus load of Poles scrambled down a bank to urinate at the edge of a stream. Some were tipsy and had to be helped by friends from falling in the mud. They were wearing their best clothes (suits and collars). Why do some people put on their finery when the rigours of a journey will ruin it?

The East German frontier foray had put all my things in disorder. I spent an hour making my van more comfortable to sleep and live in. My problem was that I was carrying too many objects: not only books and food (including my landlady Miss Parsons's gift of five two-kilo bags of porridge oats – "a minimum of seventy servings") – but countless little items from a safety pin to a candle. Everything had to be stowed in its proper place and one had to remember where this was. My most pressing concern was the state of my stretcher-bed, which I had fished out of Ingrid's attic. The hinges were broken and there was nothing to support the folding end sections. So I propped the head of the bed on my two spare wheels and the end on a stack of magazines. With a pile of clothes over my sleeping bag I felt like a trussed-up troll. But nothing, I said to myself as I dowsed the candle, would make me disentangle myself from my wrappings till it was morning and the first grey light was filtering through the window curtains.

ARRIVING IN WARSAW

I lay in the dark listening to the wind and the rain spattering on the roof. I was beginning to feel at home. Nothing unusual had happened. The landscape had been very flat; I had scarcely changed to a lower gear for two days. The roads were quiet, and when I passed road repair gangs (mittens and yellow safety jackets) they were generally idling or smoking. I had seen a few cows hobbled by lengths of rope or chain, horses pulling ploughs, tractors towing small trailers. Cemeteries were crowded with crosses and bright with flowers. Their gates and railings were in good order. Churches towered over cottages with thatched or weather-stained roofs.

In the morning, while I was shaving, I watched two farmers spraying a field. One was driving a small tractor, the other removing big stones with his hands. They seemed to be quarrelling. The washplace and toilet in the motel yard was locked. People had left excrement outside it.

I reached the outskirts of Warsaw at noon. This was the moment I had been fearing. I was not used to my ponderous van and its poor acceleration. Soon I was caught up in a whirl of darting traffic: tiny Fiats, sharply braking buses and round-abouts with converging roads. I saw that many of the old landmarks were missing. The city centre was quite changed, dominated now by a huge pile of Soviet masonry which stuck up like a mountain. Traffic police and militia vehicles were everywhere, waving down motorists and making them stand in the road while they checked their papers.

I parked on Nowy Swiat street and went for a walk. It was forty-five years since I had last trodden its pavements and I recognised immediately the long curve of once elegant shops. Yet there was something odd about the buildings. They had almost all – as I learned later – been restored from ruin and rubble. The rebuilt façades were coated with grey streaked plaster. Wandering into the courtyards behind the big arched entrances I saw that many brick walls had been roughly patched up and were still pockmarked with bullet holes and shell

splinters. But the old life within the courtyards that I remembered seemed to be flourishing. Barbers, watchmakers, tailors
and cobblers still had their tiny workshops among the hand-
painted trade signs (a lady's shoe, a hat), the dustbins and cats.
There was a smell of onions and boiled cabbage from the
staircases. Pigeon droppings whitened grimy window sills. The
grassy gardens at the rear where people took their children and
dogs were bare and wintry but looked cared for.

I made for the new silhouette of the Orbis Hotel, an ochre
tower block without grace or beauty which is recommended in
every Polish tourist brochure. The lounge was full of Arabs.
They seemed to be waiting for appointments. All the signs were
that it was a black market bazaar. I bought petrol coupons and
went into a small café. Like the Orbis lounge it was bogus. It
had a showcase of wooden peasant crafts, some stuffed birds
hanging from the ceiling, and the furniture had sharp, pro-
truding legs. The coffee tasted of chicory.

When I got back to my van I found an old man had washed
off the mud with a mop and was waiting to be paid. He was
quite annoyed when I gave him Polish money. "No Deutsch-
marks? No dollars?"

This, my first glimpse of the tourist fringe of Warsaw, was
enough for one day. To avoid it I would have to find a camping
site. A man with a satchel and bicycle gave me expert directions. Twenty minutes later I drove up to the Gromada camp
along the airport road and switched off the engine. The gates
were padlocked.

2
MEMORIES

A woman cleaner from the camp told me that it would be opening in three days' time (2 May). Until then I had to find a bolt-hole. Not far from the fence I found a space where I backed my van out of sight behind a hedge. There was a park nearby, a football field (with rugby posts) and running track. I put on my artisan's jacket and went into the park.

Joggers swished past me along the paths, there were many young parents with well-wrapped children, and dog owners. The dogs were worth looking at: expensive, beautifully cared for, sleek and clean and bursting with energy, and of many breeds: Irish wolfhounds, boxers, doberman pinschers, dalmatians and spaniels. I wondered how people in a poor country could afford to keep and feed such animals. Were they a status symbol? Or was it so difficult to find worthwhile things to spend one's zlotys on in a Socialist economy that a fine dog had become a profitable investment?

When I got back to my van a boy with a bright face and glasses was waiting for me. His father, he told me, was a university lecturer in medicine. He pointed to a complex of buildings a few hundred yards away where the medical faculty and student hostels were centred. The boy said he wanted to learn English. Could I give him lessons? The only foreign language he learned at his school was Russian. "Four times a week. It's compulsory."

"Why do you prefer English?"

"Russian gets you nowhere," he said. With English he could study technical subjects and find opportunities abroad. He had read Dickens's *A Christmas Carol* in Polish. "Do you play chess?" he asked. "Are you half-Polish?"

MAY DAY

There was a night frost and I awoke stiff and cold in the morning. Poplar trees, still without leaves, lined the fence like rows of witches' brooms. I joined the strollers in the park and felt that I could have been in Brunswick or Richmond. For the same pensioners were there, husbands holding on firmly to their wives' arms and moving with the gravity of retired civil servants. The wives had neat and sprightly legs. Near the camp gates were a betting shop, a bar and a stationer's. I asked for a newspaper but the owner said I would have to order it. He had plenty of weeklies but they were full of cultural articles and would be dull. So I placed an order for *Zycie Warszawy* which had a sports page. My transistor radio would keep me in touch with events but it was unreliable (an African servant had dropped it on a cement floor) and I couldn't get the BBC World Service till late at night. The East Berlin station, though, was both powerful and persistent, and broadcast splendid concerts from Leipzig.

At midday I went into the bar for *bigos* (boiled cabbage with lumps of sausage): it used to be one of my favourites, cheap and hot, the poor man's nightcap after emptying his pockets on alcohol. A drinking party was in top gear among a mess of soup bowls, half-eaten bread and empty bottles. One man who had been sitting quietly on his stool and who looked like a clerk suddenly toppled over and hit the floor with a thud, losing his glasses. I was about to help him to his feet but his friends insisted he should sleep for a few minutes before they propped him back on his stool. One of the party poured me some vodka from a bottle he had in his pocket.

"So you're English," he said. He squinted into my face. "You dropped Poland in the shit."

"Not, I hope, for ever," I said.

"Without a miracle nothing will change. The Russians are too strong. They could reach the Channel ports before you woke up for breakfast."

"The Poles believe in miracles."

He laughed. "Communist policy is not programmed for miracles."

*

When I move into the camp after May Day (which is tomorrow) I shall have to look again at my comfort. The two spare wheels I use as a pillow give me a stiff neck. My gas burner leaks and the kettle my sister gave me is heavily coated with fur. When I am organised I shall spoil myself. I shall feast on cheeses, pickled cucumbers and tinned carp – I have seen some in the shops. Butter, meat and sugar are rationed, and I have of course no ration card; honey is synthetic and, I am told, not recommended. But there is no shortage of milk (though it quickly turns sour), jars of jam, plain vegetables and apples.

I have decided not to join the crowds who will flood into the city for the May Day celebrations. The stationer has told me it will be a dull occasion with speeches and parades and police everywhere. "If you want to hear what General Jaruzelski has to say, tune in to your radio."

Besides, I dislike crowds. When a crowd turns into a mob it bellows "Heil Hitler!", loots shops, lynches petty thieves and roughs up women. During *Fasching* in Düsseldorf I had seen young bullies smash their fists into older men's faces in a beer hall. I remember the ugly scenes at the Shia festival of Muharram in Persia, the gashed torsoes and streaming blood. I am not yet committed to any Polish cause – though no doubt I shall be – and Socialism might even work. The Poles' vision of their own frustrated role as a free nation is so narrow that until I can identify with them emotionally – which was easy enough when we were soldiering together in the last war – I shall find their politics a bore.

When I tuned in to Warsaw radio this morning (1 May) I could hear cheering and military music from the Red Square in Moscow. The cheering was interrupted by brief addresses ending with "Hurrahs!" The broadcast then switched to an account of street fighting by students and revolutionary workers in Warsaw in 1904 against the Tsar's police and soldiers.

General Jaruzelski's speech followed. "We have gathered under the Red flag of freedom. We are children of the revolutionary uprising of 1 May 1905 when workers fought for their rights in the name of the international proletariat and the Polish nation. Freedom for the Fatherland, Fundamental

Reforms – such was our manifesto on that historic first of May.[1]

"On 1 May 1945 Warsaw was in ruins. But our heroic army and Socialist Poland had triumphed. Partisans had fought with soldiers against Hitler's Fascists. Remember our battle honours." (Tobruk and Monte Cassino were mentioned.) "The imperialists still wish to harm us, to revise the map, belittle our nation and its endeavours. Reagan has visited SS Fascist graves in Germany. I call on you all – workers, farmers and intellectuals – to strive for a better Socialist Poland based on democracy. America threatens us with nuclear weapons. But while we work for our patriotic ends the Polish army will defend our frontiers."

The speech – the Poles will read it with reluctance and out of a sense of duty – ended with restrained clapping and the playing of the "Internationale". Poland's national hymn followed. It is a lively, inspiring tune, played at a smart pace in the style of a mazurek and suited to the *élan* of light infantry and cavalry. I heard it sung countless times in many odd corners of the Middle East and Italy during my war service with the Poles. The words "Poland has not perished yet" (*"Jeszcze Polska nie zginela"*), have never failed to stir me. It was sung by hardened troops of Kopanski's and Anders's forces who, like Dabrowski's Legion with Napoleon's army in Italy, were fighting in the desperate hope of returning with flags flying to their homeland.

That night I heard a rap on the window of my van and saw two policemen and a patrol car.

"Who are you?" they asked. "This is not a parking place. It is forbidden to stay here."

I explained that I was waiting for the camp to open. "You will have to move," they said, and showed me to a place under an arc light outside the bar. "You may park on the pavement." I did what they asked. They came back twice during the night and shone their lights on me.

---

[1] In 1904 demonstrators were fired on by Russian police in Warsaw, the first open challenge to the Tsar's authority in Poland for forty years. 1905 was a year of risings widely supported by workers. On May Day thirty-seven people were killed in Warsaw. The year ended with the Tsar's promise of a written constitution for Poles.

GROMADA CAMP

When the Gromada camp opened its office in the morning the director, Pan Poinc, a military-looking man with grey hair, gave me a warm welcome, "Congratulations," he said. "You are our first visitor." He mounted a small bicycle, on which he patrolled the camp, and took me to a grassy space sheltered by trees. "No one will disturb you here. The toilets are being repaired but will soon be ready. If you stay you will meet all sorts – Australians, Finns, Vietnamese, gypsies, even a few of your own countrymen."

Half the camp was occupied by small wooden chalets with neat rubbish bins and fire extinguishers. One section was packed with little box-like caravans, Polish made. They had been standing there all winter, grass had grown round the wheels and some looked derelict. There was no hot water in the toilets. The workmen supposed to be repairing them were sitting on cement bags smoking and watching a football match through the fence.

I soon had a visitor. Andrzej was a stocky man with a full beard, blue eyes, jeans and a thick sweater, aged about forty-five. "I do odd jobs in the camp," he told me, "repair cars and drive a taxi when I can get petrol." He had spent a year in Australia and wanted to emigrate there with his son. "The trouble is the Australians treat Poles as second-class citizens."

Andrzej asked me into his cosy, kennel-like trailer which he had fitted out with bedding, lockers and a small fridge. He gave me a tumbler of vodka and a piece of sweet cake – "baked by my wife" – and seemed happy to talk.

"I used to make a living as a photographer," he said, "selling my pictures to the press. That's over now. I offended the censorship laws by taking political pictures – riots and demonstrations and police scenes – and my equipment and press card were seized."

He was intrigued when I told him about my nostalgic longing to see Poland again – the country with which my early life had been dramatically involved (I didn't mention that I also hoped to write a book).

"I understand," he said, refilling my tumbler. "But you'll be disappointed. Poland is not the country you knew. We have been betrayed."

He opened a tin of Russian sardines. "Listen," he said, "the Russians are deceiving the West with their peace talk. They could reach the Channel in forty-eight hours. They are interested only in power and will go on probing the West for weak points – as in Afghanistan – till something gives way. The Solidarity protest movement in Poland has lost its edge. It's been neutered."

A man came in who wanted Andrzej to service his car. He was even gloomier about the future.

"Perhaps the Russians will change one day," I said. "They might take to marijuana."

The visitor smiled. "As people the Russians aren't bad. Ivan is a good fellow. But the Communist party, the *apparat*, will never change. Poland," he went on, "is finished for a long time. Our history proves this. When Germany and Russia fought each other in the first war we seized the opportunity to snatch back our independence. It won't happen again. Russia is too strong. They are threatening America itself. Look at the map, at Kamchatka and Nicaragua."

Pan Poinc came in and we changed the subject. He was flattered when I addressed him as *dowodca* (commandant). He told me of his war experiences. As a youth of sixteen the Germans had deported him to work in a coal mine in the Ruhr. "Later, when the RAF came over, we used to stand outside cheering in spite of the bombs. But tell me," he asked, "what has happened to the 'English gentleman'? We had some Australians in the camp last year. Hooligans! They were drunk and annoyed the women."

We didn't pursue the subject. An Australian hooligan beating up bars on the Vistula was not a type I had met. But he might be a more interesting companion than a choir master.

Andrzej promised to help me with petrol and other small services. He seemed to be a good fellow. I was not so sure about Pan Poinc.

In the morning I walked to the city centre (*Centrum*), through humdrum streets of apartment blocks and patches of waste ground, to their junction with al. Jerozolimskie, Warsaw's Main Street. I had no town plan but steered for the tall spire of the Palace of Culture and Sciences, Stalin's unsolicited gift to the Polish nation, which towers into a murky

sky. When I drew near I was appalled at the building's enormous size and bulk. It dwarfs everything in sight. The great
steeple has no function, it hasn't even a clock. The balustrades
are cluttered with strange stone shapes that look like turbanned
heads or figures of Druids. The rows of windows reminded me
of cells. Round the base are crude statues of labour heroes.

This was a piece of Moscow, an Asiatic intrusion, deliberately intended to stamp the image of Soviet might on the heart
of Warsaw.[1] The surrounding buildings that I remembered had
been swept away, leaving an enormous Soviet-type open square
(Plac Defilad) where a gritty wind was blowing past small fruit
and vegetable stalls. The square seemed designed by military
men to provide a splendid field of fire for government troops
threatened by a turbulent mob.

Opposite the square, on a pre-war building, I noticed the
name of the British Council. I went up the narrow stairs to the
office and library. The opening hours are short (from twelve to
six) and although I had arrived early I was admitted to the
reading room. It had a copy of the *New Statesman*, as I had
suspected, but it had the *Spectator* too – for which I thought
the librarian deserved a small cheer.

Lower down al. Jerozolimskie I turned into a busy self-
service restaurant (Praha). It had long food counters, rows of
greasy wooden tables and customers balancing dollops of food
on trays as they looked for a spare stool. A woman assistant was
frying *platki* (potato pancakes) on a hot-plate. We watched
impatiently as they slowly turned brown and I ordered four (the
usual helping). The restaurant was warm, smelly and cheap,
and I saw that tramps used it, waiting to snatch left-overs from
plates.

MEMORIES

Now that I had a base I decided to spend the first days walking
through the city, talking to people in cafés and in the street,
wandering into churches and museums and sitting on a bench

[1] The Tsar had pre-empted Stalin's gesture when he erected a huge
Orthodox cathedral in Warsaw's centre as a sign of Muscovy's presence –
the Poles pulled it down after the first world war.

in the pale sun. It wasn't long before I felt part of the crowd –
that patient, nondescript Warsaw crowd in dingy clothes who
peered into shops, joined queues, grumbled (it struck me how
rarely people smiled or laughed), sucked ice-cream cones on the
pavement and ate apples at bus stops. These were ordinary,
well behaved citizens with thick, hard bodies. They bought
flowers. They took their children to toy shops. They lined up at
kiosks to buy coarse cigarettes and threw them away half-
smoked. They often stepped into a church to look at the altar
and pray. The wild-haired drunkard with dragging feet and
sunken head always had a companion to grip his arm and steer
him home. I could see that they detested queueing. But queueing was part of the system and they had got used to it – a queue
outside a fish stall or a shoe shop drew people like a magnet.
The big department stores (the Centrum) opposite the Palace
of Culture were thronged. And although the Poles are an unruly
race they waited obediently for the traffic lights to change,
knowing that the police were watching and would fine them on
the spot if they tried crossing against the red ampule.

How self-absorbed everyone looked. Not so much morose as
switched off, wrapped up in private thoughts. The gaiety of
pre-war Warsaw had gone. No elegant cavalry officers up for a
riotous week-end from some provincial garrison bowling past
the Lazienki Gardens in horse-drawn cabs. No military cloaks
or four-cornered hats, no furred Jewesses with splendid bosoms,
no Paris fashions. No night life with tempting lights and gypsy
music. Buildings were grey, the sky was grey, people were grey.
Fantasy or ostentation in dress or style was not in place.

I had so much to see in Warsaw that I knew I would need
many days to take the edge off my curiosity. So I decided to do
my exploring on foot and use the tram and bus for longer
distances. Driving my van would have made me too conspicuous. The police would spot its foreign number plate. They
would harass me for my papers, note the rust and worn tyres.
Every time I parked it in an unattended place it might be
broken into.

In any case the articulated buses (made in Hungary) and
trams (coupled together in three sections, like small trains) run
an excellent service till late at night and are very cheap. One
buys a bunch of tickets at a kiosk and for three zlotys (a penny)

one can ride from one end of Warsaw to the other. There are no ticket collectors. The passenger simply punches his slip of paper (*bilet*) in a machine near the window. But rush hours must be avoided. The service is then so overloaded that passengers have to fight for a place. Young wives with children often lift their prams on to the buses – which are roomier than trams – and are treated with courtesy even by drunks. Trams (not buses) are frequently driven by women. Drivers are skilful and are allowed to smoke.

Not everyone pays for his ride. I never saw any ticket control. But Simon, an English lecturer whom I met, warned me against trying to cheat. "I once got caught without a ticket by a chap with a beard who looked like a hippie. He flashed his badge and made me pay up: 600 zlotys on the spot. I didn't want to make a scene."

"Six hundred zlotys? Enough to cover 200 free rides! – and a profitable arrangement for the transport services if they can trap the unwary."

HOZA STREET

One of my first missions was to go to my old address at 4 Hoza Street where I had lived in the early months of 1939. Had it survived the war? The apartment had been on the second floor of a grey·19th-century building protected by a great iron-studded gate. The yard was shabby and sunless, honeycombed by basement cellars where small craftsmen – cobblers, tailors, hat makers – lived like troglodytes. My landlady was Pani Petrovna, a grey-haired widow in her sixties, short-tempered and poorly off but kind. She had lived in Moscow before the Bolsheviks drove her out and used to talk Russian with me. My room had a large brass bed, solid furniture covered with cushions, heavy curtains, faded pieces of finery and an ikon. It was poorly lit and stuffy. Over the tiled stove hung a picture of the Tsar's Cossack horsemen whirling their sabres at a crowd of fleeing people in a square.

Pani Petrovna never failed to cook me a substantial lunch: thick soup, dumplings, meat and cabbage (or swedes), and *kompot*. In those days I was always in a hurry. In addition to my classes at the Anglo-Polish School in Mokotowska street I taught private pupils and had to race round Warsaw visiting them in their homes. My room had a small iron balcony which let in the morning sun. From here I used to watch the busy life of the street: flower sellers, hawkers, drunken quarrels, cabs with priests, Jews, military officers and merchants clopping past, the slim graceful bodies of girls.

Pani Petrovna had one other lodger. He was a bad hat and I never saw him. Every Friday she used to bang on his door, which he kept locked, shouting at him to come out and pay the rent. He was several weeks behind with payments, and the landlady would get very angry. *"Lajdak,"* she cried, *"bandyta, cham!* Open up! Pay me my money!" She had a rich vocabulary of names for him: *Lobuz, zlodzei, frajer, hochstapler!* which meant "thief" and "rascal". She never cornered him. One day he disappeared.

There was an air of excitement in Warsaw in those days. Though the British press right up to the day Hitler marched into Prague on 15 March had been playing down the omens of war – Hitler, it suggested, had sown his wild oats and would settle down into an acceptable statesman and the front page of the *Daily Express* still flaunted its famous banner "There will be no war" – the Poles had no doubt that hostilities would soon break out with a German attack on their frontiers. The prospect stimulated rather than depressed them. They looked to their cavalry and to their native courage for great and gallant feats and believed the army could hold up the first Nazi onslaught until the Allies (Britain and France) had gained time to launch a counter-offensive. The Poles placed great faith in French infantry and artillery and they admired the British navy. With such friends not far away, their cause, it was thought, could not be lost. Black-out exercises and night manoeuvres by Poland's small force of monoplane bomber aircraft added to the tension. Most of the men I knew had been called up. One met them in cafés in uniform being toasted by their friends.

Now, when I went to look for my old address, I found it difficult to recognise the neighbourhood. The old street, as I remembered it, had gone. Most of the buildings were new, the old ones had been patched up and modernised (though many still had bullet-scarred walls), the street was wider, few of the little shops had survived. Of house Number 4 nothing was left.

The space where it stood had been levelled and replaced by a massive tenement block.

I felt a little sad when I saw this. My old self, whom I pictured sprinting with an armful of books out of the big courtyard gate to my next lesson, had left no ghost. Pani Petrovna with her tangled grey hair shouting "*Bandyta!*" outside the lodger's door, and the crabby porter (*dozorca*) and his wife who spied on the girls I brought back after dark and grumbled about my behaviour, had vanished into the rubble.

Towards the end of my nine months' stay in Warsaw I had moved to a bigger room at the lower end of Hoza street, near Plac Trzech Krzyzi. My new landlady was Pani Drabikowa, a smart, clever widow whose husband had been a well-known theatre painter and stage designer. As the war clouds neared – and the Poles noticed that Mars, at that time, was glowing ominously red – she warned me against marrying. "You are too young to take a wife. Wartime is for *kawalery* (bachelors). Better go off and be a soldier." Pani Drabikowa had another lodger, a delightful, toothless man, a painter, whom we called "Gandhi". Gandhi said that England had the best diplomats in the world and never went to war without emerging on the winning side. "So don't worry, my friend. Whatever happens to Poland, Albion will prevail."

Pani Drabikowa's clean, white apartment had vanished too. But an elderly woman who kept a little haberdasher's shop nearby told me that Gandhi ("a good-for-nothing – always broke") had managed to escape to England.

WILD OATS

Everything in this part of Warsaw bounded by Nowy Swiat and Jerozolimskie streets, the Marszalkowska and Mokotowska, its shops and bars, the lime trees, gardens and dingy old houses, held for me its pre-war memories. There had been days when I had earned enough money from my lessons to go to a night club and get fleeced by a stony-hearted "hostess": others when I had to make do with a bowl of *flaki* (tripe), gherkins or stewed mushrooms. Enjoying rude health and too much energy I sometimes disgraced myself. Soon after arriving in Warsaw I had (in the Oxford tradition) hired a cab and seizing the driver's long whip bowled along the street tipping people's hats off with it. No one gave chase. I stood the cabman a large vodka and we parted friends.

In those early days of the Anglo-Polish honeymoon following Chamberlain's guarantee (31 March) that Britain would do "everything possible" to resist an attack by Germany on Poland's independence, British visitors to Poland were spoiled by Polish hospitality and good will and fussed over by the ladies. Waiters gave us priority, policemen shook us by the hand, drinks were free. Beautiful housewives and elegant young secretaries enrolled as pupils at the newly organised Anglo-Polish school run by Mackenzie, a Scot, and his wife. They asked me to read old favourites that they knew in Polish translation: *Lady Windermere's Fan, Pickwick Papers*, Jack London's *The Call of the Wild*. They hadn't heard of Isherwood or Orwell or Joyce and would have been appalled by them.

I was often late for my lessons but in Poland a lack of punctuality has never been a crime. Polish men, however, were jealous of their women. It needed subterfuge and luck to make dates with their ravishing girls. There were moments of unease. Sitting with my partner in a corner of Pod Bukietem bar, with a gypsy musician twanging his violin in my ear, I imagined a Polish *rotmistrz* (cavalry captain), cloaked and spurred, bursting in with a drawn pistol to rescue his *kochanka* and retrieve his honour; or some rich rival with a fur collar and bald head appearing suddenly with a sword-stick.

The three crosses at the Plac Trzech Krzyzi were still guarding the white domed church. I went inside. People were dropping in to sit or kneel and pray. A woman attendant was arranging flowers and candles on the altar table. Under the circular roof banners were hanging, some with the word Solidarnosc. One showed the Polish national eagle still wearing its royal crown. The church had been repaired after war damage: photographs of its ruined state in 1945 were displayed in the porch. But recent gilt and paintwork had given the church a strangely new look. The nave was cold and draughty, my boots echoed loudly on the stone floor, the effect of the banners was too secular. I felt that I was in a museum and didn't stay long.

Round the corner I turned into Jerozolimskie street and

suddenly remembered that it was somewhere here, in a small eating house, that I had once stumbled on a party of twelve old Jews sitting like ghosts at a funeral. They had gaunt white faces, beards and great noses, and wore skull caps.

When I entered the parlour they had turned their lugubrious black eyes on me like sorcerers. Who was I? Some trouble-maker, a ruffian, a *ghiaour*? Feeling friendly I ordered a tray of hard-boiled eggs with a twist of salt. The crones watched in wonder. But when I passed round the eggs long grey fingers shot out and grabbed the lot. They were swallowed in a flash. When they learned that I was English some of the Jews grunted in a friendly way. One shook me by the hand. "The English (*Anglicy*) aren't bad," he said.

The eating-house has now gone – cooperative shops occupy the site; and the old patriarchs, as André Schwarz-Bart might have said, had no doubt been shot, starved or suffocated, their ashes strewn by the charnel wind that blew over Oswiecim's chimneys. As I opened the door to leave something wet and nasty struck me on the head. It was pigeon dung. A man was grinning at me. "Being bombed by a pigeon," he said, "is lucky."

CHOPIN'S MONUMENT

I have had another encounter with the past. This time a visit to Chopin's monument in Lazienki Gardens. In the summer before the war I often sat at the edge of the pond where the monument stood and read a book in the sun. There was no official English library in Warsaw at that time. The British Council had only a nominal representative (the versatile and loveable Egerton Sykes) and I had to make the most of what I could find: Dyboski's *History of Poland*, Pilsudski's *Memoirs* and a popular novel with the alluring title *Kochankowie Wielkiej Niedzwiedzicy* (Lovers of the Great Bear) which related the adventures of a band of Polish smugglers.

It was Sunday and about 300 people were sitting round Chopin's monument listening to an open air piano recital of his music. The music seemed to have cast a spell on them. They sat in silence. No one coughed. No one smoked. Many had their eyes closed. The May sun was reddening the winter pallor of their faces and there was a sort of piety in them – in the fine bone-structure and width of cheek-bones, the clear, sharp eyes of the women and their small curled mouths. The Poles were absorbed in the music, savouring every note, dreaming.

The bronze figure of Chopin sits under a sculpted willow tree, his head half turned as though listening to the wind. The branches weep. The profile is handsome and sensitive, his eyes are shut as he hears the music of the leaves.

The original statue was dismantled by Germans and has been restored. In my recollection it had a bright coppery sheen. "When I was sitting here in 1939," I remarked to a man next to me, "the willow leaves shone like copper. The colour has changed." The man looked offended. How could a foreigner know anything about Chopin?

"The patina has been affected by weathering," he replied.

Two young women came and sat beside me, eating cherries out of a paper bag. "I used to sit on this bench before the war," I told them. They looked at me as though I were an antique. I asked them about the Nazis' destruction of Polish memorials in Warsaw, including the figure of Chopin. "Why Chopin?"

"The Germans feared Chopin," they said. "His music was a symbol of Polish patriotism. They hated it. It was the sound of the Polish heart."

I walked back past the ducks. Rooks were snatching bread scraps from the pigeons, the lime trees were bursting into leaf, the chill day wind had dropped and it was getting warmer. Soon people would be discarding their padded jackets. The Botanical Gardens had opened. At a side gate a man with a pair of scales was inviting customers to weigh themselves. In the park next to Gromada camp I passed some girls with bare arms. Joggers were pounding along the gravel paths. In a fortnight it would be time for T-shirts and sandals.

3
ENCOUNTERS

STEFAN

Three cars with caravan trailers have joined me in the camp and
school parties have begun to arrive from as far as Gdansk and
Katowice. One of the caravan owners is a podgy Finn with a
beard like Father Christmas. He sits all day in his curtained box
with a TV set while his wife cooks. The school children arrive
in groups of fifty with two or three teachers. They sleep in the
chalets, eat a hot meal, and are out all day touring the Old
City and Market (Stary Rynek), the museums, churches and
national memorials. They are lively and noisy yet obey their
teachers, who are mostly dumpy middle-aged women. My van
with its GB number plate and old-fashioned shape has caught
their eye. They seem to admire it despite the rust stains and
torn seats and watch me as I wash my shirt in a bucket.

This morning a fifteen-year-old boy who had come with a bus
party from Lublin put his head through the door and said,
"When I have holidays can you take me with you?"

Looking inside my van with a boy's eyes it occurs to me that
with its jumble of objects it must look to him like a robber's
cave. The kettle and enamel mug, the torch, water can, radio, a
towel, dictionary, shorts, books and maps – at a glance, an
enticing mess to a young boy with a sense of adventure. Perhaps
that's why I enjoy the roving life and have no right to grumble.
My discomforts are of my own choosing and should be relished.

Last night a building engineer came and sat in my van.
Stefan was a tall thin man of about thirty with a tired pale face,
mousy hair, blue, lined eyes and a long nose – one of those Poles
who looks like a ravaged Prussian. He owned his own car (a
Golf) and was staying in a chalet for a few nights while the

plumbers and decorators finished work on his new flat. "It stinks so much of turpentine that I can't sleep."

Stefan had party connections and was chary of talking politics with me. But he was not a Communist. "The Russians," he said flatly, "will never let Poland go. The Soviet Union is in fact determined to expand. When the Russians talk of peace they are deceiving us."

He asked me for my impressions of Warsaw after my long absence. "The Palace of Culture is a monstrosity," I said. "Like an Asian fortress or mausoleum. Sinister."

"You are right," he agreed. "The building is meant for all to wonder at as the stamp (*znak*) of Soviet power in Poland. Like this!" He banged his fist hard on my table like an official pressing a rubber stamp. "The palace was Stalin's gift. We didn't ask for it."

He longed to travel abroad. The Germans would give him a visa without trouble but he would need permission from his superiors, and foreign currency. Many Poles would prefer to visit Italy, he explained, but that was even more complicated. West Germany was the country where Poles could most easily make money and many Poles had friends or relations living there.

In the morning Stefan took me to his flat. He drove fast, skidding round corners and punishing the tyres.

The flat was high up in a tower block and was tiny. It had a small fridge and laundry machine and was crammed with articles waiting to be stowed away in cupboards, under the beds or on the narrow balcony. Workmen were polishing the parquet floor. They had left paint stains and the doors didn't fit (Polish doors, even in the best hotels, never do).

"Nothing here is properly finished," Stefan grumbled. "Poles are poor workmen. The plumbing is sure to break down. Warsaw has been so short of housing that everything has had to be built in a rush."

He had acquired the flat through a deal, paying a deposit and some rent on his first apartment, then swapping it for the present one, which was bigger and more expensive. Such transactions, he admitted, were illegal but it was the best way if one wanted to better one's accommodation. Stefan was married but without children. Looking at his gear, the flimsy new furniture and hastily plastered walls, I thought that though his little domestic world was cramped and improvised he was decently provided for. Oddly enough, it was the pigeons he complained of. They fouled his balcony and disturbed him with their stupid gurgling. But some tenants actually encouraged them!

If this was an example of Socialist housing it was not too bad. A lift operated between the fourth and top floors. The site was sandy and rutted but there was a bus stop and a few shops. TV aerials hung from most windows. I couldn't myself have lived in such a dormitory prison among the breathing and noise of hundreds of other people. But as Stefan pointed out, Poles have an irresistible urge to move to towns and, if they can afford the higher rents, to live in the city centre. "Who wants to spend his life in mud and dust among country bumpkins with poor light and transport and the boredom of black winter nights?" he asked. I could see his point. A lodging, however cramped, with heat, light and plumbing that is near to a place of work and to a warm office, wins votes. Where housing is hard to come by the aesthetics don't matter.

I went back to the camp by bus, passing the Soviet war cemetery and getting out at the betting shop. Men were sitting outside holding their betting slips. They seemed to be mainly pensioners. When they lose they tear up the slip, throw it on the ground, swear, and go quietly home.

THE BRITISH COUNCIL

Feeling like a museum piece I walked up the narrow stairs past the jeweller's workshop to visit Barnett, the British Council representative in Warsaw. We found immediately that we had something in common. He had lived in Turkey for several years and knew about the book I had written on my journeys in eastern Anatolia. He asked me to dinner.

Jeremy Barnett lives in a small house with his family, has some good Turkish carpets and the use of two cars (his own Volvo and an office vehicle). He admires the Turks – "they don't flap". We agreed that it is a pity Turkey has always had a bad press in Britain. His wife, knowing that I can't buy meat, had roasted a large piece of beef.

Barnett finds the Poles very courteous but "great time-wasters. They do two hours work in a seven-hour day, leave jobs half done and get bored when there's no quick reward." He is sceptical about their much praised religious fervour. "It's partly bluff. They're not as devout as they are made out to be be. They use the Church as a political weapon."

He thought that Lady Donaldson's recent history of the British Council in celebration of its first fifty years of work was dull – too much like a civil service report. I haven't read her book but an indiscreet chronicler could have compiled a riveting and hilarious account of those mendicant professors who cavorted round the Balkans and Egypt during and after the war. They were an unusual gallery of eccentrics – presumably I was one myself – and I knew many of them and their friends. Durrell was one: a small chunky man with a big head and a beautiful blonde wife, living on shepherd's pie and sweet potatoes in a Gezira boarding house. Flux Dundas was another, a good-natured, failed schoolmaster with a terrible stutter who became head of the British Institute in Cairo. He ended as British vice-consul in Munich, much married and with a new spouse. Olivia Manning (Bucharest and Jerusalem) was already devoted to a writing career,[1] collecting acid observations while her husband Reggie Smith (the bumbling "Guy" of her *Balkan Trilogy*) downed beer and plum brandy and preached a half-baked sort of Communism – he supported the Soviet invasion of Finland! Geoffrey Household (who wrote the best selling novel *Rogue Male*) I remember because he made so much noise one night splashing about in a lodging-house bath tub with a gipsy girl from a Bucharest bar that I had to thump the wall. Hugh Seton-Watson, in a fur hat, was our sage and linguist. Tuckley (Cairo) had the piano, and there was "Tommy"

---

[1] In Bucharest Olivia was busy writing her first book (a life of David Livingstone) and would lock her door when Reggie brought back noisy guests. One of her remarks has stayed in my memory. "My husband," she said, "is far too precious to throw his life away in a silly war. War is for hearties!" British Council teachers were certainly not fire-eaters. In any case they could plead that they were in exempt occupations.

Thomson who decided that the British Council was not the right place to use as a bolt-hole in time of war and left Roumania with me to join the Army in Egypt. As the years went by the British Council colleagues who stayed behind deteriorated into privileged refugees moving from one sanctuary to another, and would have landed up in India with their lecture notes on the British way of life if the 8th Army had not turned back Rommel's Afrika Korps at el Alamein.

The British Council, though it had a thriving institute in Bucharest, had been slow in establishing itself in Poland before the war. Its nominal link in Warsaw was Egerton Sykes, appointed in 1938. A Polish linguist and a man of vibrant social charm he combined commerce with his cultural life, and ran an English newspaper (*Warsaw Weekly*) with an advertisement for a brand of bicycle saddles for which he was an agent. One of his hobbies was the enigma of Atlantis: he wrote a standard work on it. I came across him several times during the war when he was doing publicity work for General Anders's army. Egerton Sykes's contribution to the "Anglo-Polish relationship" was one of the greatest merit. One wonders if any record of what he did for this cause was ever kept.

I caught the last bus back to the city centre. A man with an untidy beard, wearing heavy boots and denims, sat next to me. He told me he was a failed student and had become a fireman. He also worked in a tailor's shop. It was raining heavily, streets had emptied and I had a long walk back to the camp. I found two men sheltering in a passage and asked them the way. They were too drunk to speak. When I got back to the camp the big iron gate was locked and I looked with dismay at the spikes. A few yards away was the guard dog's kennel and a notice "*Uwaga, zly pies!* Beware of fierce dog!" However, my old Oxford training helped here. I managed neither to wake the dog nor to tear my trousers, and when I unfolded my damp stretcher bed on the floor of the van I felt I had enjoyed an excellent evening.

OLD CITY

Today I made my first brief visit to the Old City. The historic market place (*Stary Rynek*) and narrow cobbled alleys behind the ancient walls are Warsaw's most famous tourist objective. In 1945 the old market was a mass of rubble. Everything has been patiently restored to the last detail, the painted gables, scrolls and carvings, the vaults, monuments and churches copied and rebuilt so faithfully, that every Pole, regardless of his politics, feels that their resurrection has been one of his country's proudest achievements.

The tourist season had not yet begun and the two sightseers' cabs stood idle, the horses' muzzles sunk in their nose-bags, the drivers, in thick caps and jerseys, dozing under rugs. Outside the open-air café a street photographer with a monkey and a barrel-organ was waiting for customers. Local artists had propped their pictures against the walls, homely scenes of Polish villages and snow-bound woods and fields. Young men who looked like students were carving and chipping away at wooden figures of peasant dancers. The souvenir shops sold figures of Jesus and the saints, stacks of crucifixes and native embroidery.

The trade in religious trinkets has of course a murky side. But there was nothing here to compare with the outrageous commercialism and vulgarity of souvenir shops trading in the precincts of the Vatican.

I went into the local history museum to see an hour-long documentary film of the Warsaw uprising of 1944, the German reprisals that followed, the deliberate demolition of vast acres of buildings and their painful restoration. The film was like watching an earthquake: walls collapsing into streets, buildings toppling in avalanches of dust, the crumpled shells of churches, fragments of monuments, shocked people shuffling through the rubble with bundles and suitcases.

The methodical destruction of so much history, the calculated attempt to pulverise a nation's soul, strikes one today as almost unbelievable. But this was not wanton German savagery. The Nazis still hoped to win the war. The core of the Reich was intact, Hitler was developing his secret weapons and the hidden enemy had to be rooted out. In this context there was a cruel logic in Nazi sanitary operations to exterminate like rat catchers the underground breeding places, the noxious sewers, of Polish resistance.

Some elderly Polish-Americans watched the film with me. They had not been in Warsaw during the uprising and left the cinema in a state of shock. The rebirth of the capital after that orgy of self-destruction and German revenge struck them as a miracle. Indeed an ignorant stranger would not have known that the Goths had ever been.

As I walk through Warsaw my mind registers odd and unconnected things. Waste, for instance: the amount of bread that is left to go stale (though it is rarely fresh when you buy it) and is thrown away: cigarette stubs only half-smoked on pavements; the fat bottoms and thick legs of policemen; poppy-seed cake sellers, priests in black berets, podgy army officers with briefcases which their wives polish. A drunk man, neatly dressed, in clean shoes, lurches into a puddle. He looks in a puzzled way at his soaking feet, says one word "*Chuj!*" and staggers on. It occurs to me that there are fewer bald heads among the Poles than there used to be. Better food, vitamin tablets, earlier nights? In the elegant Szwajcaria café the cloakroom attendant is eating spoonfuls of gruel from a tin bowl he has secreted under the counter. A few tarts are waiting outside the subway, a gypsy woman smiles at me, holding out a brown hand which glitters with rings.

It takes me half an hour to walk back to the camp. A monument to the Polish air force points the way from Wawelska. I pass under a long avenue of lime trees, turn left at the betting shop, and see my van with its blunt nose half-hidden by a tree. The van has a damp, musty smell. It is time for me to fill my bucket and do my washing.

VICTORY CELEBRATIONS

Victory programmes to mark the fortieth anniversary of the end of the last war have been dogging me for weeks on radio and television. East German television, which I watched in Brunswick, was showing Russian war documentaries while Honecker and his officials addressed peace rallies of East German youth parading under banners. Warsaw and Moscow radios were putting over the same message. Its theme is the heroic soldier-liberator, tow-haired, with iron jaw, emerging out of the steppes of Russia to fight his way through gun-fire, bullets, mud and mines to smash the Fascists and Hitlerites and hoist the flag of victory over the Brandenburger Tor. From Moscow I have been listening to eye-witness accounts of the siege of Lenigrad, of ambushes by Bulgarian partisans, the suicidal courage of Don peasants. Early this morning a Polish war veteran described how he had escaped from a German ship bombed and sunk by a British plane off the Baltic shore. The transport, said the veteran, was crammed with prisoners-of-war, mostly Indians (he called them "Mussulmans"). There were appalling scenes (he said) when the "Mussulmans" panicked and fought each other like animals to save their own skins. The Pole had stumbled ashore at Lübeck and given himself up to a British officer. The officer gave him some rations and a tin of fifty cigarettes and said, "Now get on your way!" The anecdote struck me as true : blunt words and no heroics – though I had reservations about the "panic".

Tomorrow, 9 May, is to be a public holiday: Victory Day.

It was a warm summer day and I was surprised to see that most Poles, instead of flocking to town to see the parade, were staying at home or walking in the parks. I stood among a double row of spectators at the Defilad Plac by the Palace of Culture. The crowd was thin and subdued. There was a rush for ice-cream cones and fizzy drinks but no clamour or enthusiasm. For the families standing there it seemed not an occasion for rejoicing but simply a free government show. The police, however, were present in great numbers, their vehicles parked everywhere with militia sitting in them.

There was a long wait and speech-making before the massed military band started up and the parade began. The assembled units marched past in sections according to arm of service, among them veterans of the Armja Krajowa. I was impressed by the soldiers, notably the paratroops: tough and suntanned with clear eyes and hard bodies. They deserved more than the sporadic clapping of friends and relatives. An infantry unit broke into the goose step for a short distance. Their officer, a tall handsome fellow with a black moustache, had recognised someone in the crowd and ordered his men to make a gesture. For sixty yards they stamped the ground like pneumatic drills.

These were the sort of fighting men the Russians, Poles and Germans can produce in their hundreds of thousands whenever their military machine switches on the human conveyor belt. Such disciplined coordination of mind and muscle, under good leaders, can achieve human miracles. I remember watching Hitler's SS Leibstandarte Guard march through the old town of Nuremburg during the Party rally of 1935. Tall men in black uniforms and pudding-basin helmets, sweat trickling down their faces, smelling of sweat and leather. Those silent striding giants had filled me with awe. They cast a black shadow across the crowds and the little Dürer houses. Along the route military bands were pounding out the Badenweiler march with fife, drum, cymbals and brass as though willing the Volk to join in the march towards that "rosy dawn in the east" where the black soil of the Russian Ukraine was waiting for the new Reich. The Arbeitsdienst formations, in their own way, were equally impressive. Here was Hitler's golden youth, stripped to the waist, brown skinned, torsoes corded with muscle, shouldering burnished spades. As military ballet the parades were splendid. But they reeked of war, and I remember thinking that nothing now could stop the thud of those marching feet.

THE BRITISH COUNCIL

Since writing this chapter I have read Lady Donaldson's *The British Council: The First Fifty Years* (1984). Her brief, quite rightly, is to justify the good work done by the organisation since its inception in the thirties. An entirely different sort of chronicler, a satirical diarist, would be needed, however, to acquaint us with the real-life gyrations of the Council's far-flung network of overseas employees. For me the paradox at the heart of the British Council was that by the time it had been installed to sell British culture abroad as an arm of British diplomacy (without, however, being made to suffer the conventional diplomat's inhibitions), its recruits belonged to a generation of youngish university intellectuals, liberal to leftish, Left/Book Club readers or Kingsley Martin fans, that had already lost its faith in the Establishment and the Empire. Such alienated people found it distasteful to speak up for a "British way of life" – let alone boast about it from a lecturer's desk – whose record was tarnished by slums, mass unemployment, the class system and the Raj. No wonder Lord Beaverbrook hated them; when war broke out they rarely joined the armed services.

One might mention here that both in Warsaw and Prague there were scandals of defection. Lady Donaldson mentions the case of C.G. Bidwell, the Council's representative in Poland, who defected to Russia in May 1949, alleging that the Council was a London agency of political and economic imperialism working against the interests of Poland and the working class. A little later Dr Arna Ride's defection from Prague led to further embarrassment for the Council.[1]

My experience is that British Council visits by VIPs, *savants* and entertainers have little relevance to its real task, which has been to fund libraries, book supplies, scholarships and academic research and to organise language courses. Most of the donkey-work of teaching English under British sponsorship insofar as it has not been taken over by native-born teachers has been done with chalk and blackboard by the unsung ones: ODA and VSO teachers, and British residents paid in local currency.

[1] Polish friends tell me that Bidwell has settled in Poland, where he earns a living as a sheep farmer and writer of text books.

4
FAITHS

In the street, in a shopping queue, in the tram or coming out of church the Pole seems to be preoccupied, uncommunicative, switched off, almost glum. Yet he readily responds to any chance remark I make to him. Older people expecially seem willing to talk – and to grumble. The rentier is not pressed for time, and he probably feels lonely.

In Teatralny square I stopped to look at the monument to the Heroes of Warsaw – the challenging figure of a war-goddess with powerful breasts and a brandished sword, a sort of hell-cat, leaping from a plinth into space. Then I sat in a small public garden outside a tenement block near Grzybowski square and watched a white-haired lady feeding the pigeons with stale bread rolls. Warsaw's large pigeon population is greedy and spoiled – people favour and constantly feed them with scraps. Citizens would feel lonely without the birds. A man in a good suit came and sat beside me. He was in a bad mood. He was having trouble with the police, he said. They had forbidden him to park his car in the yard outside his own apartment (he lived in the housing block behind us). So he had to find another place. "But once my car is out of sight thieves will break into it. Car thieves in Warsaw are the devil. They won't steal a car but they will strip the parts."

I walked across to the Saski (Saxon) Gardens where the seats were occupied by people tilting their faces to the sun. It was siesta time. Some were dozing, women were knitting, children were playing on the grass. Suddenly I heard shouting and looked round. A line of militia vans and trucks had appeared from nowhere and soldiers and police were jumping out of them. "*Uwaga! Uwaga!* Attention! Attention!" a sergeant was

calling through a loud-hailer. The men had already cordoned
off the paths and roads. "Everyone must leave immediately!"

Looking aggrieved and upset the crowd collected its picnic
things and walked away. An old woman who was the last to
leave spoke angrily to the sergeant. "Shame on you!" Perhaps
an official visitor or another parade was expected. Near the
Palace of Culture traffic had been slowed down to allow about
300 young athletes to pass in procession. They wore shorts and
track suits and had banners and a band. "*Nie ladny!*" I heard a
woman say, "*nie zgrabny!* They can't even march properly." It
was true that the young sportsmen were not in step. They
looked utterly bored. Perhaps they had been up all night in
some country bus and had had no breakfast.

On my way home I went into the Church of the Holy Cross
in Nowy Swiat. It was wrecked during the 1944 uprising and
has been expensively rebuilt. Over the entrance is a prominent
figure of Christ holding a tilted cross. A huge Baroque high
altar, above which a white Polish eagle has been placed, dominates the nave like a golden throne. The aisles and chapels
gleam with gilt. The effect of the burnished metal is sumptuous. Urns contain the heart of Chopin and of Reymont, who
won the Nobel prize for literature with his novel *Chlopi*
(1924). Tombstones and epitaphs commemorate the famous:
the writers Prus, Kraszewski and Slowacki, and General
Sikorski. The pews are polished, the stone floor spotless. The
figure holding out the cross over the entrance seems to beckon
passers-by: a mendicant friar, stained with grime, half in
shadow. Before the war I had passed the church a hundred
times but rarely stepped inside. The Roman ambience was too
strong for me. If, however, you have faith, this is the place
among the flaming candles and splendour to brood on Polish
history and its unfinished sadness and to take another draught
of what jeering Marx dubbed the "opiate of the people".

At the bus stop outside the central railway station an elderly
man came up and said, "Let me sit down – I'm an old fellow
(*starik*)." He had just come out of church.

"I should give up kneeling at altars," I said jokingly, pointing
to his arthritic legs.

He started to grumble. "If you have enough to eat," he said,
"life is sweet. But if you're hungry this bugger complains (he

slapped his belly). The belly is never satisfied. It always asks for more."

"Like a Russian."

"The Russian is a beast," he said with sudden fury, "a wild animal, a barbarian." He spat and clambered on the next bus.

The school children who stay at the camp for a day or two brighten the place up. Yesterday fifty deaf and dumb youngsters arrived by bus. They are cheerful, athletic, skip and chase each other and play football, and have lively faces that light up as they mime and gesticulate. The boys wear jeans. Some of the girls are pretty and have boy friends. The Deaf and Dumb institute is in Plac Trzech Krzyzi. I often see the inmates strolling in town. They have enough money for a meal and a glass of tea at the Praha restaurant.

A schoolboy has been chatting with me at the camp. He comes from Szczecin (Stettin). I told him I had visited Stettin and Stralsund (now in East Germany) before the war. They were beautiful old Baltic ports with fairy-tale buildings from the world of Grimm and Eichendorff, and had a northern history, entirely German.

"The Germans," said the boy, "have all gone from Szczecin. Only Poles live there now." His parents came from the eastern border provinces now absorbed in the Soviet Union. They were homesick. "But I was born in Szczecin and I am proud of it."

On Sunday morning I listened to a church service broadcast by Warsaw radio. The priest was using the slightly archaic Polish of the Scriptures. His message was simple. Christ would forgive and Matka Boska, the Mother of God, would show compassion. Life on earth is brief. But the Christian faith is for ever and we (in Poland) are its shield.

Here again was the Polish problem stated by a Roman priest. He confronted us with the sad, dusky Goddess of Czestochowa and with Poland's vision of herself as the last outpost of Christendom in Europe. To the east – Soviet atheism. To the west, in the Democratic Republic of East Germany, a hybrid form of the true faith, a church that is largely Evangelical strangled by Marxism.

Later I went to communion service in a large red-brick church near the camp in al. Grojecka. The church was fitted with loudspeakers and crammed to the doors. Woman of all

ages, some with prams, outnumbered the men. The singing and
responses, led by a choir, were beautiful. I stood throughout,
leaning sometimes against a pillar. Constant kneeling on a hard
stone floor is not for me. When I see the old folk – thin, stumpy,
bent, obese – bowing and kneeling for over an hour (Polish
services are long) I wonder at their toughness.

After the service the priest went round the pews offering a
fragment of consecrated wafer to those who wished it. When I
went out into the street I felt that I had been in another world:
disembodied among the candles, the prayers and the watching
saints.

Either one whole-heartedly accepts these demonstrations of
faith by a devoted congregation in a suburban Polish church: or
one rejects them as a brand of Polish folklore presided over by a
sorcerer in vestments. Or should one cynically dismiss them as
a symbolic gesture of defiance by a naturally unruly people
against government coercion and interference in their lives?
The fact remains that Warsaw policemen, security agents and
leading party officials, never set foot in a church: but the mass
of decent Poles regularly do.

Later, on my radio, I listened to a service from the United
Evangelical church in Warsaw. This was a different present-
ation of religion. The pastor spoke in homely terms of gratitude, forgiveness and reconciliation. He was like a schoolmaster.
"Should a man thank the Creator for giving him an ugly crooked
nose?" he asked. "Yes. For God in His wisdom has also given
him the greatest gift of all – the gift of life and of the sun to
ripen his bread."

SYNAGOGUE

Warsaw citizens are rarely at a loss when I ask them for street
directions. But I had to stop half-a-dozen people before I found
one who could tell me where the Jewish synagogue was. It
turned out to be a plain, drab building near Grzybowski square,
tucked away behind some tall tenement blocks where television
aerials hung over balconies.

I approached the synagogue with a slightly uneasy conscience,
a feeling of Gentile guilt. For I was one of a generation that had
been alive when Nazi butchers slaughtered a whole culture and

people and we had done nothing, or very little, to prevent it happening. The present synagogue was put up after the war to replace its predecessor in Dzerzhinsky square which is now the site of a huge high-rise tower block. By a strange irony the new tower block remains unoccupied, a conspicuous white elephant. I had heard rumours that the Jews had lodged a successful objection to the new block because it desecrates a holy site. This is rubbish. Engineers have condemned it as structurally unsafe.

A notice on the synagogue wall indicates that the building is a protected monument (*objekt zabity*). The notice was partly hidden by a message scrawled in chalk and partly erased: "The Jews should clear out!"

A few Jews were sunning themselves on a low wall. One of them joined me when I sat under a tree. He was a small brown-faced man in his late sixties with a hooked nose and upturned nostril slits like a bird.

"You are English? Protestant? Good, Protestants are good people." (Catholics, who accuse the Jews of killing Christ and who have tolerated pogroms, are presumably not.) He took out his wallet and spread out five certificates. They were his records of army service, one in Russian.

"I fought in the siege of Leningrad," he said. "I marched from Leningrad all the way to Berlin and I was wounded. Look at my hands." He showed me his two small hands; they were stiff and crooked, the fingers bent like claws.

I congratulated him, though I am wary of such anecdotes, and he looked so small and frail that I could hardly believe he had slogged all that way from Leningrad via Lenino, Warsaw and Frankfurt-an-der-Oder to the *Siegesallee* in Berlin. When I told him I was travelling alone in a camping van he was astonished. "You are taking a risk, and you are not young."

He told me that the Jewish community in Warsaw was very small – about 500, though the number fluctuated as visitors came and went. The average attendance at the synagogue was thirty. He lived alone, in a small room with only a few sticks of furniture. He was a bright, cheerful man and I liked talking to him. But he didn't intend to let me go without asking a favour. He wanted dollars, "just a few, to help me".

As the synagogue was closed I walked round the corner to the National Theatre. I used to know it well but it had been entirely rebuilt and today faces a big windy square. It was here, at the theatre door, in the late summer of 1939, that I used to wait for Wanda after she had finished her show. She was a regular member of the cast, small, dark and vivacious, a friend of artists and writers, her late father a famous poet.[1] Standing in the night in the shadowy street with cabs clopping past I had thought Warsaw an exotic and exciting place, far from my humdrum Saxon world, alive with strange cries and curious sounding words, with priests and men in fur hats and women with tiny feet. The future had stretched out unknown, infinite, adventurous. Poland was surrounded by enemies, which gave a dangerous edge to life and brought people together. The cabman taught me how to swear. The night watchman, the street cats, the watchmaker in the yard were my friends.

One could look back now and try and count the cost. Warsaw, not long ago a ruined city violated by its own hand as it struggled to free itself from Nazi occupation, has risen again in imitation of its past. A new population of peasants has come to town, setting up in business and trade, as officials, shopkeepers and clerks, manning the police force and security services and the army garrisons. But they are stuck with a regime that censors, mistrusts and watches its citizens, gripping them round the neck. No wonder there is so little laughter and animation in the streets, and the nights are dead, and the Pole feels he is beleaguered in his own land.

[1] Boleslaw Lesmian died in 1937 and I didn't meet him. While Wanda accompanied me to Bucharest and Cairo on the outbreak of war, her mother and sister stayed in Warsaw until the Germans sent them as factory workers to Mauthausen. When fighting was over the Polish Red Cross moved them to Porto San Giorgio in Italy, where I traced them in a refugee centre. They left for London and then settled in Buenos Aires. Wanda herself fell ill with pulmonary tuberculosis in Cairo. With the help of the army medical corps I arranged to evacuate her by hospital ship and train for a protracted cure at Dr Wolff's sanatorium in Davos. During his lifetime Boleslaw Lesmian (who was brought up in Kiev and had Jewish blood) was neglected and abused by critics as *avant garde* and an exponent of "decadent symbolism". After the political thaw of 1956 Poland rehabilitated him as one of her greatest poets and streets are named after him. See Maria Mazurowa's memoir *Wspomnienia o Boleslawie Lesmianie*, Lublin 1966.

PROFESSOR NIELUBOWICZ

Before I left for Poland Edward Lowbury, a medical professor of Birmingham university, and also a poet, had given me the address of a Polish colleague whom he had met while doing research work in a Warsaw hospital. I was glad of the introduction as I knew no one at all in Poland. When I telephoned Professor Nielubowicz at the university hospital I learned that he was the Rector himself and a very distinguished person. He sounded puzzled. "You are a traveller and writer? Not a medical man? This is unexpected. But I will meet you."

The professor had a chauffeur-driven car and took me to luncheon at a hotel. I was not at my best. I was wearing two coats – it was a very cold day – and in the presence of this eminent surgeon I felt like a charlatan.

Professor Nielubowicz had a striking appearance. He was quite bald, with a short powerful neck, white face, piercing black eyes with very clear whites, pitch-black eyebrows and an immaculate set of dentures. He reminded me of Boris Karloff. He was very solemn. We spoke English.

"I have never talked to a literary man before," he said. "My field of interest is surgery. I am a specialist. Are you," he asked, "a professional writer?"

"No – writing is my hobby."

"I have no hobbies. I meet only medical colleagues."

He ordered steak and beer. "This meal (*obiad*) is our dinner," he explained. "In Poland we don't eat lunch like the English." He looked at his watch. "I must be back at the hospital at 3.30. I have a kidney operation to perform."

He was astonished when I told him that Professor Lowbury wrote poems. "I've never heard of a medical specialist who was a man of letters – let alone a poet."

"What about Chekov?"

"General practitioners are different."

The professor began to thaw and asked me about Africa. "I have seen only one African patient. It was in Cairo. The patient was rather drunk and was behaving irresponsibly. The Egyptian doctor slapped him hard in the face and the man sobered up immediately. I thought that an unusual thing to do but it worked."

Professor Nielubowicz planned to retire in two years' time and would live in a flat. "Poles are not accustomed to buying their own houses. Too expensive."

He laughed when I told him how Captain Emil Mentel, the former Polish cavalry officer on whose farm I had stayed in Rhodesia, had opened a bottle of vodka and got drunk when he heard that a Pole had been elected Pope. Captain Mentel had also got drunk when two Polish women climbed a terrifying Himalayan peak, breaking a record. But he had shown no interest when I told him one day that the Warsaw-born novelist Isaac Singer had won the Nobel prize for literature. "Singer," he said, "is not a Pole. He is a Jew."

The bill was rather steep (550 zlotys each) – "but not *fatalny* (it won't kill me)" I heard the professor say in Polish to the waiter. I gave him a copy of Lowbury's collected verse. "If ever you are in need," he said, "come to me." There was no doubt that the professor was a nice man and had treated me with more consideration that I deserved. I walked back under the lime trees. Magpies were flying over the camp, dipping and straightening as though they were skimming hurdles.

BRITISH EMBASSY

I have been to the British Embassy to sign the visitors' book. The Embassy is one of a row of fine villas on the al. Ujazdowski facing Lazienki Gardens. The entrance was at the back and I followed a British wife with a shopping bag but found I had come to the wrong door. There was a notice "British personnel only" and I felt a stab of envy when I saw the treasure stacked inside: cartons of whisky and Danish lager, All-Bran, butter, cheese, tinned ham, Marmite and shampoos. The warm breath of caring Britian had reached this outpost on the Vistula but it was only for the few.

The receptionist, a Londoner, was dealing with a Norwegian who wanted to buy a car – the Embassy staff, I gathered, sometimes had cars for sale. I asked him if he followed the football. "No," he said crossly, "we don't get many facilities here." A chimney sweep came in with his long brushes and was shooed away. "In Poland," I said to the receptionist, "chimney sweeps and hunchbacks bring good luck. They are invited to weddings."

Stoneman, the Information Officer, took me to meet the Ambassador. Mr John Morgan had served in China and Russia and was relaxed and informal. I apologised for being scruffy. "I live in a caravan."

"You're not scruffy at all," he said nicely. "What brings you to Poland?"

"Nostalgia. I was in Poland when war broke out and I have always wanted to come back and complete the circle."

I explained that I hoped to write a book but that the mental adjustment from my simple life in Africa to the complex politics of eastern Europe would be difficult. "It needs an intellectual not a traveller's approach to understand them."

When I left the Ambassador closed his remarks with a neat saying. "The Poles are interested in only three things. The Polish past. The Polish present. And the Polish future." I was invited to luncheon in two days' time.

A strange Pole in his twenties and his girlfriend called at my van in the evening with a bottle of Jugoslav wine. He opened it by thumping the bottom with his fist. They came quickly to the point. They wanted a favour.

The girl, it appeared, owned a large consignment of apricots ripening in the south of Poland. They intended to sell them in Gdansk, where prices were high, and use the money to buy a Mercedes car in Hamburg. To get his travel passport the man needed a sponsor. Would I go to a lawyer they knew and vouch that I had invited him to stay with me in Germany? "Any address will do. You simply sign the declaration, the lawyer pockets his fee, the Polish authorities will give me a passport and the Germans – who never refuse – issue a visa. Will you help?"

I wasn't very keen on the idea. It seemed facile and fishy. I told my visitors I would think the matter over.

More visitors have been arriving at the camp: two Dutchmen who sleep in a little toad-shaped tent: a Polish family from Katowice in a Mercedes caravan – I can see its television screen flickering after dark; eager schoolboys who dash straight from their smoky Diesel buses to the camp restaurant as though famished. The poplar trees have put on leaves, the limes and willows are green, the damp is drying out from my van. Mr Poinc has told me again how he used to stand outside cheering when the RAF dropped bombs in the neighbourhood of his labour camp in the Ruhr. But he can't forgive the Allies' "treachery" at Yalta. "Churchill was a brave and gallant old man," says Mr Poinc. "But he was a child when it came to understanding European politics."

With the increase of visitors the camp toilets are so smeared as to be (for me) unuseable, and the old cleaning women with faces like wrinkled winter apples are constantly grumbling at the mess. Field hygiene, I recall, was a sacred cow in the British Army when conditions permitted. There were thunder-boxes looked after by Indian sweepers with twig brooms: small private chapels screened by hessian for officers; trenches for the men, lime and creosote issues, fly swats, latrine buckets. Polish soldiers never bothered with all this. Sanitary duties were a shameful chore, to be left to others or not done at all. In Gromada camp the pipes are blocked and there is a smell of sewage. But this was not a subject for Polish gentlemen to discuss.

At night the camp is quiet except for a few bursts of pop music from the nearby medical students' hostel and some drunken cries when the bar empties by the betting shop. The camp is in fact a staid place (though Mr Poinc warns me it will liven up when the gypsies arrive). Sometimes a police car or ambulance flies past with sirens howling. But no bats squeak in the cherry trees, no jackals howl as they stalk poultry. It is pleasant to lie on the grass and watch athletes tearing round the running track beyond the fence. I look forward to seeing a Polish rugger match.

The British Ambassador's residence is in Bagatela. His luncheon party was small and informal. I was wearing my black plastic boots bought in Stratford. Lady Reddaway, widow of a former British Ambassador to Poland, and Rod Haden, an English teacher of linguistics at the university, were among the guests. The controversy over the siting of General Sikorski's grave was discussed. The Polish government is anxious for the general's remains to be transferred to Poland but the Poles in England flatly refuse to allow this.

I was asked to describe how I made my way from Poland when war broke out – I had walked over a Dniestr footbridge into Roumania – and I recounted the Polish frontier policeman's last words as he stamped my passport. "Come back to Poland, Panie Profesorze, in a bomber". Alas, I had betrayed his trust. I had come back, but forty years too late, in a clapped-out old van.

I mentioned how in those sanguine days after the fall of Monte Cassino and capture of Rome (1944) my old Polish batman, an illiterate peasant from Grodno, had said to me, "Panie Kapitanie, when we march back to Poland with flags flying I will give you a plot of land." His fantasy had turned into a nightmare. Grodno had been clawed back into the great Russian maw and the Yalta agreement was to degrade Anders's soldiers into alien fugitives hunting for jobs in English biscuit factories or potato fields in Scotland. Sitting in the Ambassador's comfortable house I felt how ironic it was that I, a foreigner, should be breathing air that belonged rightly to those exiled soldiers. The Welfare state had offered them consolation. But what is a Knightsbridge bed-sitter or a council house in Stoke compared with a home in one's native land?

Stoneman has promised to introduce me to some of Warsaw's intellectuals and perhaps a few war veterans, and has put me in touch with Kevin Ruane, the BBC Warsaw correspondent.

Kevin has an office in an old building at the corner of Mokotowska, Marszalkowska and Wilcza streets. Dingy windows overlook a courtyard that smells of sour rubbish, cabbage and fried onions. There are small shoemakers' and tailors' workshops on the ground floor and a basement printers'. Kevin had two comfortable rooms above a pedicure salon. Two attractive girls watched me as I picked my way up the dark stairs.

KEVIN RUANE

Kevin comes from Everton (he follows the football results) and was a Russian linguist before switching to Poland. We found we had friends in common: Charles Harrison and the BBC monitoring team in Nairobi, and Tom Heaton, who not long ago completed a marathon foot and bicycle safari from the Indian

Ocean to the top of Lake Rudolf and back (I was Tom's back-up man on the Tanzania stage, driving his Land Rover and preparing camp sites – at night he would fall on the ground and sleep in his underpants with a scrap of muslin over his head to keep away the early morning flies). Kevin thought it would be difficult for him to introduce me to Polish *literati*. "Writers and people of that sort don't band together. They know they're being watched." He had met a few war veterans – "they are bores". Polish security methods did not bother him. He was experienced enough to spot agents, even those lurking in crowds. "They are often roughly dressed and many have beards."

Kevin took me to lunch at the Press club in the American Embassy. "You must have noticed great changes," said Kaufmann, a New York journalist.

"The Jews and cab horses have gone, the soldiers look different, even the Polish navvy wears protective gloves. Perhaps it is I who have changed most," I remarked.

Kevin took me in his car to the controversial Katyn massacre memorials in the two large municipal cemeteries. We walked past Gomulka's grave – it is marked by two large blocks of different coloured stone, one (I was told) representing Gomulka's identification with the east, the other with the west – and Bierut's memorial shrine. Here the Katyn victims are commemorated by a massive stone cross. The inscription records that they were murdered in 1941. The date is significant. For it implies that the executioners were Germans.[1]

---

[1] In April 1943 4,321 corpses of Polish officers were disinterred by the Germans in Katyn forest on the bank of the Dniestr near Smolensk. They had been shot in the back of the head. About half of them were reserve officers, among them many professional men. They represented a large slice of the Polish intelligentsia. An international medical commission of doctors from the nine countries of German occupied Europe, also one from Switzerland and one from Italy, concluded that the men died in March-April 1940 when the Russians and not the Germans were in possession of Katyn. The Russians counterclaim that the Germans committed the atrocity in the winter of 1941 after they had crossed into Soviet territory. The political significance of which date to put on Katyn memorial stones is therefore all important. The date 1941, which is used by the Russians, implies that the Germans were the perpetrators – for at

The Katyn memorial in the second cemetery bore no date, leaving the identity of the killers "an open question". For Poles the truth behind the Katyn memorials is a matter of great sensitivity. No Pole believes that Germans shot the Polish officers. It is engraved on their hearts as a "Russian crime".

Kevin is known as a level-headed and tenacious journalist. The Polish authorities don't make life easy for him and he has fallen foul of Urban, the official government spokesman, by needling him with awkward questions. Urban himself (he is a Jew) is a caustic and wily performer and respects Kevin as a shrewd protagonist.

JASKEWICZ

Jaskewicz was one of the war veterans Mr Stoneman suggested I ought to meet. He lives high up in a new block of flats in the Centrum near the Palace of Culture, which soars above it like the Tower of Babel. Jaskewicz was in his late sixties, well preserved, with spiky white hair and a prominent veined nose. Sitting among his books he reminded me of a parrot. He made coffee and held forth for a whole hour, entirely about himself.

After the German invasion (Jaskewicz told me) he was imprisoned in Warsaw. His father disappeared and was later reported killed. He escaped by ship to Denmark whence he made his way to England. "I had one aim, and that was to fight Germans." He joined the Polish army in exile, was trained for secret missions, and after two abortive attempts (the planes had to turn back) he was dropped into Warsaw in 1942 with two other agents. There he went into hiding in a safe house which he shared with two British officers, a Polish woman with a child, and a Jew. One of his tasks was to prepare false documents. When the house was eventually raided the Polish woman and child were shot, the Jew vanished, and Jaskewicz was sent to

that time the district was occupied by them. But all evidence points to the guilt of the Russians. Even if this were not so, no Pole will ever believe that anyone but the Russians carried out the murders. The Poles say that it was deliberate Russian policy to destroy "the cream of the class enemy" and thus facilitate their control over Polish territory.

Colditz prisoner-of-war camp; the two British officers had already preceded him there.

Jaskewicz had studied architecture and he returned to Poland after the war to help with the rebuilding of Warsaw. The book in which he has recorded his experiences has sold out. "But I have the addresses of 400 people who want to read it," he said. "I will buy as many copies as I can and sell them myself, keeping the profit."

Jaskewicz was clearly a courageous man, a survivor in a tough school. But he had no sense of humour and made the recital of his one-man war sound tedious. His adventures happened too long ago. The part of Warsaw where he hid from the Germans after 1942 has been levelled to the ground. Today's Polish army points its bayonets towards the west. It is Soviet planes and helicopters that patrol the Polish borders. Red Army war memorials with five-pointed stars immortalise Communist liberation. Russian is taught in junior schools and Moscow radio crackles through the air. Perhaps the time has come to keep quiet about one's wartime adventures. Do young people want to listen to them?

I walked down from the ninth floor passing corridors which had many doors. There were cooking smells, brooms, prams. Domesticity, the tyranny of carpet beating and the shopping list, had caught up with the lonely parachutist.

5
THE FIVE-POINTED STAR

ART MUSEUM

Warsaw cherishes its many museums as evidence of the nation's history. In the National Art museum I found that a part of the Polish historical section was closed. Matejko's painting 'Battle of Grunwald' was not on view and I wasn't in the right mood to appreciate the Dutch and Flemish masters. Rubens's giant women with their great hips and breasts and buttocks were too much like naked *Hausfraus* in a Hamburg *Freibad*. One would have to be in prime health not to be discouraged by their size. These were the Bacchic fantasies of rich Amsterdam merchants whom the master had satirised as half-goats with wrinkled bellies. The Slavs in art are decently clothed. They cover themselves in armour plate, uniforms, jewelled robes. Peasants wear hose, smocks and fur caps.

The early mediaeval art collection was on the ground floor, much of it harrowing. The paintings, ikons and figures express the Christian vision of early Polish craftsmen. Christ in agony, the hanging head and rictus, the matted beard, the body pierced and stained with blood, the pallor of the grey skin. Works of peasant horror from Torun and Silesia.

One painting shows the devil flying like a vampire bat over the head of a nun as she kneels in prayer in a convent garden. The symbolism would have amused my old African students. They understood witchcraft and would ask me jokingly, "Can one see the devil?" In the African sub-world of superstition people dream of evil imps scurrying about a man's hut like tiny rats. "Can't you see them? There's one climbing up Mwanga's neck!"

I shall visit the museum again. While I was sitting outside on a bench a priest came up and I made room for him. He was pale, clean and had a thin, intellectual face. I told him this was my first visit to Poland after forty-five years. "You will notice great changes," he remarked.

"Warsaw is bigger and much busier," I said cautiously.

"I don't mean that," he said. "We are not satisfied."

"You mean economic problems?"

"They're not important either." He raised his voice. "We are not free. *Nie ma wolnosci!*" He got up, a big cross swinging over his breast. "Poland is not free!" he repeated and hurried away. He was wearing a beret, and his black shoes twinkled under his robe.

SOVIET CEMETERY

I was thinking of the priest's words when I visited the Red Army cemetery near my camp on the road (Zwirki i Wigury) to the airport. I walked there past a row of delightful little summer cottages with allotments and flower gardens. There are two separate burial sections: one for officers, the second for other ranks. The war memorial is a granite obelisk (110 feet high) with a black star looking down on the figures of two Red Army soldiers with machine-pistols succouring wounded comrades. The monument, according to an inscription in Russian and Polish, was erected in 1950 "in honour of the heroes who fought for the independence of Poland and the liberation of our capital".

The officers' graves are neatly terraced, with flower beds (pansies) and metal plaques on headstones, of which I counted about 250. Each plaque was inscribed with up to three names and a five-pointed Soviet star. The other ranks – about 20,000 of them – have been put into the earth without names. Each of their burial plots has four small concrete blocks as markers. The stars cut in the blocks are eroding.

It is a very orderly cemetery, planned like a parade ground, carefully levelled and planted with trees and shrubs. Only half-a-dozen people were there – young couples enjoying the sun. Two policemen were lounging on the ramp under the obelisk, smoking, and there was one old man. I spoke to him. He was seventy-three, arthritic, blind in one eye and partly deaf. He told me he had never been to school. The Nazis had taken him

off with a slave labour transport to Königsberg where he looked
after farm machinery. He had seen Poles seized and shot. When
he returned to Poland his first wife died and he remarried.

"I come to the cemetery every day," he said. "I go to the betting shop and wait here for the results. Sometimes I win a bit,
usually not. One must do something to keep an interest in life."

I observed that the Red Army officers' graves were named,
the other ranks were nameless. "Ah," he said, "that is the
Russian way."

He explained that the Soviet Embassy kept a close eye on the
cemetery. They organised visits and placed carnations at the
foot of the obelisk. Helpers were sent to cut the grass and
prepare flower beds. The two policemen smoking near the
obelisk were there to prevent misbehaviour and damage.

I left the old man and sat on a headstone. Not only were the
Red Army officers' graves named; tablets gave dates and places
of birth, rank and unit, in Cyrillic script. The other ranks were
not named. They were nameless and unknown. Perhaps, in
Communist countries, other ranks don't count very much: or
there are too many of them – a mass of anonymous ants. Yet it's
always the brave Russian soldier – Ivan with his red peasant
hands, his greasy forage cap and shirt held in by a leather belt
– who is figured (it is the great propaganda line of Soviet
patriotism) fighting to death against Fascism and now American
imperialism. It is a truism that no army, unless it is a rabble,
can function without a clearcut distinction between officers,
who bear the responsibilities, and their men. But in the
Red Army cemetery, under the Soviet insignia, there was no
equality even in death.

NEW ACQUAINTANCES

People look younger and slimmer now they have cast off their
heavy winter clothes and put on light summer dress and footwear. Their winter pallor is turning brown in the hazy sun, hats
have been left at home, fresh green leaves are concealing stained
grey walls. This morning, counting the people who pass by, I
note that roughly four out of ten have dark hair and eyes, the
rest are fairer. Balding heads are common. Gold teeth have
almost vanished.

The crowds don't hurry. They have time to window-gaze and sit on benches. They don't smile much or greet each other. How different from the warmth and animation of an African city. Some Poles have finely carved faces with wide cheekbones, a firm mouth and clear, often deep-set eyes that narrow at the corners into a tiny crease. Others, especially country women, have peasant faces, fleshy and round, with small blue eyes, or thin and furrowed with craggy noses. Polish city women want to be smart. But a truly elegant person would be out of place here. Handbags are shoddy. The military man or official carries a briefcase, shoppers a plastic carrier. Still, there are compensations. The tram and bus service is quick and cheap. There are flower stalls everywhere, and like the churches they are always open. There are little basement shops where you can get repairs done while you wait: green spaces to walk the dog, pigeons and ice-cream.

Continuing my social round I had dinner with Rod Haden, the linguistics lecturer whom I had met at the Ambassador's house. He has a French wife (from Lille) and they live with their daughter in a building scarred with bullets and splinter holes. The stairs are dark and mouldy, the little iron balcony hangs by a thread, but the apartment – which is provided by the British Council – is dry and comfortable and the Hadens are permitted to use the families' shop run by the Embassy.

Haden confirms that recent British Council policy has been to reduce or cancel English teaching posts abroad and to concentrate on the narrow field of linguistics. It is argued that native-born teachers can deal adequately with the literature: and that it is the teaching of the language itself, the words, not the vision and thoughts of Shakespeare or Dickens, which is the key to spreading the use of English throughout the world. Today's expert tells us that Shakespeare was a malignant racist (he invented Shylock, Caliban, and a crazed Moor who murdered his beautiful wife) and that Dickens's heroines were silly innocents who allowed men to behave like monsters. Haden thinks it wrong of the British government to economise on British cultural activities abroad – its cheese-paring attitude, for instance, towards the external broadcasting services. English text books for schools and libraries are a certain way of strengthening British influence – and indirectly trade – abroad.

Haden comes from Cumbria. He is small and good-natured –
Punch with a beard. Enjoying a secure post, nutritious groceries
from the British families' shop and a splendid French wife to
organise his life, he can sit back at ease while colleagues, at the
mercy of local contracts and foreign employers, worry about the
vulnerability of their jobs.

Through Haden I have met Emma Haynes, who came to
Poland eighteen years ago and has stayed on through turbulent
times as lecturer in the university's English department. Emma
is half-Scottish, her Polish is flawless, and she is clever and
good natured. "If there's anything you want to know about
Poland," said Haden, "ask Emma."

The Szwajcaria is one of the best cafés. Men with the raddled
good looks of retired army officers, women who might have had
something to do with the stage, eat their rich sweet cakes here.
Businessmen walk in with briefcases, young people in jeans, an
occasional drunk in working clothes who is quietly shooed
away. A strolling gypsy band drops in on its tour of the bars.
The violinist has sleepy black eyes and a cap to put the takings
in, usually ten-zloty coins. The cello player has a long red nose
the shape of a bottle (what Germans call a *Biernase*). The
accordionist holds himself like a wrestler. When they have
played enough they sit down and are treated to coffee. They
come from Roumania. The police barely tolerate this moth-
eaten relic of private enterprise and constantly move them on.

The coffee in Szwajcaria is black and bitter and I prefer tea –
which is served with a tea bag marked "China black tea:
Shanghai" and four small cubes of beet sugar. Everyone smokes
furiously. In the tradition of old Vienna men come here to read
their newspaper, which requires two hours' close study if it is
one of the ponderous cultural weeklies. The women long to be
elegant but their clothes are of poor quality and their handbags
are ugly. The toilets are closely watched by a woman in a white
apron.

Roger Boyes, the *Times* Warsaw correspondent, has a small
cluttered office in the same building. I met him in the café. He
is in his early thirties, chubby and blond ("I have Danish
blood"), went to Keble ("that ugly red-brick place"), has a
precise sense of words, and is casually dressed – he looks indeed
as though he had just strolled in from the High after a tennis

match. He has a clever and delightful Polish wife. With Solidarity quiet for the moment Roger finds the news front rather dull. He has to keep alert for government changes, police abuses, human rights and the treatment of dissidents, and the repercussions of Father Popieluszko's murder. He has been commissioned to write a book on the case.

He is, I think, a little envious that I knew Poland in her glamorous days. Discussing the Pope he says that, as a Pole, he is vested in the popular mind with a sort of divinity. Yet despite the Pope's strictures, abortion is common. Polish hospitals will do the operation but wards are crowded and women frequently have recourse to a private doctor ("in some back room"). General Jaruzelski never goes to church. This would be against his principles and ideology. The Poles – though at the best of times they are a difficult people to satisfy – are a frustrated nation. "What pains them is that they can't write, speak and travel freely, and they are exasperated that the Polish economy and standard of living lag so far behind the West's."

Roger has the use of the *Times* flat but lives for the time being at his wife's home. I look forward to meeting him again, but I don't want Poles to get the impression that I hob-nob with western journalists.

VISTULA

From the café I walked past the Army Museum towards the Vistula, and stopped for a few minutes in the Museum compound. It has a collection of World War Two guns, tanks and aircraft. An inscription on one Soviet tank says that it was driven all the way from Lenino to Warsaw (some 750 kilometres). Schoolchildren are taken to see the exhibition but seem bored by it. The tanks that drove back the Wehrmacht are out of date, the small fighter planes are antiques.

I crossed the Vistula over the Poniatowski bridge. The river is some 300 yards wide. The right bank is wooded, the left bank covered with scruffy grass where anglers sit on stools. Praga, across the river, is densely populated and industrialised with a skyline of stacks and high rise buildings. As I walked across the bridge I could feel it trembling as heavy vehicles passed. I have heard that the bridge is soon to be closed for urgent repairs. It

was in Praga that the Red Army paused after its advance from
the east and stood by while Warsaw was ground to dust during
the June 1944 uprising. The Vistula, which flows through
Cracow to Gdansk, from former Austrian territory to the
Pomeranian plain, is an axis that historically and culturally
divides east from west. The countless little *shtetls* on the eastern side were part of the Pale where hundreds of thousands of
Jews used to live. Ignorant, isolated, deceived and fatalistic,
this vast colony of women and children, merchants, rabbis and
scholars, musicians, prodigies and craftsmen waited as if mesmerised while the Nazi avalanche gathered momentum and
then swept them away. The mark of their debasement was that
only their gold dental fillings and the women's hair survived.
The bodies' ashes were thrown on beet fields and into lonely
forest clearings – humus for green and stagnant ponds.

I come across drunks in surprising places – on benches, at bus
and tram stops, hanging round the railway station, warming
themselves over hot water pipes, quarrelling in bars, jostling
people in the subways. Some are temporarily paralysed, a few
have keeled over. They are not all working class men. They
may be clerks who have just knocked off work, artisans or
youths. Yet they are not as desperate as the homeless *clochards*
of Paris. They are not allowed to sleep under bridges or in parks
(too cold anyway). Pedestrians treat them with tolerance, but
keep their distance. A drunken man can retch suddenly or drop
burning cigarette ends on your clothes.

In Praha café the other day I noticed a clean, smart young
man with a satchel brooding quietly over his coffee. He was
staring at the cup. Suddenly, without warning, he collapsed,
hitting his head on the floor, knocking cup, saucer and bottle of
fruit juice on to the ground, where fragments of glass shot
between our feet. He got up very slowly and sat dazed for a
couple of minutes. Then he began to tidy up the mess. A party
of schoolgirls were laughing at him. I felt sorry for the young
man and (in my school master's voice) told the girls to shut up.
The young man went away looking groggy. He must have
swallowed his vodka ration not long before and it had felled him
like a ninepin.

POPIELUSZKO'S CHURCH

Mr Poinc has reminded me that I am discourteous not to pay my respects to the late Fr. Popieluszko. His church, St Stanislaw Kostka's in Zoliborz, has been promoted into a "small Czestochowa". It was here that the priest, before he was murdered by security agents, used to spread his rebellious message to a rapt congregation. Since his death the church has become a place of pilgrimage and his grave, lit by guttering candles and swamped with flowers, is now more widely known and honoured among Poles than the Unknown Soldier's Tomb in Warsaw's Victory Square.

Fr. Popieluszko may or may not have been a good Christian cleric. He was certainly brave and outspoken to the point of rashness. As contemporary Poland's model of a turbulent priest he blended fierce opposition to state atheism with impassioned Polish patriotism.

I joined about a hundred people standing or praying in the churchyard. The tomb rests under a great slab and the air is pungent with the smell of wicks burning in little pots of oil. The cross over his grave has a curious shape. It has been roughly carved to look like a piece of charred black wood with a blood-stained hole in one arm representing a wound. Hanging in the yard and on the fence I counted fifty Solidarnosc posters brought from all over Poland, notably Danzig and Silesia – the lettering turned inwards, not facing the street. Near the tomb is a sculpture of two boys with baby faces under huge helmets carrying ammunition: one has a Sten gun strapped to his back.

The church is an ugly, modern building with two concrete steeples and a clock. The clock works. People come and go all day and long after dark. No one smokes. This is not common sightseeing. The faces show deep piety. The church interior has been decked out as a museum and is full of banners and bric-à-brac. A gallery of photographs shows Fr. Popieluszko at various stages of his life as he treads the road to Calvary. As a young man, laughing with children and youths. As a sportsman, bare to the waist, sun tanned, sitting in a boat on a lake. Preaching. Officiating at Mass. The final photograph shows a car with smashed windows and a flat tyre. In the open boot and back seat two dummy infants have been placed with outstretched arms – dead.

The grisly pathos of this exhibit and a picture of the dark dam where the priest's body was dumped are calculated to perpetuate anger and a desire to avenge.

One wonders if it is right to build up the murdered man into such a hero, a sort of Hollywood star, to be ready to canonise him. But the Poles worship their heroes, their warriors and their poets even though the cause they fought for was often lost, a victory in defeat. (I sometimes think that the only thing the Poles really envy the English for is the charge of the Light Brigade!)

Andrzej told me later in camp that he had known Fr. Popieluszko personally. He was a "splendid fellow, very sociable, liked parties and young people, a sportsman, brave and popular." He had met him in Torun and recounted how the priest had told him of a red-hot brick someone had hurled through his flat window in Warsaw – "he burnt his hand removing it and was wearing a bandage. The government eliminated him because he was too troublesome."

Another Pole spoke to me about the priest with some reservations. "He was a powerful but crude speaker, a peasant not an intellectual – which of course is just what the mass wants. His brutal death has presented it with a new myth."

EMMA

I have been to Emma Haynes's flat: two small rooms, kitchen and bathroom, a little cramped but cosy. The lift works. Many of her neighbours are pensioned officials with loyal wives of the sort who outlive their husbands. Emma's flat looks out on a handsome square (Plac Zbawiciela) surrounded by solid apartment houses and overrun by pigeons. At the back there are chestnut trees, a colony of rooks and a school playground.

As the flat belongs to the university the rent is very cheap (400 zlotys a month including heating and light). But it is not easy to get repair work done quickly. Emma showed me a damp patch on the ceiling. "To find a workman you have to pay him extra. Many Poles have two jobs – one on the side, that's how they make ends meet. They say they're too busy."

Emma knows all the secrets of shopping, from finding new shoes to fresh cherries, and says that living conditions have improved over the last two years. With consumer goods becoming more plentiful people have been getting rid of their surplus money. The queues in butchers' shops are mainly for pork, which Poles prefer to beef. Cheap New Zealand mutton sometimes appears but most people won't look at it. "In some ways the Poles are rather spoiled."

Emma has excellent relationships with her teaching colleagues at the university. English was considered of more practical use than Russian ("looked on as a waste of time") and is spreading under American influence. The British Council has given the English department modest help. They made a £1,000 grant some time ago but the Americans are more generous.

Emma took me to the university shop this morning where I was permitted to buy food without a ration card. I carried away a large parcel of liver paste and butter. At lunch we were joined by Galina of the African studies department. She longs to visit Africa but postings are rare and they are limited to African countries with socialist regimes (Angola, Mozambique, Ethiopia). "I have met only a few negroes," she admitted sadly.

I told her that I missed the gaiety and elegance of Warsaw's old night life and the cavalry officers with their four-cornered hats and beautiful riding boots and breeches. "The moment they came into a night club it was time to go home," I said. "They bagged all the best girls."

"Polish officers are not so handsome as they used to be," commented Galina.

"Nowadays," I said, "they carry briefcases as though they were all in the Pay Corps and if you look at their trousers you'll see that the bottoms are frayed."

URBAN'S PRESS CONFERENCE

Roger Boyes has invited me to go with him to the weekly press conference, at which Jerzy Urban, the government spokesman, answers correspondents' questions. I had, of course, no press card. "But the security people won't check you," said Roger. He was wearing his white trousers, rubber pumps and a summer shirt as if he were at the seaside. About sixty journalists were present.

Urban dealt first with the latest foreign press reports on Poland, commenting on their "accuracy" with touches of sarcasm. Then the correspondents put their questions, which concerned police violence, a coming political trial, and trade statistics. Urban, a Jew of about sixty with a bald sun-tanned pate and a fringe of white hair at the sides, handled the questions calmly and efficiently. He denied the allegations of violence, said that the reported incidents had not been substantiated, admitted nothing and clearly knows his job.

As an outsider I found the meeting boring. For the time being nothing eventful is happening in Poland. The Solidarity movement is dormant, the Popieluszko murder trial is over, the news items under discussion were trivial. The language difficulty was evident, most of the journalists using headphones to follow the interpreter. A cynic might have seen us as a roomful of highly paid gossips with nothing to write home about. Still, it is journalists who keep the world aware of what is going on. They are an intelligence machine with antennae always on the alert. Embassies and High Commissions operate through different channels: it is often said that they are more likely to be wrong in their diagnosis and advice than the best correspondents, who have the advantage of more varied and closer contacts with the man in the street than a diplomat.

I stayed the night at Roger's unoccupied flat. After lying on the floor of my van for several weeks I looked forward to a real bed. The apartment block on Rozbrat is pitted with bullet holes. But it is pleasantly situated at the edge of Lazienki Gardens and tall trees brush the balcony. The porter, said Roger, was a scrounger. "Give him a few razor blades to keep him happy and a tip if you come back late. He is of course a police contact."

The flat has a large library of Polish books (many in translation) belonging to the landlord, a Pole, and books on east European affairs left by previous occupants. To start with I looked at the gruesome pictorial account of Trotsky's murder in Mexico (his skull pierced by a short-handled ice-pick) and an illustrated book of Russian erotica *The Love Dreams of Russian Venuses* published by an émigré press in Paris. Here were lumpy bodies matted with pubic hair, fornicating Cossacks, bestiality and satyrs. The pictures were in praise of male virility; there was nothing effete or Lesbian about them.

Mayakovsky's *Poems* were in an edition published by Progress Publishers, Moscow (1976), in an English translation by Dorian Rottenberg. The verse on Lenin's death was a piece of insufferable toadying;

Yesterday's dumb pawns
                            he led
                                      to a war of classes
Until a human
                working-class dictatorship
                                    arose
to checkmate Capital
                  and crush its prison-castle.

The poem goes on:

Today
        I want to infuse
                    new glitter
into the most glorious of words: PARTY.
Individual –
              what can he mean in life?
His voice
            sounds fainter
                    than a needle dropping.
Who hears him?
              Only, perhaps, his wife.

The ending lines are:

Over the world-wide forest
                  of factory
                        stacks
Like a giant banner
              the huge
                  Red Square,
millions
        of hands
            welded into its staff,

Soars
    with a mighty sweep
        into the air.
And from that banner
        from every fold
Lenin,
    alive as ever,
        cries:
"Workers,
    prepare
        for the last assault!
Slaves,
    unbend
        your knees and spines!
Proletarian army,
        rise in force!
Long live
    the Revolution
        with speedy victory,
the greatest
    and justest
        of all the wars
        ever
           fought
           in history"

The account of Trotsky's gruesome murder, the erotic Russian Venuses, and Mayakovsky's doggerel were enough for one night's reading. When I put out the light the flat seemed eerie. A street lamp shone ghost-like through the window and a tree scraped and sighed against the balcony.

In the morning I read Timothy Garton Ash's *The Polish Revolution* (1983). He gives a step by step account, in great detail, of the Solidarity movement and its sudden brutal end. The Poles, says Ash, were taken by surprise when the government finally took measures to crush the movement through martial law and arrests. Ash complains that foreign governments did too little to support Solidarity. Foreign bankers wanted their money back and were relieved when the strike was broken and "law and order" restored. Trade Unions in Britain thought the strikers had gone too far and were wrecking Socialism itself.

Ash points out that the church, throughout the troubles, preached non-violence. Only about fifteen people are known to have been killed – evidence that the Poles maintained excellent self-discipline. Had they resorted to violence there would have been massive bloodshed.

Ash emphasises that "Yalta" is still the bogey word ("the Allies sold Poland to the Russians. We are not free").

EMMA'S FRIENDS

I am meeting Emma's friends and adjusting myself to their tastes and interests. They are generally university lecturers, students or people connected with the arts. Conversation jumps rapidly from one subject to another. One is not expected to be a bore. The political undertones to what is said and irreverence for the authorities are not disguised.

The six guests at Emma's last night discussed living costs, English football fans, the Black Madonna and censorship. Living standards are admitted to be higher in East Germany than in Poland but West Germany is of course the Mecca. Officially there is no unemployment in Poland. Everyone is entitled to and can claim work. After three months without a job a man will be ordered to take one. This leads to overmanning and is enormously costly apart from devaluing the "work ethic" and quality of performance. Yet shops and restaurants are always short of staff ("hard work, long hours, poor tips").

Polish television had been showing lurid pictures of the violence of English football fans at the Liverpool – Juventus match in Brussels. The guests wondered why the Belgian police didn't use tear gas and water cannon. But what interested them most was that "the best footballer on the field, Boniek, was a Polish forward."

A radio engineer at the party described Father Popieluszko as a "peasant who had lost his way" and that his "hearty life style" was not a recommendation for canonising him.

Walesa-type moustaches (the old RAF bomber pilot sort) have become a fashion, one of the women said. "I notice that some of the police wear them too," I remarked. The soldiers on duty in Warsaw, she added, were bluffing the public. "Their guns are not loaded."

No one knew for certain how the painting of the Black Madonna at Czestochowa came to be gashed. Emma said a Swedish soldier had slashed her face. One lady blamed the Hussites. Another a Tartar horseman. A teacher from the African studies department remembered how a black student who had seen the ikon had told her that "the scarified cheek was a copy of African tribal marks".

We discussed censorship. My copy of Kazimierz Brandys's banned *A Warsaw Diary* had not been spotted by the customs at Frankfurt-an-der-Oder and I have promised to lend it one of the guests. Pasternak's *Dr Zhivago*, Solzhenitsyn and some of Orwell's writings, *Animal Farm* and *1984* for example, are banned. But cheap Russian classics printed in Moscow are plentiful in the bookshops.

No one thought that Gorbachov ("a slippery fellow") would change the party line or moderate Soviet foreign policy.

I was to enjoy many such parties in the flats of friends. They were never dull, the hospitality was sincere and there was always something to eat, vodka and Balkan wine. With the clamp-down on night life under the Socialist government, Poles prefer to do their entertaining at home; and if they don't have guests, television keeps them indoors.

Censorship, queueing, corruption among officials and restrictions on travel are major irritants in people's feeling of frustration. Lucky is the Pole with relatives or friends abroad who can send him money and sponsor an invitation to visit them.

With Emma I have been to an exhibition of paintings by Marian Czapla, a university art professor. It was an unusual setting. Czapla had hung his canvases, about fifty of them, in a derelict factory that used to make gun barrels. We had to climb over rusty machinery to view them. All but one of the paintings showed the violent martyrdom of St Peter. They were done in crude colours, red, black, and ochre. Peter was dying like a dog, his great muscular body twisted in agony, his face contorted as though he were howling. These were nightmare pictures: visions from the Inferno or from a death camp. Crosses had been daubed over the canvases like bloodstains. The exception was the sombre painting of a dead working man. The symbolism was obvious. Two martyrs: the murdered Father Popieluszko, and an industrial worker shot by police – the Church and Solidarity. The bizarre setting too – a grimy factory workshop – made its point.

Marian Czapla was a hairy, heavily built man in an open shirt looking like a stevedore. I asked him if he painted his violent pictures at night. "No," he answered cheerfully, "I like to work in the sunshine."

To avoid embarrassment with the authorities the exhibition had not been advertised. There were about fifty guests and glasses of cheap vermouth and Bulgarian red wine.

CAMPING

A Pole from Opole with a caravan and a red-haired wife is pestering me for "a small sum of money – £40". He claims that he needs new shock-absorbers and as these are foreign-made the dealer is demanding hard currency. He repeats his request several times a day: *"Pomysle Pan?* Have you thought about my proposition?"

The fact is that though the black market rate in zlotys for English pounds is five times the official one, I have more Polish money than I need. And pound notes are my life-line. I must husband them. I have put off the Opole man. He doesn't seem to be offended, and I think he is a gypsy. His wife's red hair has been coarsely dyed and when she prepares food she squats like an Oriental.

The camping season is now well under way. Young people squeeze into small tents. They have guitars and footballs. The car owners seem to have brought their domestic chores with them. Meals take hours to prepare: simmering stews, salads, mushrooms and pickles. Camping equipment is shoddy with plastic buckets that break, skimpy ground sheets, wobbly chairs. Neighbours borrow my foot pump and jack. There is nowhere to swim but I like living here. We may envy our neighbours' possessions– their German car or Swedish tent – but we're not snobs. Magpies fly over my van. Bees hum and there is a smell of blossom. The uncertain weather – a downpour one morning followed by a day of sultry heat – keeps one alert. I have more than enough books to read: Gorky, Grosz, Singer, Heine's *Reisebilder* and Horst Krüger's *Ostwest-Passagen*.

A huge red pantechnicon the size of a small house with a row of tiny windows, towed by a Mercedes Benz bus, has arrived from Passau (Bavaria). I watched forty Germans tumble out, elderly men with bellies and stout women. How many tons of potatoes, pork chops, Bockwurst and cream cakes it must have taken, over the years, to produce that distended flesh! When they mount the stairs to their bunks I imagine rows of human bolsters snoring in the night like bullfrogs. Ferrying them all the way to Moscow and back and handling their bowel, bladder and sleeping problems needs a triumph of organisation.

In a café near the camp the same three or four seedy men spend most of the day on the fruit machines. They hammer, thump and shake the knobs hoping desperately for an orgasm of cascading coins. From time to time they go to the barmaid to change their paper money for coins. They seem to be spivs; or perhaps they have some sort of bogus night work. Schoolboys also play the machines, looking for the price of a Coca-Cola.

I have given up going to the Praha restaurant. The greasy air and smell of unwashed clothes has put me off. But I sometimes use the toilet. A woman is in charge of it. The other day I heard a man crying for lavatory paper. "Am I expected to use my bare fingers?" he shouted at the woman. She swore at him and came back with two tiny sheets. "Take it, you hooligan, and clear off!"

I have been sitting in the park next to the camp. Within an hour four drunks have passed by. Each had a comrade gripping him by the arm. Without his support they would have fallen flat on their faces. They were quiet and half-dazed, reminding me of walking wounded, or ragdolls being returned to their box. With the warm weather people are escorting their little boys on bicycles and exercising their dogs. I note doberman pinschers, Alsatians, red setters, dachshunds and schnauzers. The old married couples look happy and relaxed. They have survived their crises and infidelities and are bound in happy unison for the family grave.

Their gentleness makes me think. If this were Germany, and

these good citizens (with their kind, weather-beaten faces) had
been Germans, I would have wondered what grisly secrets they
might be hiding in their breasts: the Jew-bullying they surely
witnessed at school and in the streets, the smoke billowing over
Russian ghettos when they were soldiers: the sealed freight
trains they must have glimpsed, crammed with staring eyes, as
the box-cars clanked to lonely forest stations where potas-
sium cyanide pellets, furnaces and pyres awaited the victims.
Because this ugly suspicion still lurks at the back of the mind
(one scarcely sees a Jew in Poland, yet one is conscious of the
ghosts of the Jewish people) – because it was among the Poles,
in the neighbourhood of their small towns and villages, that the
German death camps went to work, and the Poles were witnesses – would it not be more comforting to put a taboo on the
whole villainous past: or else to declare one's own guilt by
association for policies that bombed Hamburg and Dresden into
soot and ashes, sank refugee ships in the Baltic, and while there
had still been time to help, denied Jews asylum across the
Channel?

Every morning unless it is raining a Polish woman with a rosy
face brings her small granddaughter to play in a corner of the
camp. She likes talking to me. Today she asked if I would care
to rent a room in her apartment. "My last lodgers," she said,
"were African medical students. I couldn't stand them. They
brought in street girls and I was afraid they would steal my
things."

Pani Zofia, who comes from the old West Prussian town of
Poznan (Posen), speaks both German and Polish. "I can feed
you, do your washing and darning, and give you a real home,"
she said.

It is a tempting offer. But I must guard my independence,
and I see she is a great talker and has strong prejudices.

In the meantime several gypsy families have arrived with
cars, tents and piles of bedding. The men pitch the tents then
go off to town, leaving the women on their own. At night they
drink, raise their voices, and the wives tease the men. One
young woman throws her shoes at her husband. When the lights
go out in their tents I hear them quarrelling.

The gipsy women have fine swarthy profiles, restless eyes,
long black hair tied with ribbons hanging over their shoulders,

and shapely legs hidden by trailing skirts. The younger wives change their dresses three or four times a day, put on high-heeled shoes when they feel bored and flick their legs provocatively. They have shrill voices, sing like dancers, and are constantly washing clothes and sheets. The children peer into other people's caravans, join in their games and steal their toys.

The gypsies speak an impure Polish but amongst themselves the gypsy tongue. They say they come from Roumania and the Poles don't like them. Pani Zofia complains that gypsies always have plenty of money but never do a stroke of work. "They are all thieves. The children are worst, so keep an eye on your things." Mr Poinc admits that the gypsies are unwelcome visitors. "But it is government policy not to turn them away. It's the same situation you have with your Asians." Mr Poinc, however, is simplifying the problem. There is the matter of guilt too. It was in Poland, in Oswiecim, that scores of thousands of gypsies were rounded up and dragged by Nazi executioners to the furnaces. Surely, after that, their descendants have earned the right to wander freely in the towns of Poland without being harassed by the police and watch committees.

I like the gypsies. Like old soldiers they know how to make themselves snug and comfortable on a patch of grass. They can always find wine and know where to pick up a little money. Their lithe bodies, white teeth and cheerful impudence bring life and colour to this dull camping colony of Polish dumplings. They greet me warmly and the two prettiest girls have twice climbed into my van to size up its contents and suggest a currency deal. I have disappointed them. These days, alas, I am a milksop without machismo.

QUEUEING

I try to avoid queueing by buying little. I go to the shops only for milk and cheese, groceries (bread, pickles, jam) and for books. Without a ration card I am unable to buy butter, meat or sugar. Poland has always been reputed for her dairy products – and for mushrooms, ham and conserved fruits. I have a choice of half-a-dozen cheeses: cottage cheeses (sold in large hunks), Tilsiter, cheddar, goat cheese or soft Gorgonzola. Jams, alas, all taste much the same and are too sweet (the best are exported). Bread is rarely fresh: much of it is unconsumed and wasted. I go to street stalls for apples, pears, cherries, tomatoes and gherkins. Pastry counters have poppyseed cake and dough-nuts (*paczki*). I get my Carmen cigarettes, stamps, bus tickets and newspapers from kiosks. To buy shoes or a hat I would have to wait until supplies arrive at a store and quickly join the queue; and even then they might not have my size.

There are queues at the butchers, which have rows of sausages hanging from hooks like truncheons. The rush hour for shop-ping is after work when people, who may have been up since dawn, are tired and short-tempered and push you aside if you let them. Supplies of fresh cherries and strawberries are instantly sold out: customers buy large quantities to share with friends. There are plenty of mushrooms.

This morning at a department store in the Centrum I bought a Russian watch stamped with the name "*wostok*" (the east). I have seen only two street clocks in Warsaw and none in public buildings, and people are always stopping me to ask the time. This has been embarrassing because my watch seized up weeks ago. The shop had only one size of watch strap and it didn't fit. At the same counter a queue of twenty people were buying Russian cameras, which had just arrived. Some of the cust-omers looked poor and shabby yet bought two cameras each (to resell at a profit). I also bought cotton vests and ball point pens that produced only a faint scratch. You are not allowed to try on clothes for fit. You take your cellophane-wrapped packet, pay and vanish.

My circle of acquaintances widens. At Emma's I have met two lecturers, Breeze and Doyle, from the Roman Catholic university of Lublin, who call on her for a meal and a bath when they are visiting Warsaw. Breeze teaches Celtic and English mediaeval literature, Doyle Irish studies (literature, mythology and language). Welsh and Irish! Strange, even out-landish, disciplines, I would have thought, to be imposed on hard-headed Polish students in a Communist country. Breeze tells me that the linguistics department at Lublin has only recently been opened; and that the initiative for introducing Celtic to the syllabus comes from its new head, who had devel-oped a burning enthusiasm for Celtic culture and filled his study with works that no one is allowed to borrow. But there may be method behind his choice. Celtic is the tongue of rebels

– and in Ireland of Catholics: a challenge on behalf of a minority culture: a quixotic protest against the domination of linguistics by conventional Western languages. It's a gallant Polish gesture against totalitarianism, with a Catholic slant.

Breeze is dark-bearded, precise and pedantic, with a sad solemn face: a tireless expounder of abstract cultural themes. Doyle has not yet recovered from the shock of being transplanted from distant Cork to an Iron Curtain country with unfamiliar politics and an unrecognisable language. He has brought with him a brand new wardrobe – suit, snow-white shirts, genuine woollen underwear – which everyone envies.

I often listen to Warsaw radio. Its excellent fourth programme, which is modelled on the BBC, has schools' features, language courses, literary readings and talks by experts. I have been informed about Hinduism, Soviet war poetry, partisan memoirs and bilharzia. There was an abstruse talk on Creole. An American preacher on Radio Evangelicum, Zürich, has warned us, "Never marry anyone who is not a Christian and not of your own religion. If you do you will be untrue to God. Your partner must share your beliefs. Have nothing to do with pagans."

Chopin is played persistently throughout the day, to the point where I get bored with him. The Poles use the piano as a patriotic bugle, the instrument par excellence for expressing their national spirit through the music of Chopin's Polishness. No pianist is admired in Poland if he cannot play Chopin well.

Mrs Renishaw, Labour MP for Wolverhampton, interviewed on East German radio (East Berlin International) gave her impressions of an exhibition of old musical instruments in Halle. "Halle is wonderfully rebuilt. Astounding, fascinating, an absolutely marvellous exhibition."

Asked if she had met any politicians she said, "Yes, we had highly satisfactory talks though there were some language difficulties."

"What are your views of the political situation?"

"We are, in my party, against the star wars programme, which is absolutely horrendous. When we are in power we shall remove our nuclear weapons."

Mrs Renishaw was glib and gushing. The East German interviewer seemed well pleased with his guest.

6
OKOPOWA, GYPSIES AND SAMIZDAT

PUSHKIN

The Warsaw History museum is a fine old building with creaking wooden floors and stairs – the "Little Negro" house in which it was set up in 1947 is the only one in the old Market Square that was not destroyed in the war. The other visitor to the museum that morning was a Swede with a sophisticated rucksack. One section of the museum shows maps, prints (some by Canaletto) and documents relating to the ancient history and development of Warsaw as a fortified city on the Vistula. There are exhibits of mediaeval craftsmanship, tools and wrought-iron work.

The modern section contains dramatically enlarged photographs of Warsaw as a city of jagged ruins in the aftermath of the war: collapsed churches and buildings, mountains of rubble, broken statues. The tall column of King Sigismund III holding up a great cross (it was knocked down and smashed by German tanks in 1944) is shown lying in fragments at the foot of the pedestal, a dismembered corpse in armour.

A special section had been arranged in honour of Pushkin. The prints of his portrait were the familiar ones. Some of them accentuated his negroid features: the thickened nose and mouth, the curly dark hair. Others brought out the brilliance of his expression and eyes.

Pushkin's short and tragic life has a special appeal to Poles. Like the Poles of old, in the 19th century, he attacked the autocratic establishment and police state of the Tsar, was exiled, his writings and letters were censored, and he was closely watched by the secret police. He was eventually goaded into challenging a worthless French officer Baron D'Anthès to a duel. They faced each other behind a hedge. D'Anthès's first bullet pierced Pushkin's thigh-bone and lodged deep in his abdomen. He was carried home in unbearable pain. Shortly before he died he asked for some cloudberries; he ate two or three and swallowed a spoonful of juice. His last words were "Life's finished ... Can't breathe."

I mentioned the episode of Pushkin's wanton and tragic death to the museum attendant. The details were new to him. He knew that Pushkin and Mickiewicz had been friends and had once lived in the same house in al. Jerozolimskie. But for him Pushkin was not part of Polish history.

WAR MUSEUM

On my first visit to the War museum I left the earlier historical exhibits (armour, colourful uniforms, weapons and Kosciuszko hero-worship) for another time and looked at the section concerned with the last war. The overwhelming theme is victory: photographs of Polish units marching into captured cities and of soldiers clustered round battered German monuments. The apotheosis shows a Polish detachment parading in Moscow's Red Square with the Red Army.

Among the trophies and mementoes were a pile of German helmets and swastika banners, busts of Polish military leaders, their medals laid out beside them, and wartime uniforms including those worn by Polish troops in the Middle East and Italy with 8th Army flashes and 2 Polish Corps insignia. I was happy to see the familiar baggy khaki shorts – the Russians, when they saw our bony British knees in the streets of occupied Vienna thought we looked like an army of boy scouts. A blurred photograph shows two Polish soldiers hoisting the Polish flag over the monastery ruins at Monte Cassino. It brought back memories of wind-blown sand, stony ridges where the dead lay, some blackened and rotting, others fresh and young, the brief elation after a battle was over, and peasant vino.

One section recalled the Nazi prison and death camps with show-cases of convicts' blue-and-white striped "pyjama suits", broken spectacle frames, babies' and children's clothes and shoes from Treblinka and Oswiecim. A horrifying picture (which has been widely used) shows a young Jewish mother shielding her baby against her breast while a German soldier shoots her in the back with a Mauser.

The theme of these exhibits is victory, heroism, destruction and the despair of the defeated. Soldiers strut through the pitiful remains of liberated cities. What is war? Televised battle scenes show D-Day beaches and bombs hurtling down on the Ruhr. Untelevised war is a private experience that a soldier shares only with his mates. The real picture is found in field hospitals among the maimed and amputated, in the lice-covered families hiding in ditches and in villagers lying among smashed carts and dead horses. A liberation soldier drunk and looting a peasant home while another tosses sweets to wild-haired children are the authentic twins of war.

Real and lasting victory seems to have eluded the Poles in their kaleidoscopic history of partitions, uprisings and spells of repression. Glorious battles are no substitute. Stalin has been visualised boasting about the "beautiful regions that he with his own hands had wrested from the Germans and served up to the Poles, to eat and relish till the fat ran down over their chins. Yet the Polish intelligentsia are ungrateful, consumed with self-pity, tragic emotion, and theatrical grandeur". Does this mean that the Poles should accept and embrace their neighbours instead of pursuing their special brand of freedom, independence and irredentism? Or must Europe go to war again over Lwow, Wilno or Allenstein?

Nevertheless, the irony of the War museum is that it enshrines only a part of Poland's memories of the last war. The record of Poland's sufferings at the hands of the other enemy – the occupation of the eastern provinces, the Katyn massacre, the betrayal on the Vistula – are passed over as though they never happened; they are not the right material for a museum that functions under Communist rule.

Poles don't visit the Lenin Museum but Orbis coach parties of Russian tourists are conducted there as a matter of duty. I joined a group of them under a Russian guide who was holding forth on Lenin's activities in Cracow (1912–14) during his exile from Tsarist Russia. We stood in front of an enlarged photograph of Lenin that accentuated his Asiatic features – the pronounced cheek-bones and tigerish eyes under a proletariat cap. The Russian tourists were wearing their customary cheap print dresses and shirts. Some had cameras. They were very solemn, as though attending mass. The guide, who was a woman, ended her script by describing the western imperialists' criminal and insolent efforts to destroy the Bolshevik revolutionaries in 1918–19.

I went into the garden to eat apples with a kitchen knife, putting the remains tidily into a paper bag. The Russian tourists were watching me curiously. Was I a fellow traveller? An informant checking on the number of pilgrims who came to pay homage to Lenin? A football fan?

The Jewish History museum is nearby, off Dzerzhinsky square. It is tucked away behind a huge high-rise building that stands, a conspicuous white elephant, locked and shuttered on the former site of the old Jewish synagogue as though the ghosts of the departed Jews have laid a curse on it.

The museum was under repair, a dark and dusty place with only two of its rooms open. They contain macabre souvenirs and photographs of Nazi guards manhandling Jews, corpses, a Jew crucified on an electric fence, two youths slipping through a hole in the Warsaw ghetto wall – and that snapshot of a bemused little boy, in cloth cap, shorts and socks, his hands raised, stumbling past a German guard who is pointing his Schmeisser at him as he and his family are driven out of their home. An incalculable number of people must have seen this photograph. The boy and the beast have been immortalised. One wonders what happened to that German guard in his steel helmet and jack-boots aiming his gun at the helpless and the weak? He would plead, as they all do, that he was merely doing his duty for Führer and Fatherland. Or should one blame it all on the indifference of God? A Jewish survivor from the death camp at Sobibor is quoted as saying, "I don't believe in people any more. Nor in God. Children are supposed to have angel souls. How could God allow them to be murdered? They were just angel souls."

A Jewish woman on the museum staff told me that the camp photographs had been taken by Germans: "they were gloating". The museum had in addition a small collection of striped prison clothing and rotting canvas shoes. It is evident that the museum lacks resources. I shall return there another time.

Mrs Theobald, an American lecturer at the university, gave a farewell party last night (twenty guests). We drank Gilbey's gin, cinzano and Hungarian wine. I talked at length with a Polish school teacher whose family comes from eastern Galicia (Polish Ukraine), an area now incorporated in the USSR. He claimed that during the war the local Ukrainians had behaved like barbarians to the Poles. They committed horrible atrocities. His father had told him how he had seen a Ukrainian soldier wearing a necklace of dried female teats. The Polish Ukrainians, said the teacher, hated three things: the Poles, the Roman Catholic church (especially Jesuits), and Jews. He admitted that the Ukrainians have had a sad, miserable history. Their ancient longing for an independent state has been frustrated by the Russians and the Poles. Hence their hatred for them and their desire for revenge. Hitler's invasion gave them a chance to get their own back. Thousands of young Ukrainians volunteered to fight the "Bolsheviks" under their own national flag. Nevertheless as a Pole he thought they were "an extremely thwarted and ill natured people"; and there can be no doubt about the savage record of the Ukrainian guards whom the Nazis recruited to help run their death camps and of Ukrainian anti-partisan units in murdering Polish resistance fighters and civilians. Survivors' accounts mention them with scorn and hatred.

I listened with especial interest to what the school teacher had to say, as I have my own memorable experience of handling Ukrainians as prisoners of war (the so-called Galicia Division) as well as many other Russian nationalities during my army service in Italy. My position as a British major under orders to carry out the repatriation clauses of the Yalta agreement was invidious. Was I to support the harsh policy of handing over these 10,000 Wehrmacht auxiliaries of the Galicia Division to Moscow as dissidents, traitors and criminals – or bend the rules? I resolved to give the Ukrainians the benefit of the doubt and classify them as non-repatriable, non-Soviet citizens. The end result was that the whole division, instead of being escorted back to Russia in sealed box cars under armed guard, was released (1947) to civilian life in England, whence many emigrated to Canada. I think this decision was right and the British were justified in resisting Soviet efforts to get their hands on these bewildered peasants, who had surrendered to the Allies after being defeated in battle. The dire fate of many Ukrainian guards employed at Nazi extermination centres is another matter. The Red Army had every reason to execute these hirelings and tormentors on the spot. Had they been allowed to filter through the war criminal cages many more would have escaped.

Then there were the Keelhaul and Eastwind operations carried out by the British military authorities in Italy, which resulted in 170 Soviet citizens being forcibly repatriated from Rimini (May 1947) and handed over to the Red Army as a token sacrifice in place of the reprieved Galicia division. A strongly worded report on this action which I wrote to GHQ (CMF) was leaked some years later (1973) to the American press and caught Solzhenitsyn's eye while he was compiling the material for his *Gulag Archipelago*.[1] For him "this one random little document" (to quote his own words) disclosed "the last secret or one of the last, of the Second World War," namely, "the hitherto concealed history of forced repatriation to the Soviet Union." What Solzhenitsyn had particularly in mind was the forcible sur-

---

[1] Indexed under Epstein. In my report to GHQ (CMF) on operation Eastwind I wrote: "The decision to repatriate one category (military personnel) and not the other (civilians) was essentially an arbitrary one, based on the principle that an adequate number of bodies should be handed over to the Soviet authorities in order to appease them ... Now that the damage has been done, it is essential that constructive measures be taken immediately to release and rehabilitate the surviving Russians in this enclave. Our prestige is at stake."

Solzhenitsyn quotes these words that I used in my report: "After having remained unmolested in British hands for two years," I wrote, "they had allowed themselves to be lulled into a false sense of security and they were therefore taken completely by surprise ... They did not realise they were being repatriated ... They were mainly simple peasants with bitter personal grievances against the Bolsheviks." I added that "They were given treatment reserved in the case of every other national for war criminals alone – that of being extradited and handed over against their will to captors who, incidentally, are not expected to given them a fair trial."

"They were all sent to destruction on the Archipelago," Solzhenitsyn comments. To us who were on the spot, the Russian men and women were not just names on a nominal roll. They were human beings, sometimes our batmen, cooks and orderlies. This of course is what the higher authorities, who never set eyes on the men whose fates they were controlling in faraway offices, ignored or did not sufficiently recognise.

render to the Russians of thousands of Cossacks (some of them White Russians) whom the British army had rounded up in Austria after fighting ceased in May 1945. But he didn't know or mention all the facts: the reprieve of the Galicia Division, and the deceptions deliberately practised on Moscow (and on our own Allied higher authorities) to save as many as we could of those who had been originally set aside for sacrifice under operations Keelhaul and Eastwind – the patient whittling of the lists of the condemned from 500 to 170, the doctoring of nominal rolls, the contrived escapes.

In their post mortems on Allied repatriation policy both Nicholas Bethell[1] and Nikolai Tolstoy[2] quote from my leaked report and from my meetings and correspondence with them after I came back from Africa. Their books raised a great fuss and were seized on by the media; and even today the responsibility for the fate of the Victims of Yalta is still a matter of recrimination and discussion.

I also talked to a lawyer, who mentioned the war-time role of the Polish underground resistance and the partisans. Their presence, he said, often brought trouble for they had to be fed from scant resources and their activities provoked brutal reprisals on local people. I remember that in Italy partisans had been unwelcome for a similar reason. They ate up food stocks and alerted the Germans, who in reprisal lined up local dignitaries in the village square and shot them. In Smith's Rhodesia the prime aim of the guerrillas was to intimidate, cow and force villagers to cooperate. This was done by torturing headmen as "sell-outs". Their ears and noses were cut off or they were flayed alive in front of their wives. The "burning necklaces" used by young South African blacks are part of the same tactics of terror.

STONEMAN

Stoneman, Information and Cultural officer at the British Embassy, has given me lunch at the Actors Club. He is married, about thirty, modest and helpful. But I think he is curious

---

[1] Nicholas Bethell: *The Last Secret*, Futura 1976.
[2] Nikolai Tolstoy: *Victims of Yalta*, 1977 and *Stalin's Secret War*, 1981.

about my real motives for swanning about Poland. In a police state everyone is suspect and no one can be taken for granted. I learn that the British Embassy staff numbers about fifty; there are ten British Council employees, ten other teachers, and a business community. Talking of the past, I described how Hitler's panzers had flushed out a strange bag of British citizens who had been lying low for years in eastern Europe. Many were married to local wives and when they had been forced out into the light of day they had caused untold confusion among consulates. Some were ex-servicemen who had taken wives while working as prisoners-of-war on Polish and German farms. One I had heard of had been left a sawmill in the Steiermark. The British Consul in Constanza, I recalled, had an extremely stout Bulgarian wife. During their evacuation to Cairo in 1940 they were caught by an earthquake tremor in a Bucharest hotel, the wife panicked, the bed collapsed and she got stuck. Stoneman had no details of old timers who might be staying on in their old age in Poland – but there must be some.

Robert Maxwell is due to visit Warsaw to arrange for the publication of General Jaruzelski's speeches. They have been translated and the collection is to appear in July ("very quick work"). I suggested that Maxwell might have financial interests in Poland. As a generous man he might well give some help to the poor Jewish community.

The embassy, Stoneman said, had no trouble with hitch-hikers – "they keep well away from us". The black market rate for the dollar varied according to the price of a bottle of whisky. He agreed about the Polish obsession with past military exploits – "vital to their self-respect". We were served greasy pork cutlets and soggy vegetables which neither of us could finish. "Poles eat too much," said Stoneman.

Later I had tea with an unmarried Polish woman who works for the radio. Her remarks interested me. Though many Poles were eager to emigrate, she said, they were often apprehensive about adjusting to life in a foreign country. Poles had become conditioned to government and state control over their daily lives and would find it strange to fend for themselves as individuals. Poles would willingly leave Poland only if they had relatives or friends to help them through the early stages of displacement.

Polish wives, she complained, have a hard life, often leaving early in the morning for work then coming back to look after the home, cooking and children. "Polish husbands look very loving when they are pushing a pram on Sundays with their wives, but don't deceive yourself." She smiled. "They have other interests." Women brought up in the countryside – as a great many town dwellers are – expect a life of toil. Divorce and abortion are frequent. The Pope denounces abortion but for modern Polish women piety is not enough to dissuade them from the operation. The government of course does not accept the Pope's teaching in this matter.

Discussing anti-Semitism my companion made it clear that she could not acknowledge even Polish-born Jews as "real Poles". Jews always stressed their own distinct culture and custom and their rabbis, she said, were to blame for their insistence on preserving this difference. A Polish-born Jew might achieve world fame, like Singer, Sabin, Rubinstein or Menachem Begin. But he was still regarded as a non-Pole. He could die as a martyr in the cause of Poland; but that would not make him into a Pole.

JEWS

I have revisited the synagogue. An old man with a stick greeted me while I was standing in the garden. He said he was born in 1908 and worked as a cobbler and shoemaker. He offered to take me into the synagogue. "Just give me a few dollars and your life will be blessed."

The caretaker also had a stick and limped badly. He let me in and gave me a black paper skull-cap to cover my head. The first thing I noticed inside the synagogue was an open Talmud on the lectern and a beautiful and costly Persian carpet. I was warned not to speak. The old shoemaker motioned to me and said, "Touch the page of the Talmud with your open palm and you will have luck in your life – in your whole life."

"I'm already seventy-two," I said, "my time is almost finished."

"That's nothing. I am seventy-five." He asked me again for dollars – "a gift will bring you happiness (*szczescie*)."

Outside the synagogue we sat on a bench and I gave him a

pound. He was suspicious of it as he couldn't decipher the value (700 zlotys in the black market). "I was the finest shoemaker in Warsaw," he claimed. "I made the best shoes. That is why the Germans didn't kill me."

Another man joined us. Neither could understand why I, "a gentleman and a professor", was living in a van and sleeping out at night. "It is dangerous. And you are a respectable gentleman." I explained that I had been living in a camping van in Africa for four years. This was too much for them. I was a liar.

On the ground floor of a new block near the synagogue are a Jewish social club, the editorial office of a Jewish newspaper (written mainly in Hebrew, with sections in Polish), and the Jewish theatre, which has a team of Jewish actors. I was admiring some cleverly designed posters in the foyer of the theatre when the porter, a burly man with a face like a potato pudding, called out "Are you English? What about the massacre in Brussels football stadium?"

"They were just drunken louts."

The porter seemed to be very angry. "You English! You send your own hooligans to massacre innocent spectators at Brussels. Yet in the war you used other people to do the killing for you – Poles, Frenchmen, negroes."

"The football fans were unemployed drop-outs."

"Nonsense," he scoffed. "Unemployed men can't afford boat fares and hundreds of dollars just to see a football match. These were ordinary English people – a very bad lot!"

After he had cooled down he said, "I don't blame you personally. You're too old for that sort of hooliganism." He added that he had served as a soldier under General Maczek in Germany. I gave him some cigarettes.

As I walked home I passed many queues. Poles try to do their shopping early as bread goes stale by the afternoon, milk (bottles or plastic packs) and cream (*smietana*) quickly turn sour and fresh fruit is soon sold out. Despite shortages people are frequently overweight. Men grow thick and women spongy. Emma says this is due to too many carbohydrates in their diet – potatoes, noodles and pancakes, groats, heavy bread, milk products and sweet cakes. But food in any case doesn't interest me much. The hideous rustling of packets of crisps in buses and shopping precincts in England, the smell of fried chips, have put me off potatoes for ever.

There's no doubt that hunting for simple purchases in the Warsaw stores, standing in the rain against shop fronts, barging and pushing and the frustration you feel when the last loaf of bread or tin of sardines is snapped up in front of you, ruin the citizen's temper and make him morose, quarrelsome or envious according to his disposition. Some customers are rude, and push past you through the shop doorway. Some are greedy. Heavy-breathing ones with ponderous bodies reach over your shoulders. Little old ladies can't find their change and waste time. There are so many coins and crumpled notes to be counted out, checked and put safely away in your purse. Parcels and packages have to be stuffed into plastic carriers that break. Look carefully when you step out on to the pavement: there may be a puddle or a hole. Hold your purchases tight as you battle through the late afternoon scrum to board a tram. You won't find the luxury here of people shopping from car parks. Since I am an outsider the discomforts of life under Socialist rule scarcely bother me. But one senses the humiliation and depression. The Poles know that by comparison with their own country, the West is a consumer's paradise. They look for scapegoats: the Russians; corrupt and inefficient government; the great burden of armaments. They feel there is an age-old conspiracy against the Polish nation. Conditioned to control their feelings, the crowds move on with grey, set faces, self-absorbed,uncommunicative, to seek refuge in the kitchen with their families, in the parks, in churches, in the vodka bottle.

GYPSY MANNERS

The camp has been filling up with caravans, school parties and gypsies. Three families of Finns have arrived, crossing by ferry to Gdansk and motoring to Warsaw. One of them, a fat white-bearded man, tells me he has been coming here for the past five years: "the damp Polish air is good for me". He spends much of his time lying on a long bench in his nightgown, then strips off to his underpants, pats his great belly, waddles about a bit, sits down for food, and goes to sleep again.

The gypsies, like any primitive society, have an ideal division of functions. When they are not in the city doing "business" the men lie on the grass under trees until it is time to drink. Their women are always busy – washing clothes, airing the bedding, which is excellent (soft warm quilts that are white and clean), scolding the children, stirring cooking pots, chattering and singing in the toilets. Their high harsh voices, raven locks and physical grace belong not to the misty beet-fields and swamps of Poland but to the warm south-east where the grapes and the Indian corn grow. In the evening the men get drunk. Shoes are thrown and there are scuffles with wives. In the morning everything is quiet again. One of the men, a short tubby fellow in a T-shirt with a big Lech Walesa moustache pokes his head into my van and says "I am sorry" – he means "good morning". They talk to me about prices, the value of my van and my possessions and offer to buy whatever I have (pump, tools, transistor). They joke about Poles, calling them "a foolish people, always in trouble with their neighbours". The tragedy of Polish history, they say, has been the Poles' refusal to come to terms with the Russians – "the flea biting the elephant". They should settle with what they have and start to earn money. "The Poles know nothing about making money but always complain they are poor. We are gypsies," they add, "and the Poles look down on us." Then they laugh. "But we're clever. We can earn as much as we like. We know our way through the regulations. If you're caught, bribe your way out."

Mr Poinc naturally doesn't like his gypsy colony. They leave empty beer bottles about, throw rubbish behind the tents, and the men drive their cars recklessly, skidding and cutting deep ruts in the grass. They bring new toys for their children every day. I have to keep an eye on one boy of about five; he is intrigued by my van and its contents. They remind him of a travelling shop and he is waiting to pinch something.

Mr Poinc has been shocked by the television pictures of English football hooligans in Brussels. "They did a terrible thing. What has happened to the English gentleman!" I am made to share in their disgrace. But the young lawyer who exercises his dog in the camp, a sleek Weimeraner with yellow eyes, has told me not to feel upset. "The football rioters," he said, "showed the right spirit, only they attacked the wrong people. They should have a go at the Russians."

Pani Zofia, who comes every morning with her grand-daughter and her knitting, has also seen the riot pictures and thinks of the English now as pirates who cross the sea into foreign countries in raiding parties. She too can't stand gypsies. "They are thieves and speculators (*hochstapler*). The Germans would have known how to deal with them – and with football hooligans." She shows concern for my health ("You will get a stiff back sitting in that tin box"), disapproves of my wandering life, and lists the delightful dishes she would prepare for me if I took a lodging in her apartment (*pierogi*, sour soup, cutlets, *kasha, smietana*). She would keep my clothes spotless and I would not be disturbed in my reading. I think of her as a kind woman. But the fear of being coddled, watched and no doubt rebuked discourages me.

Summer visitors keep the camp staff busy. The wooden toilet seats are smeared with excrement as though some people squat on top of them like mullahs at prayer. The workmen have not finished rebuilding the bath house. The cement bags lie out in the rain. After a spasm of activity they sit down and smoke. They are heavily built, good-natured men, like the old English navvies, and move like tortoises. Yesterday at midnight a school teacher called on me with a bottle of wine. He was in charge of twelve boys from Gdansk. They had two small tents and a heavy shower had made them wet and miserable. "They are fine boys," he said. "But Poland is a shit country. Not all of us can milk the system and I shall never earn enough to buy a car – let alone maintain one." He would have liked to get drunk, but I gave him coffee and he went unwillingly back to his waterlogged tent.

The weather has turned cold and wet. People have gone back to woollen pullovers and padded coats. The chill camp air seeps through the rusty chassis of my van. In the night I wrap myself in spare raincoat and duffle bag with extra newspapers and cardboard sheets under my body. At such times I am tempted to make my way back to Africa. The cold has scattered the campers.

Walking along Hoza street past my old address at Pani Petrovna's I found a small antiques shop. Among the old leather straps, war medals, statuettes and fishing tackle I recognised some snapshots of Polish soldiers taken in the Western

Desert and Italy. Farther along I went into a small dressmaker's to shelter from a shower. It was damp and stuffy inside. The woman in charge, who was in her sixties, gave me tea. She didn't remember my two former landladies. "All the old residents have gone. Why is Poland so unlucky?"

"It's a matter of geography," I said.

"Not at all. The Germans are right when they call us an improvident people. Poles don't have the knack of saving so our economy is always in trouble."

"But do you want to live like *Hausfraus*? You would die of boredom!"

The rain has filled the roads with puddles. Passing buses and cars throw spouts of muddy water over pedestrians walking near the gutters. I notice how many of the rebuilt frontages of buildings conceal shabby, unplastered courtyards and walls still scarred with holes.

Late in the evening – it was after 11 p.m. – I was waiting at a deserted bus stop on Wawelska street when I saw a large brown envelope lodged in a corner of the seat. I picked it up. "Don't be afraid. Pass on", was written on it in large letters. I opened it and found six duplicated copies of a Solidarity news sheet. I was alone and unobserved and took a copy to read at my leisure. But I mustn't get caught with it.

OKOPOWA CEMETERY

Today I took a tram to the big Jewish cemetery at Okopowa. It is surrounded by a high brick wall. I entered through an iron gate, passed the caretaker's office and went along a path through the most recent part of the burial ground. The tombs are dated up to 1940, they are in fairly good condition and the epitaphs are bilingual, in Hebrew and Polish, using both sides of the headstones. Many are elaborately carved with roofs and railings and costly marble steles.

I then turned into the older part of the cemetery. Here the sun never penetrates. The headstones are rotting and choked by bushes and brambles, slabs lie at random as though toppled by a typhoon, the ground is sodden with humus, the inscriptions (they are in Hebrew only) have eroded. Trees sprout through the graves, forming an abandoned scrub. When a breeze blows they rub and grind against each other and their angled branches creak like skeletons.

I sat down on a headstone. There was no human sound. Only the creaking of wood, the chirping of sparrows, and magpies calling to each other, their long tails fluttering like fans. Here was nothing but dereliction: a scene of wreckage that was being swallowed up by plants and obliterated by winter frosts. One expected to see snakes coiled among the debris.

When I walked on a wild-looking youth came from behind a crumbling tomb. He said he had lost his way, and seemed highly strung and nervous. He showed me a horrid scar on the inside of his arm – "I was beaten up because I am a Jew".

Back in the new section of the burial ground there was sunlight and I could see that someone had been tidying up. The gravestones have been built to last – many are made of granite and marble – and their impressive size and elaborate workmanship are intended to remind one of the former prosperity and importance of the deceased. In this sense they show hubris and imply bourgeois virtues. All the familiar names are to be found: Feigenblat, Strumpfmann, Szpacenkopf, Finkelszteyn, Sukierman, Goldman, Fliederbaum. There are mineral names (Silberszteyn and Diamant), vegetable names (Weinbaum), animal names (Hirschbein), occupational names (Schneider), rustic names (Taubenhaus) and names deliberately chosen by Gentiles long ago to brand or humiliate them.

Relatives or close friends have added fresh names and words to some of the steles: "Family burnt in Treblinka". "In memory of the victims of German bestiality". "Killed by a Fascist bullet". "Tortured to death". These are cries of anger as well as compassion. But it is too late to avenge them. The generation of Nazis who were responsible are now dead or in their dotage.

I saw about a dozen Jews in the cemetery including a group of mourners. The men had covered their heads – some wore skullcaps and one man was holding a satchel over his head. I had brought my own headgear – my balaclava – but it was so hot I took it off. At the gate I spoke with the attendant, a young Jew. He told me there had been no serious vandalism, "Nothing to complain of – just a few youths, louts, not Germans". But proper upkeep of the cemetery, he complained, was beyond the resources of the Jewish community in Warsaw. "We are poor.

Most of the Jews are old, living lonely lives in small rooms.
Having survived for so long we are determined to go on to the
bitter end."

The ritual carvings and the decay are sad and beautiful. The
memory of racial murder has left its trace in the messages cut
out by relatives in the stones. But those lying here knew
nothing of the holocaust. Their remains were not dragged out
of Nazi death pits or scooped up as a handful of ashes from a
prison swamp. Only the few who have added fresh names to the
steles speak for them.

Next day I revisited the cemetery at Okopowa to look again at
the carved stones that with the passing of Polish Jewry are fated
to become rarities and mere relics. The steles (the older ones
are generally of sandstone) are of various shapes: arched, rec-
tangular or triangular. Among the decorative motifs are plants,
animals and birds, objects relating to the deceased's profession,
symbols of death and the Star of David. There are carved
wreaths of flowers: the lion (symbol of the tribe of Judah), tiger
and eagle and beasts of the Apocalypse; two hands joined
together in the gesture of blessing – this is the mark of a priest
(*kohen*); a hand holding a quill (a scribe); candelabra (*memorah*)
or seven-branched candlesticks symbolising the temple of
Judah; the elaborately chiselled epitaphs with their Star of
David (two triangles).

It is not until you leave the ornate plots facing the cemetery
entrance and wander into the wilderness of tumbled slabs and
weed that the destructiveness of time becomes so wantonly
apparent. Graves and sepulchres split by birch trees, fragments
of eroded stone, nettles, brambles, darkness and damp. Jews
say that as the body returns to the earth so the earth must be
allowed to take it over. Even so, nature seems to have re-
sponded with devastation and cold indifference.

SAMIZDAT

The *samizdat* bulletin I had found in the bus shelter late at
night was poorly duplicated and the print was smudged. The
articles dealt with Solidarity and internal politics. After my visit
to the Jewish cemetery at Okopowa the item on "Polish attitudes

towards the Jews during the War" especially interested me. It was as follows:

I have not seen Lanzmann's film *Shoah* which has recently caused such a storm in the Polish People's Republic. But I am aware that the majority of both Poles and Jews view the Jewish problem in terms of stereotypes. The Polish stereotype may not care to admit it, but solidarity or fellow-feeling with the Jews was limited. Yet, whatever the Jewish stereotype may say, Polish anti-Semitism was not a vital factor in the implementing of the German plan of extermination.

Offering help to the Jews carried the risk of death. In the face of this risk it is astonishing how many Poles did bring themselves to offer disinterested help.[1] Religious houses had a particularly good record. But giving help in return for money was more frequent than purely disinterested help. This was entirely understandable in the circumstances and is nothing to be ashamed of. Several tens of thousands of Jews are alive today thanks to the good offices of Poles. Or, to be more precise, to certain Poles and despite others.

The death camps were located in Poland where most Jews were to be found and where the occupation was most tyrannical and complete. Yet there is nothing to suggest that the Germans counted on local anti-Semitism. No Polish organisation took part in the extermination campaign. In this sense the Poles bear no guilt. There was, however, a plague of blackmailers who tracked down hidden Jews: it was because of them that when a Jew ventured out into the street he risked being denounced. Again this was only a marginal factor. Most of Polish society was passive, and in view of the Nazi occupation terror it was an entirely understandable attitude. Anyone who fails to appreciate this is either ignorant or bears ill-will. But things did not end with passivity. Indifference, a feeling that "it's none of my business," was widespread. And there were those who felt pleased that the era during which

[1] The film director Roman Polanski, a Jew, survived the war in Cracow as a young boy being sheltered by a family called Wilk, who later gave him into the care of the Buchalas, a poor couple living in Wysoka hamlet. See his autobiography *Roman* (1984).

Jews had "ruled the roost" was coming to an end, and that Poland's Jewish problem had been taken out of her hands and was being solved by non-Poles. Finally the disappearance of the Jews brought material gains to Poles who took over their shops, houses and possessions.

The occupation of Poland did not end Polish anti-Semitism. When the Polish flag was hoisted over the ghetto during the Jewish uprising in Warsaw, the underground newspaper of the Stronnictwo Narodowe wrote: "Even the Jews now fighting for their lives realise that it is not their own fate as Jews – a hundred times deserved – that can move the world, but that of the Poles." Statements like this did not occur in the official AK press yet they testify to the atmosphere. And Jews who lived through the occupation in Poland remember it well. Their experiences were often nightmarish: one doesn't need a martyrdom complex to describe them; they were the truth. The Jews felt constantly threatened. Blackmail, hatred and robbery were so common that they dared not trust anyone apart from a few friends. Some armed Polish units regarded the Jews as enemies and murdered them when they came out of hiding even when they had crossed the battle lines. Jews who managed to escape from the ghettos and transports found themselves in a tragic plight. Usually the AK forest partisans units refused to accept them and they had no one to go back to. When they were forced by necessity to steal food they risked being killed by the partisans.

The walls of the ghetto really did divide. Attempts made by the Polish underground to provide cooperation and help deserve Jewish gratitude, but when they came – towards the end of 1942 – it was too late. By then the majority of Polish Jews had been taken off to be exterminated. There was no underground campaign to organise escapes from the transports moving from the ghettos to the death camps – this was probably impossible yet Jews, often bitter and resentful, did not want to believe this. Nazi occupation extended over so much territory that millions would have died anyway, even if all Poles had been philo-Semites.

However when it comes to the conduct of individuals, things could have been different. That sympathy for the Jews was by no means general can be seen from the work published by

Borwicz, who immediately after the war, under the auspices of the Jewish Historical Committee, began to collect lists of people who had helped Jews. Many of these people complained that their actions had got them into trouble or had involved them in reprisals.

Tragic experiences are often the basis for unfair generalisations. If Lanzmann's film is really one-sided, painting an exclusively black picture of the behaviour of the Poles, then this is an insult to all those who acted honourably and innocently. It debases them to the same level as those who really deserved to be condemned. It is unjust and harmful if films, discussions or propaganda make use of terrible experiences to reinforce negative prejudices and stereotypes. But it is clearly impossible to give a full picture of that period without emphasising the Jewish experience and for Poles this requires the courage to face up to bitter truths. It is irrelevant for Polish newspapers to point out things that the French should feel guilty about. We have just seen that unlike Polish publications and commentators their counterparts in France manage to talk openly about the attitudes of French society towards the extermination of the Jews.

Abel Kolner

It seems that the writer is trying to strike a balance. The Poles didn't like the Jews: and helping them under the Nazi occupation would have endangered their own lives – though money talked. The result was an attitude of "it's not my business". Unfortunately denunciation of Jews and their deliberate rejection were all too common and led to many deaths. The film is a challenge to Polish self-esteem. But it should be openly discussed, not dismissed by critics and newspaper editorials as unfair or untrue. One might add here a comment on war-time relations between Poles and Jews that was made by Czeslaw Milosz, winner of the 1980 Nobel Prize for Literature, in his autobiographical *Native Realm* (1968). Referring to the slaughter of some three million "non-Aryan" Polish citizens by the Nazis, he says:

As an eye witness to the crime of genocide and therefore deprived of the luxury of innocence, I am prone to agree with the accusations brought against myself and others. In reality, however, it is not so easy to judge, because the price of aiding the victims of terror was the death penalty. Individual behaviour depended upon too many circumstances and motives to be able to establish for certain the connection with prewar anti-Semitic tendencies. Religious motives (convents particularly distinguished themselves in rescue operations), personal courage, neighborly ties, or greed for money clashed with physical impossibility, fear, or apathy. Blackmailers, recruited from the scum of the citizenry, constituted a grave danger for refugees from the ghetto, who presented an opportunity for easy plunder. If some political organizations in Poland had openly collaborated, as they did in other countries Hitler conquered, the picture would be clearer. But Polish collaborationists were simply killed. So any Nazi sympathizers (and there were some) had at least to keep up the appearances of noncollaboration. The extreme Right had not, of course, disappeared; it fed the ranks of the underground Home Army and the National Armed Forces (a not very numerous Fascist group). If the Home Army permitted more than one furtive slaying of Jews who had taken cover in the forests, it was a decision made by individual officers or soldiers, and it depended on personal attitudes. The National Armed Forces, on the other hand, officially planned many of their raids. As for the Left, both Socialist and Communist parties entered the war either weak or divided, and it was not they who set the tone for the Resistance movement.

Milosz ends with the bitter conclusion that the Old Poland has gone, replaced by a new organism with different borders and almost clear of its minorities. "Flames consumed the old synagogue: the foot of some passerby in the city suburbs trips over the remains of a gravestone with Hebrew letters – all that is left of the old cemeteries."

Soon after reading the samizdat article I came across a passage in Janina David's *A Touch of Earth* (1966) in which two Jewish girls are discussing the theme of Polish anti-Semitism. Janina survived the holocaust in the care of nuns and became a

Catholic. Sabina was hidden by a Polish village family. She is still afraid of being recognised in the street as Jewish and hides her face in public.

"The Poles hate us – they wonder how we survived and they wish we hadn't. If they had a chance of sticking a knife in us, they'd do it!"

"Oh, Saba, really, pull yourself together! The Germans are gone. No one sticks knives in Jews any more."

She looked at me as if I had gone mad. "No one? So you don't remember what happened in Kielce as soon as the Germans were out? There was a pogrom! Yes, a pogrom. Just like in the good old days before the war. They were sorry the Germans didn't have time to finish off the last few Jews and they weren't going to let them escape. That's how they love us, your Poles!"

I stood before her, quite helpless. It was true. There had been a pogrom. There was anti-Semitism as there always had been and always would be. There were Poles who still openly regretted that Hitler had had no time to finish us all off. Only the other day a man had followed me on a bicycle, driving close to look at my face and then with a hissed 'Jew' he spat at my feet and drove off. And no one intervened.

"How you can go over to their side now, after all they've done to us, is quite beyond my understanding," continued Sabina. "Don't you feel odd in a church? Don't you feel all those eyes boring into your back: can't you see that they don't want you to be there, that you don't belong? Everybody knows you in this town. They know you are Jewish and no matter how often you go to church, Jewish you'll always be. And they'll tell you that one of these days if they haven't already. I'd rather die than run that risk. All I want is to leave this country and while I'm still here to keep away from them as much as possible."

"But Saba, they can't all be bad. Look, I was hidden by the nuns who knew who I was and your family were also saved by Poles."

"The nuns thought they'd got your soul, which was all they were interested in. If you had been recognised and arrested they'd have felt that you died as a Catholic, which made

everything all right, even though you'd have been murdered
for being a Jew! And as for us, we were lucky. I don't deny
there were some brave Poles who took enormous risks. And
don't forget that they had to guard against their fellow citizens, not against the Germans who hardly ever recognised a
Jew anyway. But the good were few. Too few. They would
not have saved Sodom and Gomorrah and they did not save
the honour of this country!"

There is a bitter realism and helplessness in this dialogue
between two young Jewish girls. In the pogrom in Kielce (4
July 1946) that is referred to, forty-two Jews were killed. This
was the climax of murderous incidents that had been going on
since the end of the war. Following the Kielce murders 100,000
Polish Jews, more than half the survivors, fled abroad.

7
EXPULSION

PEKING MAN

An English couple with a baby have arrived at the camp on a tandem bicycle pulling a two-wheeled trailer. They pedalled past my van looking like an animated haystack, and the sight of the baby peeping out like a small pink animal caused a sensation among the campers. They have a tiny tent and a tarpaulin to protect them from the elements. I went to see them. The man asked me for toilet paper. "I haven't used toilet paper for months," I told him.

The baby (Katy-Jane) is only a few months old and is healthy and smiling. The mother is slightly built and pretty. The father – his name is Greenhalgh – has a scarred face and flattened nose and is made of stringy muscle. He is wearing a workman's cloth cap and a T-shirt marked "Wicked Wolf". He tells me he is a self-employed plumber. They come from Colchester and intend to cycle to Peking. Various firms – the bicycle manufacturer and food suppliers – are sponsoring the journey. They are carrying (in my opinion) an enormous weight, but as the north European plain is flat from Holland to the Urals they have chosen favourable cycling country. The baby, harnessed to the carrier behind her mother, smiles and gurgles.

They are cheerful and in the best of health. But they have had problems and I fear there will be more to come. The East German authorities not only refused to let them cycle across the Democratic Republic but said it was against the regulations to load a tandem and trailer on the Berlin train. After persuasion the East Germans relented and the family were allowed to camp at the end of a corridor. The Poles too had refused to let them use their bicycle. Again they had to take the train. "It looks as if we shall be sitting in a train all the way to Moscow," said the man. "It may be different in China."

"Perhaps the Chinese will let you cycle along the top of the Great Wall," I said.

The Polish staff and some of the campers are concerned about the couple. "It's foolhardy to expose a baby to such an ordeal," they complain. Pani Zofia says the baby will fall sick and die. "It's criminal. It shouldn't be allowed."

But the mother is admirably calm and confident. "When people tell me 'Your baby will get sick' I point to their own babies and say 'My child looks much healthier than yours.' That shuts them up."

"Having the baby with us actually helps," the father told me. This in a way is true, for people will be kind to daring freaks. I wonder if they will complete their marathon journey. They have money and the good people of Colchester are sponsoring them. But what will the dust, the glare, the endless bumpy miles and tainted water do to the young mother's fresh face and graceful limbs? I wish them luck.

At one of Emma's parties the British Council came in for criticism. The library opening hours are too short (from midday to 6 p.m.) and the premises are shut down for two months every summer. Not long ago the library got rid of 30,000 books. The British Council policy of discouraging English literature courses in favour of linguistics was also deplored. In consequence, in the English studies department (*Anglistyka*), which has 400 students, only thirty have opted for literature, with fifty doing linguistics. Sensitive governments naturally suspect foreign literatures. Their political message may be unwelcome.

An architect and a girl who had studied for two years in Moscow had some interesting things to say about Russia. They are convinced that the USSR will never willingly relax its hold over Poland. But for Poles a united Germany as a counterpoise to Russia would not be welcome either. Poles tend to look down on Russians as backward children, but they fear German efficiency and organising ability. A united Germany would want to boss the Poles: *Befehl* in place of *prikaz*, a Prussian drill-sergeant instead of an *apparatchik*.

The girl had been impressed by the strength of Russian patriotism. Russians were proud of their achievements under

Communism in missiles, space research, satellites and international sport. But they had a paranoid fear of being encircled by the West – a fear drilled into them day by day by massive propaganda.

Emma's parties usually go on till midnight. The last buses and trams cease soon after 11 pm. There are few taxis, so the guests walk home. I have walked the two miles back to camp many times. The experience is rather eerie. Street lighting is dim and one walks through caves of black shadow. The bars have closed, the cinemas and churches are empty, working-class people are squashed for the night in their crowded tenement blocks in the outer suburbs. There are no street cats. But a few dog owners take their spaniels and Alsatians for a late walk round the squares. My friends warn me about the risk of being "mugged" but I note they take no precautions themselves. Soon after ten, in fact, Warsaw is dead. The shadows and the quiet give one a sense of comfort as well as loneliness. People who haven't much money are bound to go early to bed. And there is another deterrent to late hours. Patrol cars and plain-clothes police agents are never far away. No one wants to be questioned and harassed by them after dark.

Yesterday I went to the opera to see 'La Bohème.' It started early, at 7 p.m., to enable people to return home before the streets became eerily empty. The audience had put on ties and well-worn suits, their best coats and jewellery. The atmosphere was correct and rather solemn, the foyer spartan and draughty. Later, at Emma's, guests called and there was much discussion over bottles of wine. One of the subjects was the role of foreign cultural influences, especially the French, on Poland.

Poland has never had colonies. She has taken a European, not a world view of history. Before the war the Poles showed scant interest in British culture. Conrad, who settled in England and wrote in English, was an aberration. It was the culture of the French which the Poles admired, its intellectualism and revolutionary spirit. The Poles often found themselves fighting on the opposite side to the British. Kosciuszko fought for the American rebels. Dabrowski's Polish Legionaries were raised in Italy (with two other Legions) to fight for Napoleon in the hope of a restored Poland. They were misled, crushed in battle (1799–1800), and the reserves sent off to quell a slave rebellion

in Santo Domingo where they perished of fever: those who
survived surrendered to the British army. In June 1812 almost
100,000 Poles marched with Napoleon's Grande Armée to
Moscow. After the battle of Borodino they reached Moscow in
September. (As a boy Alexander Herzen's nurse used to tell
him how Napoleon's dragoons galloped down the street with
horses' tails tied to their helmets.) A month later, after the
burning of the capital, the French began their disastrous retreat through blizzards and ambushes. Napoleon abandoned his
troops and left them to die in the snow, hurrying back through
Warsaw like a ghost, without even calling on his Polish mist-
ress, Countess Walewska. Of the 100,000 who had crossed the
Niemen six months earlier, only about 20,000 Poles survived.

Chopin lived in Paris. So did Mickiewicz (London, alas, had
Karl Marx). The Poles admired Byron, Dickens, Oscar Wilde
and Jack London, an American. Today everyone knows of
Orwell, though his *1984* is banned. But for the Poles, the
British stood outside the main European stream. We were
thought of as merchants, seamen and imperialists. We fought
best at sea or in remote colonial campaigns against natives. We
were envied for our steadfast patriotism and for our monarchy.
It is a French soldier General Weygand who used to be cited as
one of the saviours of Poland at the Miracle of the Vistula
(Pilsudski's defeat of the Red Army in 1922).

After the September 1939 campaign the bulk of the Polish
soldiers and airmen who escaped were routed to France. The
Carpathian Lancers went to French-administered Syria. Again
it was the French connection that let the Poles down. When
Vichy betrayed them the Lancers had to move to Palestine. The
Poles in France had to be evacuated to Britain.

The French were elegant, chic, gallant and intellectual. The
Englishman used to be caricatured with a pipe, a tweed jacket
and a shot gun (Carton de Wiart, who lived for years as a
country gentleman in the Pripet marshes, was looked up to as
the eccentric prototype). The Poles would have preferred fighting their war from France. Instead they got Scotland and
Grimsby, Earls Court and Kensington.

As for Germany, there is no denying the lack of empathy
between Poles and Germans. For the ordinary Russian, Poles
have much fellow feeling. They are both Slavs. Germans,

however, stir up the Polish inferiority complex. The Pole can't bear the thought of Germans breathing down his neck and ordering him about – *"Laufschritt*! At the double!" It seems the Germans have been corrupted by having as neighbours people they have historically looked down on as "inferior" – notorious (in the German view) for their *Schlamperei*. Contiguity has brought out the worst side – the bully – in the German. "Inferiors" must be bossed!

One of the best-known Jewish public figures Nahum Gold-mann wrote of the Germans (*Mein Leben als deutscher Jude*, 1983) that they have the vices of their virtues. Without their singular qualities of discipline and respect for authority, their lack of revolutionary courage, their thoroughness and perfec-tionism, they would never have tolerated the Nazis' crimes or been capable of organising such scientific butchery. Theirs was "barbarism based on an index card system".

All these, of course, are for a Pole self-evident truths. But it is disturbing to hear them brought up again.

Emma and I have seen a Yiddish play at the Jewish theatre. The house was half full. Headphones with simultaneous translation from Yiddish to Polish were provided but the confused doubling of voices spoiled their effect. The play, a comic satire, opened with a boastful young Nazi official in a brown uniform with swastika armband and jackboots strutting about in a fever of self-importance. Suddenly his world collapses. He discovers that through an appalling error – the mixing up of two newborn babies in a hospital – he is a Jew! The hysteria and trauma that follow are finally resolved by both the Jewish and Christian relatives involved in the scandal agreeing that it was, after all, "a matter of no importance. Jew and Christian share a common humanity. They are both 'people'." It was an idealistic and, I think, improbable solution.

After the play we walked into the Old Town looking for a bar. Only one was open, a small wine parlour selling expensive red wine for tourists. We walked back through a city that had gone to sleep: dark stones, silent churches, dripping trees.

A VISA PROBLEM

June was almost over. I had stayed in Warsaw longer than I had planned and it was time to start my journey to Cracow and

Czestochowa. I reclaimed my passport, which I had entrusted to the camp office for safekeeping, and made an appointment with the visa department to pay the balance of zlotys required to cover my stay in Poland and extend my visa. The office secretary said there would be no problem as long as I had the cash.

The visa department is in a grimy building in Okrzei street across the river in Praga. I waited in a corridor with a Greek, a Hungarian, a Somali, some Turks and Arabs and helped them fill in their forms. There were five doors. Every time an official left his little office he had to lock it. As the locks were stiff and the doors ill-fitting the effect was comical and irritating.

Pani Dyrektor, the head of the visa office, was a handsome, severe looking blonde in her thirties. Her shopping bag hung over a chair. She gave me a cigarette and we chatted amicably. She asked me about my previous connections with Poland and my life in Africa and smiled. "You have had an interesting life." She gave me an application form to fill in and told me to come back the following day to collect the visa.

That night – it was after midnight – I was awoken by a tap on the door of my van. It was the young Polish lawyer whom I had often spoken to in the camp. His face looked white and serious in the shadows. He beckoned me to follow him behind a bush. "Don't wake anyone," he whispered.

"Panie Denisie," he said, "you are in trouble. In serious trouble. You must be very careful what you do."

I asked him to explain. He was reluctant to say more but repeated his warning and added, "There is a spy in the American news office (ABC). *They know about you.*" He wouldn't elaborate and was nervous. I went back to my stretcher bed wondering what I could have done to blot my copybook with the authorities. I had in fact been keeping a deliberately "low profile". I had turned myself into a bore. I lit the candle and ran through everything I had done in Warsaw.

I had been once to the British Embassy – to sign, like a loyal subject, the visitors' book – and I had had lunch with the Ambassador at his residence and attended the Queen's Birthday party. I had eaten a vile pork chop with Stoneman in the Actors' Club. I had dined with Barnett, the British Council representative.

After a meal with Kevin Ruane I had taken a Sunday

afternoon walk with him through two cemeteries where we had
discussed Everton football and Polish women ("they are very
good," said Kevin, "and have self respect"), and he had shown
me the two Katyn massacre memorials. Roger Boyes of *The
Times* had taken me as a guest to one of Urban's weekly press
conferences in which trivia had been discussed, and I had then
gone with him to eat a hamburger at the American news office
(ABC). Later I had stayed three nights in Roger's empty, eerie
flat browsing through his books and had been perturbed by
Mayakovsky's doggerel lines on Lenin. I had not written a
single word for a newspaper and I didn't intend to.

I had drunk Balkan wine with Emma's university friends at
jolly parties, discussed African literature with some lecturers
and students, walked in the parks, eaten tepid food at the
Praha, wandered into churches, visited the Lenin, Jewish and
War museums, discouraged black market touts – I had behaved
in short as a model foreign guest of mature years, smug, respectable, savouring a nostalgic return to former pastures. I was not
a conspirator, neither a "spy" nor an agent. I was not interested
in Polish politicians or the underground stirrings of Solidarity.
I was baffled. I felt aggrieved.

I left early to catch a bus to town. The lawyer's warning had
alerted me and I looked at the people at the bus stop. One
young man in a wind jacket, carrying a shoulder bag, had
walked behind me from the camp gate and seemed to have his
eye on me. I had to change buses twice to get to Praga and wait
in the rain, and when I saw the young man still standing behind
me I realised he was following me. I envied him for he had an
umbrella while I had to walk through a downpour to the visa
office where I arrived drenched.

The blonde woman was waiting for me. Instead of smiling
she gave me a grim look. Two officials came in – an older man
and a younger fellow with a policeman's moustache. They
invited me to take off my wet coat and, as I had expected,
started to interrogate me.

The session lasted for an hour and a half and I felt as though
I was being probed with a strong but badly focused light. The
older man, who had a large, pale expressionless face asked the
questions, his colleague wrote down my answers. Pani Dyrektor
looked at me as though I had jilted her. The pale man started

with a few formal inquiries about my previous work. Then the pattern began to emerge. What were my *real* motives for visiting Poland, my contacts in Warsaw, who was paying me, what was I writing? I listed the questions – not all of them – later in my notebook. Here they are:

Who paid your salary while you were working in Gdynia before the war?
Was it a British or a Polish posting?
Who arranged for you to make your way to Cairo after September 1939 and why did you go there?
What were your duties as a British officer attached to the Polish forces during the war?
Were you present at the Monte Cassino battle?
What happened to your wartime Polish friends when the war was over?
Why didn't you return to Poland straightaway?
Why did you choose to go to Germany to work for the Germans?
Why have you decided to come back to Poland?
Are you a journalist?
What connections have you in Warsaw?
Who were the lecturers you met at the university?
What did you discuss with them? How have you spent your time in Warsaw?
Why did you go to the British Embassy to sign the visitors' book?
What is this book? Where is it kept? Whom do you know at the Embassy?
Where did you learn Russian?
You claim that when you were in Africa the students respected their British teachers. How can that be? You were imperialists!
Are you writing about Poland? I prevaricated here. "I am not a journalist," I said, "and I am not interested in Polish politics. I have written nothing for the press."
Why did you have this desire (*tesknota*) – it is your word – after over forty years, to see Poland again?

I was not surprised that the interrogator found it hard to make sense of my *curriculum vitae*; lecturing to young German

"Fascists"; eight years among the Mussulmans (Turks); four years in Smith's imperialist Rhodesia: fifteen years in Uganda – a country steeped in blood; living in a camping van in the heart of Warsaw. What puzzled him was what I was really doing in Poland and the nature of my connections with the British Embassy and the university. I was clearly up to no good. My camping van was a cover. I must be an agent or a spy.

There was no hint of a smile or a joke during the long questioning. The interrogator was persistent but icily polite. The blonde director watched me closely. When it was over the two men left the office. I knew that my answers had failed to convince the interrogator – it seemed he had already made up his mind about me before the session started. Still, I thought I had done quite well.

When the official came back, spread my passport on the desk and restamped it, I felt for a moment that I had been accepted. Then the shock. "You have forty-eight hours to leave Poland."

I wasn't going to give him the pleasure of seeing me make a scene, of humiliating myself. "You are being discourteous," I said.

"We have made our decision."

"And my thousands of unspent zlotys?"

"You can buy souvenirs," he answered grimly and went away.

As I was leaving I told Pani Dyrektor that I intended to reapply at a Polish consulate for a return entry visa. She was sour and unhelpful. "That would be for others to decide," she said.

It was past noon when I left the grimy police building. To reach the border by midnight on Sunday I had to start next day. The police had been crafty. The British Embassy was already closed for the week-end.

I went immediately to see Roger Boyes and to use his phone to speak to the British consulate. Roger offered to tell his newspaper of my expulsion order but I asked him not to. His secretary, an English-educated Polish girl, warned me to be careful what I said on the phone. "It is bugged."

The consul was away and his deputy, a veteran woman of many years' service, made it clear that as it was a week-end it was too late for the embassy to look into my case. She gave me the routine advice. "Declare all your Polish money at the border, insist on a stamped and signed receipt for it – make sure it is signed, and make a photocopy of it – and you may then authorise someone in Poland to reclaim the cash within twelve months." I would have to leave behind 70,000 zlotys, most of it the unspent part of my visa fee. For me this was a small fortune, equivalent to four to five months' salary for a middle-class Pole.

Emma and her friends were astonished when I told them of the expulsion order. Either I was some sort of impostor – which was unthinkable – or the Poles had made a great nonsense of my affair. I felt very sad to be leaving these splendid people. At a farewell gathering someone said that the police and security interrogators were boors and peasants. One of the guests replied, "Don't blame the police. They have been briefed from above and have their orders. If the *apparatchiks* have the slightest suspicion that security is at stake they show no mercy. What follows is a set-piece. There is no 'human angle'."

Late that night I said goodbye to Andrzej, who was about to leave with his small white trailer and family for a summer holiday at Sopot. He had heard from the camp office that I had been told to go. As we shook hands I looked him straight in the eyes and asked, "Andrzej, what have the police got against me?"

"You are," he said slowly, "a *korespondent* (newspaper man)." After a pause he added, "And perhaps more than that." He declined to say anything further.

I had no time to shop or buy souvenirs: the interrogator had cynically suggested that I might blow my zlotys on "silverware" (which the customs would have confiscated). Emma, Rod and Bogna came to see me off at the camp. Bogna gave me a cold roast duck filled with rich stuffing to eat under a tree by the road side. Mr Poinc didn't say goodbye. He had been watching me suspiciously and was relieved to see my van lumbering through the gate. I was sorry to leave the gypsies and their laughter and absurd quarrels. As I turned into the Zwirki i Wigury road I said to myself, "The Poles can't get away with this. I will be back."

THE ODER

There was not much Sunday traffic. My first stop, Poznan, was 300 kilometres away. The engine beat steadily, the tyres hummed, the fields sparkled under small drifting clouds. Then suddenly – I had feared this moment, for I'd had no time to check the engine – the motor faltered and died. The distributor had given up.

As I was fiddling with it a peasant came up on a bicycle and helped push my van off the carriage-way. He was no mechanic (nor am I) and smelt strongly of vodka. "*Cholera*!" he exclaimed. "But don't worry. There's a mechanic in my village."

"How far?"

"Five kilometres." He pointed across the fields towards a distant blue haze.

Luck seems to favour drunks and careless travellers. A small truck appeared and the peasant waved it down. The driver, a clean young man in his best clothes ("I'm on my way to a wedding"), was the very man I needed. He took off his jacket, rolled up his sleeves and plunged his hands into the greasy black tangle under the bonnet. He worked for half an hour repairing and securing the leads. When the engine fired again he laughed, cleaned himself and drove off to the wedding. The peasant wanted vodka. I gave him money and left him waving in the road. "*Na przod*!" he was crying. "Forward!"

Late that night I camped in a forest layby near Poznan. I was boiling tea next morning when a Fiat car pulled up and the passengers unwrapped cutlet sandwiches. One of the women gave me a large piece of meat and a lump of dark buttered bread. How much nicer ordinary people were than the Warsaw police.

The approach road to the border crossing at Frankfurt-an-der-Oder had been sealed off for repair work and after several diversions I found myself at a sentry box at the end of the bridge. I had been warned that I would need a pass which the NCO now demanded. "You must go back to town and collect one from police headquarters," he said. Then he changed his mind. "You may go."

Outside the police and customs sheds a queue of vehicles was inching its way forward whenever a gap appeared. The official who took my passport gave me a curious look. "What have you done?" he asked. "Did you steal something?" I thought he was joking and asked what was wrong. He pointed to the stamp inserted at the Warsaw visa office. "This is a *wiza administratcyina*, a deportation order."

Neither the British consul's deputy nor I had realised the significance of the entry. It branded me as an undesirable, a sort of malefactor, and I would be closely searched. But I had anticipated trouble and had already put on my long johns by the roadside and stuffed my four travel notebooks inside them. To cover the bulge I was wearing my heavy American raincoat. It made me sweat.

The next thing was to steer into a bay and unload everything on to tables. The official was a stern woman with a thin face. As she examined my books she put a number on one side. They seemed to be a strange choice. Among them were a simple guide book to the stars – it had a picture of a planet and constellations on the dust-jacket (a star wars manual?), a 1918 White Paper on German barbarities among the Hereros of South-West Africa dated 1918 which I had bought as a schoolboy (dismal photographs of manacles and hanged negroes), a Polish émigré newspaper from London, *Dziennik Polski* (banned in the Socialist republic), *Memoirs of a Consul's Wife in Turkey* published in 1879 (harem secrets?) which Emma had picked up in a junk shop, some German Rowohlt paperbacks and a dozen copies of the magazine *Baltic and Scandinavian Countries* which I had helped to edit in Gdynia before the war.

She came back an hour later with a senior official. "We are confiscating these," he said, and wrote down their titles. I protested but was wasting my breath. But Davies's *God's Playground: A History of Poland* and Kazimierz Brandys's *A Warsaw Diary 1978–81* had survived the search.

Handing over my wad of zlotys was like surrendering my purse to a mugger. While I was waiting for a receipt a bus load of Polish tourists going to East Germany drove up. They were told to line up in the road and four of them were taken into an office to be stripped to their underwear. They trotted back grinning like schoolboys.

I went back to my van and looked across the river at the city and the shore. It no longer beckoned. I saw a mass of scarred brown buildings merging into grey prison-like blocks, a dark river and a low sky. It depressed me. Here was a manic instance of hatred and division between nations. The German beast of prey, beaten down and snarling in captivity, crouched on one river bank. The Polish wolf, neutered, sullen and quarrelsome, glared on the other. The country to the west looked back to Bach, Kant, Goethe and Schopenhauer; its Slavonic neighbours to warrior kings and leaders, poets, saints and revolutionaries and the derelict ghettos of Lublin and Lodz. A nation of artisans, organisers and philosophers confronted a race of knights, priests and peasants kneeling before the sad face of a miracle-working icon. Behind the customs sheds stood the garrisons, the flags and battle hymns. The Oder flowed between, vanishing in muddy fields and forests.

The Oder barrier, the searchings, the guards, the guns and tanks camouflaged and deployed among trees and fields, the radio harangues and propaganda, the discordant sound of two rival tongues, were proof that, as in tribal outposts, we live in stealth and suspicion.

The East Germans let me go through without a word. At a lay-by near the Berlin Ring turn-off I talked to a Polish family on their way to Weimar and told them how some of my books had been confiscated. Why were the Polish officials so concerned about a Victorian wife's memoirs and black men hanging from hooks? The explanation turned out to be quite simple. Polish regulations, I learned, state that printed matter or objects manufactured before 1945 are antiques and cannot be taken out of the country. Moreover a pre-war book may be ideologically unsound. But why had the officials picked on my London street guide and the primer on constellations? Military maps? Satellites and Reagan's space war?

I reached Brunswick after midnight the following day, slept in my van and was awoken by the dawn chorus of small garden birds. By 7 a.m. people were going to work (Germans are early risers) and I spoke to Emma by phone. I arranged to meet her in Berlin in a few days' time. She will bring a carefully drafted letter of application for a re-entry permit into Poland which I am to take to the Polish Military Mission in West Berlin. We are to meet at the Friedrichstrasse crossing-point.

II
EAST
GERMANY

8
BERLIN

Ten days later I arrived at the holiday resort of Wannsee (West Berlin) where I parked in a leafy road a few hundred yards from the lake. Summer was at its height, the northern nights were cold and clear, the lake dotted with sails and motor boats. Brown people in shorts packed the ice-cream bars, sausage stalls and beer gardens: beaches and parks were filled with sun-bathers and picnickers; pensioners with dogs and knitting women had taken over the shady benches. Everywhere I saw splendid cars and young men in leather uniforms on superb Japanese motor-cycles. Poland had nothing to compare with this.

I watched a man assemble his canoe from sections which he carried in ingenious containers. Another unzipped his fishing tackle, bait and canvas stool from a sort of conjurer's case. Nearby six Turkish families were sitting on the grass eating flesh-coloured water melons. The older women wore head scarves and were squatting like barrels. The younger wives were still slim, with dark hair hanging over their shoulders. Two of their children had small bicycles. The men had macho moustaches. I greeted them in Turkish and said to a silver-haired lady sitting beside me, "The Turks look happy enough."

She grunted and put down her knitting. "The Turks," she said irritably, "are a nuisance and shouldn't be allowed to come here. Wherever they go they leave their *Dreck* (rubbish) be-hind. Some park authorities have warned them to keep away.

"We come here to enjoy the trees and the water," she went on, "not to pick our way through melon rinds."

"And to foul the grass with dogs, which is a much greater nuisance," I felt like adding.

I went to look for a camping site and saw a line of caravans parked near the Teltow canal at the Bäkestrasse bridge. The gates were closed and there was a notice *Ruhepause* (siesta time). As I walked along the fence I was suddently brought up with a shock. It was as though a door had been violently slammed in my face. The Wall, the *Mauer*! I had come face to face with it, the knife-wound that severs Berlin's heart. I was very angry. The insolence, the brutal negation of this heartless barricade, smashing through a society's civilised life, blocking off half the capital and marooning it in a Chinese dungeon.

THE WALL

As a piece of engineering the Berlin *Mauer* was dull enough: just a blank white wall crudely coloured by graffiti with a rounded top disappearing into woodland. But coming across it unexpectedly, along a quiet lane, it exuded mystery and menace. Behind the graffiti were guard dogs and watch posts, the staring eyes and ruthless fire power of Vopos, part of a human barrier that stretches from the Baltic to the Black Sea, from Batum to the Caspian.

A tubby man was resting under the wall and I sat down with him. He was a Danish tourist waiting for the camp to open. "The Germans are very punctilious," he remarked. "They've eaten their *Mittagessen* and are sleeping it off." We talked about the Wall. "Devil's work, *Schweinerei*! Still, the West Germans have done better than the English. You lost your colonies and now you're poor. The Germans are too *tüchtig*, too *fleissig* for most of us. They work harder."

Two Jeeps on routine patrol each manned by four American soldiers with a machine gun came round the corner of the street and drove slowly along the wall. They were back in five minutes. I left the Dane and walked under a railway bridge to the Teltow canal, where the wall reappeared on my right. A mile along the towpath I came to another caravan camp which had been ingeniously laid out on a disused bridge at the old Dreilinden control post where the Helmstedt—Berlin *autobahn* used to enter the city. The check-point has been shifted, the vacated area blocked and wired off, the approach roads sealed, and it was here, on an overhead ramp in no man's land, looking across the wall to the watch towers and canal, that I decided to stay when Emma came.

From here the towpath continued a further 300 yards till it stopped at a wire-mesh barrier bearing a notice: "End of the American Sector". Just inside the barrier was the wall, dominated by watch towers, and a boom across the canal to control barge traffic. A few yards behind me, on the towpath, a plain wooden cross had been stuck into the ground. I read, "Hermann Dobler, 28.10.22. Shot here on 15.6.65."

As I walked back to the ramp I passed a Berlin archery club range which was hidden by trees but which had impudently hung its target in front of the wall. I returned the way I had come, the wall now on my left gleaming white among pines and abandoned gardens. The silent canal (private motor-boats turn round and go back half a mile from the boom), the birds and grassy banks and pine trees were so peaceful that the watch towers and armed Vopos seemed grossly melodramatic. West Berlin residents, however, as I soon learned, are so used to living in a trap that they scarcely notice or comment on it.

It was somewhere here, in the canal, that the legendary Kohlhase, whom injustice had turned into a famous brigand, jettisoned his stolen silver treasure – it has never been recovered – before he was caught and broken on the wheel with forty of his band in Berlin in 1540. An oak tree with a plaque (the Kohlhas Eiche) commemorates the spot where the hoard is said to have disappeared.[1]

For a last close look at the wall I climbed a fence and scrambled towards it through bracken and thorns till I came to a point where the solid concrete wall was interrupted by a section of wire mesh giving me a clear view of a watch tower almost on top of me. Between the wall and the tower I recognised the familiar double-apron fence, the strip of ploughed

---

[1] Kleist has immortalised the outlaw in his story *Michael Kohlhass* whom he represents as an honest horse-dealer driven to commit murder and arson with a band of followers in avenging the wrongs done to him by the authorities. "From one of the most upright of men he became one of the most terrible of his time" (*einer der rechtschaffensten zugleich und entsetzlichsten Menschen seiner Zeit*). Kleist's Kohlhass was beheaded. Kleist shot himself (and his companion Henriette) on the bank of the Wannsee (1811).

sand and the chain of powerful lights on pylons that I had seen
so often in my earlier travels along the Soviet frontier in eastern
Turkey and in Iran. The look-out cabin above me had a search-
light and six windows through which two heads were moving. A
dog was barking.

The cement-coated wall was topped by cylindrical pipe sections. Some were cracked, revealing brick and rubble filling;
the wall also showed erosion. I had heard rumours that the wire
mesh was so sharp it could sever a climber's finger. I tested the
small diamond-shaped interstices with my hand. They were not
sharp enough to cut but it would be difficult for a climber to get
a finger- or toe-hold in them.

I sat behind a bush to smoke and collect my thoughts. I had
spent most of the day prowling about like Alice in Wonderland
in a labyrinth of enclaves, walls and wire guarded by watchful
dragons. The whole place was a folly, a *Riesenspass* (a huge
joke), to quote a graffito I had seen on the Bäkerstrasse wall
(*Die Mauer ist ein Riesenspass*). It was also a horrible prison in
which gardens, fields, roads and housing settlements have been
cut off, split and isolated and prevented from communicating
with each other. One thought of a West Berliner waking up on
that morning of 13 August 1961 to find workmen sealing off his
back garden with a great fence over which Vopos would look
from a raised cabin into his private life.

Yet it is not the East German people, not the Vopos, who are
the real perpetrators of this crime. It is Big Brother. There's
hardly anywhere in Russia, travellers report, in which watch
towers are not in evidence. They are as much a part of Russian
history as *blinny* and Tolstoy. Russia is motivated by fear.
West Berlin represents a hole in her defence dyke. It must be
constantly watched.

I went back to my van in the leafy Conradstrasse, near the
lake. The damp night air brought out gnats and a smell of dog
shit. Soon after seven in the morning the dogs appeared, with
owners in shorts and flip-flops. Obese and slow, the dogs had
disgusting habits, sniffing and crouching among the faeces
while their masters looked on with a fond proprietorial eye.

It was another glorious summer day, the sky watery blue, the
lake chequered black and green, the birch and chestnut trees in
magnificent foliage, and clusters of slender masts sticking out of

the water like palms. In the Eichendorf sanatorium pink and
fleshy patients, surfeited with food and medicines, reclined
under parasols. Beer was flowing in the pleasure steamers, the
Condor, Wappen von Berlin, Ernst Reuter and *Lichterfelde*.
From the bridge I looked down on an unbroken procession of
motor boats. Beefy men with folds of fat round their bellies,
over-tanned girls in bikinis, men like satyrs or hobgoblins
with prominent paunches and flat buttocks, slim and beautiful
youths.

A motor-cyclist club was setting off from the Bahnhof
restaurant with girls clamped to their backs like Siamese twins.
When they put on their leather jackets, goggles and helmets
they changed into spacemen. They gunned their Hondas with a
roar and were off like torpedoes.

EMMA

To make certain that I didn't miss Emma I drove first to
Checkpoint Charlie and left a message for her with the British
military police and the West German control officer who operate with the Americans and French from sheds at the barrier.
Checkpoint Charlie is a sinister, seedy place in the Graham
Greene mould. It attracts touts, hippies, Arab layabouts and
tourists. A souvenir shop shows films and photographs of violent incidents at the Wall. There are *Imbiss* (refreshment) stalls
and a viewing platform for rubber-neckers. As they mount the
steps with their binoculars and cameras and peer over the Wall
these visitors from Europe, America and the Far East – many
are Japanese – have an air of suppressed excitement as though
they were doing something forbidden or even risky that might
disturb the Medusa's head lurking behind the gaoler's chains
and locks. Yet their first view of the Communist paradise must
be disappointing. All they see are grimy unrepaired buildings,
the dingy premises of *Die Neue Zeit* newspaper squeezed
against the Wall, and a maze of bollards, barriers and control
sheds designed to prevent a driver from crashing through at
speed. Many of the cars that pass through belong to foreign
embassies and are given favoured treatment.

As there was no sign of Emma I took the underground to
Friedrichstrassebahnhof. It was thronged with people passing

through the controls between the two zones and I was afraid I
might miss her. I was lucky to find the right door. And there, to
my relief, was Emma sitting on her suitcase with a parcel of
Polish delicacies.

Two Germans run the Drei Linden camp on the *Autobahn*
ramp. We parked next to a Swedish family and were given a key
("always lock the gate, and put your rubbish in the can outside"). A double-decker busload of New Zealanders had just
arrived, healthy young people built like tree trunks and flushed
with vigour and proteins. They had travelled from Moscow
via Leningrad, Smolensk and Warsaw. "Moscow was a boring
dump," one of the bronzed Amazons told me. The month's trip
cost £560 excluding personal spending. The leader, a massive
girl built like a boxer, was disapproving when Emma told her in
the showers that we were camping inside the caravan park.
"With all those bloody Germans? Come and join our mob."

We drank with them in the camp restaurant where they
stayed till midnight downing sconces of lager from a big glass
jackboot (*Stiefel*). The only Maori, who seemed to be the
party's mascot, stuck to a purple mixture of pernod, vodka and
beer ("a sort of punch"). When the lights were turned off there
was a little retching, then silence from the tents. It was an
admirable evening. No breakages, no blows, and rich takings
for the two proprietors.

Emma had brought my application for a new Polish visa in a
letter carefully drafted by a Polish lawyer friend, stressing my
old ties with the Poles and asking why I had been expelled. We
joined a crowd of petitioners pressed against the gate of the
Polish Military Mission in West Berlin. Tempers frayed as
people waved their passports and tried to force themselves into
the courtyard, and it was two hours before I found a bearded
official to look at my letter. He was polite but discouraging.
"This is not my *rejon* (field)," he said. "According to the
regulations you must wait another year before you can apply for
a new visa." He declined to elaborate, but clearly my eviction
order was a very black mark. "You can if you like petition the
minister for Foreign Affairs personally."

There was no point in arguing and I had had enough of the
charade. People were thumping the gate and calling angrily for
attention as we pushed past them. Over a cool drink I decided

to post copies of my letter of application for a new visa to the Ministry of the Interior in Warsaw and to the Polish Consulate in Cologne. While waiting for an answer I would visit Leipzig and Weimar. I looked forward to a glimpse of the East German Democratic Republic. It might help me to judge Poland within the wider pattern of her relationship with another Socialist system.

We walked back through Charlottenburg and the Tiergarten. On the east side of the Wall the Brandenburger Tor stands lonely and scarred under its winged goddess, a despoiled war trophy, object of pity or contempt, railed off in a square guarded by armed police. Hard against the Wall on the West Berlin side, which marks the end of the British sector, is the old Reichstag. The Wall here is covered like a children's blackboard with graffiti: "Stop live animal experiments"; "The Walled City"; "Celtic F.C."; "Liverpool F.C.". At the foot of the Wall a space has been reserved for ten simple crosses with the words "Victims of Violence 1961–84". Three of the crosses are marked "Unknown".

STEINSTÜCKEN

A mile from the Bäkestrasse bridge, along the Königsweg, is the village of Steinstücken. When the Berlin Wall was built the village was left with no direct communications with West Berlin except through the East Berlin zone. The Königsweg road was subsequently built to provide this direct access. It runs through a narrow corridor between two parallel sections of the Wall, forming an enclave.

The Wall dominates the village. It cuts through plots and gardens and isolates houses. To walk to the inn you have to brush along the Wall following a footpath. The railway runs through fenced-in embankments as though operating within a cage. In the village outskirts there is a memorial in the shape of two crossed helicopter blades with the words: "Until 31 Dec. 1976 this site was a helicopter landing zone of the US armed forces. Since the construction of the wall in Aug. 1961 it served to protect the former exclave of Steinstücken."

The landing pad is now used as a children's playground. On

the Wall nearby someone had sketched a face with a long nose peering over it, and the words "Kilroy was here".

Steinstücken's unenviable position – squeezed like a cockroach in a cranny of the big white Wall – attracts curious visitors and the innkeeper does well out of them. He has a dove cote and duck pond and a tree-shaded beer garden. Being a good German he has stuck notices everywhere: "It is forbidden to lean or leave bicycles here"; "Do not feed the ducks"; "Do not molest the pigeons". To reach the village along the Königsweg you have to pass through a mile-long gauntlet of watch towers with guards showing through the windows. The walk is enlivened by painted blood stains and graffiti: "Fuck off DDR!" "Dogs!".

During the time of tension when the Wall was first built the village's exposed and vulnerable situation led to property and plots being abandoned and houses were offered at bargain prices. With the construction of the Königsweg access road the present residents have got used to their plight. Yet they feel the strain. No one likes living within a few yards of armed Vopos. People have to watch their children and keep the dog from straying. The difference between "us" and "them" – those that live *drüben* – has hardened over the years. Rival ideologies and constant media pressure have driven a generation of schoolchildren apart.

Going back to the camp along the Königsweg Emma and I caught up with two old ladies in black straw bonnets walking slowly with sticks. They seemed oblivious to the guard towers craning over the walls of the enclave and passed a wooden cross stuck in the pavement without giving it a glance. The cross was marked "Willi Marzahn 19.3.66. *Auf der Flucht erschossen* (Shot While Fleeing)." At their time of life the old ladies must have seen enough of watch towers and crosses. The guards too, I thought, must be bored with their daily stint as Peeping Toms with nothing to divert them but a few cyclists and some old people on their Sunday afternoon stroll.

The New Zealanders are leaving. I said goodbye to the Maori, who was sitting on his pack with a bottle of Soviet champagne having his hair trimmed by a beefy girl. A bus party of Australians are expected later in the day. One of the German campers has told me they came here to rest (*um sich auszuruhen*) and don't like the English. "Very dirty, rude people. They mess up the toilets and are noisy and drunk." I thought he was being silly and unfair and said, "The Australians will be here tonight. Watch out! (*Pass mal auf*)."

Emma has left. I took her to the Friedrichstrassebahnhof and watched her disappear through the Wall. It was as though she had dropped through a hole on to another planet. The station was swarming with East German police and soldiers. I walked up the stairs to catch a train back to Wannsee. The platforms were dingy and drab with a grimy roof and windows. Over-loaded peasants from the east were sitting on their baggage, Turks and spivs were hanging round the Interflug shop. Three Vopos patrolled the platform and there were others in the roof, scrambling among the girders like apes. I pointed them out to a man who might have been a Greek. "*Gück mal da, die Affen!* (Just look at those apes!"). He took alarm and walked away.

Sitting in the S-Bahn taking me back to Wannsee I wondered what had happened to Georg Grosz's obese, bald Berliners. Grosz had drawn savage cartoons of them during the infla-tion years of the early twenties when feverish extravagance and debauchery flourished in a Berlin that teemed with war cripples. They were gross men of the "boar's neck" type. They wore waistcoats, heavy watch chains and rimless spectacles, had shaved heads and smoked thick cigars. In Berlin in 1933 I had seen many of them. Where are they now? I hadn't spotted any. Are they extinct? The answer seems to be that they have dis-guised themselves. Instead of waistcoats and fur collars they wear casual or sports clothes. Instead of a perfectly shaved skull like a pumpkin they plaster their wisps of hair over the scalp or let it dribble over the fat-folds in the neck. They may wear beards. But they want to look youthful. Grosz made his Berliners repellent. They looked, he said, like pigs and he drew them like pigs. He despised their greed. Greed accounted for their fat white hands, their rasping voices and whoring. With the passing years Grosz's frogs have turned into Vikings.[1]

---

[1] Georg Grosz: *A Small Yes and a Big No*, 1982. Grosz despised the masses. "To me," he wrote, "Hitler was no more than the Germans deserved; after all they had picked him." Grosz drew horribly mutilated war cripples with crab-like prostheses and no noses – which fitted in with the mood of Remarque's anti-war *All Quiet on the Western Front*. These

AUSTRALIANS

The Australians have arrived at the camp – fifty of them – in a double-decker bus with a Cork number plate. They are bigger and hairier than the New Zealanders and are extremely good natured. The two German proprietors made another small fortune in the evening, filling up the great glass jackboot with ice-cold frothing lager. Nothing was broken and the bill was paid, though there was some yodelling in the tents. The next callers will be Vietnamese. The two German campers are relieved to hear this. "The Malays," they said, "are a polite and studious people. They walk on tiptoe and don't fall asleep in the showers."

EAST BERLIN

This morning I crossed into East Berlin to the travel office in Alexanderplatz to collect my vouchers and visa for Leipzig and Weimar. I had last been here in the summer of 1933 and almost everything has changed. The Alexanderplatz and Marx-Engels-Platz have been turned into huge squares surrounded by high-rise blocks in the portentous Socialist style. A new landmark has sprung up – the 365 m. high Television Tower as symbol of Communist technology. A crowd was watching the guard of honour standing outside the unknown soldier's tomb. The remains of an unknown resistance fighter has been added to the memorial (with a plaque against Fascism) and it has been renamed in honour of the victims of Fascism and Militarism. The three sentries in their white gloves and belts stood like frozen dolls, one soldier's boots incorrectly aligned. Opposite, in Bebelplatz, the figures of generals and heroes of the Wars of Liberation (to use the official phrase) face each other round

and similar nightmare pictures by disillusioned artists I saw exhibited by the Nazis during the annual Party rally in Nuremberg in 1935. The exhibition was labelled "Degenerate Jewish Art". To ram home the point Egger-Lienz's virile canvases were hung in an adjoining room as true "German Art". They showed blond farmers sowing corn and strapping peasant women with sheaves.

a green lawn: Scharnhorst, Gneisenau, Yorck and Blücher.
Blücher occupies the biggest of the plinths and has turned
his head as though trying to catch a last glimpse of Paris. A
little lower down Unter den Linden are Humboldt (formerly
Friedrich Wilhelm) University and the statue of Frederick the
Great. He has been put back with his horse on his old site and is
covered in verdigris.

At the end of Unter den Linden the triumphal arch of the
Brandenburg Gate marks the end of the East Berlin zone and
the beginning of the British sector. The great gate is protected
by railings and a police guard. Beyond it I could see the faces of
people staring back at us from a viewing platform next to the
old Reichstag on the West Berlin side of the Wall. It was a
grotesque situation to be in. Here we were being looked at like
animals in a zoo by rubber-neckers who struck one as morons.
For there is nothing melodramatic about the Wall to those who
live behind it. The Wall is a fact, and the East Berliner has
adjusted his life and his habits to it. Besides, who likes being
gaped at as an object of curiosity, of pity or of dislike?

After several days I am getting used to the camp, its bizarre
situation on top of a ramp looking down into no man's land, the
anglers sitting on stools on the canal bank, the barges passing
the security boom, teams of racing cyclists who tear along the
towpath with bottles of glucose drink clipped to the handlebars,
the fat thighs of campers, and the silent white Wall with its
peering watch towers. The Berlin air is sharp and invigorating,
northern and dry and scented with pine needles, the soil sandy.
It is possible to forget, though not for long, that we are an
island of nonconformers surrounded by Communist land.

Below the bridge, near the Wall, is a summer colony of small
plots with little chalets. I am astonished at the junk the campers
have brought with them. All they really need is a strip of grass
and some trees, a tent, water and a rubbish pit. But they have
brought garden tools and a mower for their few feet of grass and
sandy earth, a kennel for the dog, pots of paint, ironing boards
and a pump to inflate the air mattress, door mats, gongs,
toasting racks, coat stands and garden sculpture – a concrete pig
or a donkey carrying a pannier filled with geraniums. In the
centre of each plot is a tiny bathing pool just big enough for a
family to sit in. This is the West German consumer society.

They have come to this green and sunny spot to throw off their clothes and hear the wind sighing over the canal. Yet they have brought their suburban chores and their impedimenta with them. The Polish campers at Gromada had nothing to compare with this: a few plastic buckets, a portable cooker, a radio and football and a store of vodka. There was no compulsory siesta after *Mittagessen* and they didn't mind noise.

HERR MARK

Most of the people thronging the long wide boulevard running between the Marx-Engels-Platz and the Brandenburger Tor were tourists, many of them on package tours from Czechoslovakia and the Balkans with little money to spend. I didn't notice any punks but I saw a sweaty Englishman take off his shirt on the pavement. From the Brandenburger Tor I turned back to the university and found a bench in a grassy garden with ivy-covered walls behind the entrance hall where it was peaceful and quiet. I had been looking forward to this moment, a moment to awake memories, for I had last sat here in 1933 during my stay with the Mark family in Eggersdorf twelve miles to the east of Berlin. Herr Mark was headmaster of the village school and he had a son at the university who was writing a thesis on Dickens's use of slang. Heinz sometimes took me to student meetings in the Siegesallee where we listened to political speeches and everyone cheered Hitler. The German students were older than I was and more mature. They were much more earnest and without the fashionable Oxford frivolity. They were thrifty, carefully counting the coins when they took out their leather purses to pay a bill. Their clothes were well worn and carefully pressed. Many had faces marked with duelling scars.

Three of Herr Mark's four sons were involved with the Nazi movement. The eldest owned the village hardware shop and was in the Party "for business reasons". Heinz was under pressure from Nazi student organisations. Friedl, the youngest, was in the Hitler Jugend and had to practise route marches with a heavy pack loaded with stones. Ernst was an engineering student at the Technische Hochschule. He would have nothing to do with the Nazis and because of this his colleagues bullied and ostracised him. He had a harelip. It was Ernst who opened my eyes to the menace of Nazism and warned me, two years later, that the next war would start with a German attack on Poland; it was this prospect that made me decide to go to Poland after leaving Oxford.

In those days Berlin seemed rather terrifying. I was shy. I was still learning German (I carried a tiny Lilliput dictionary in my pocket). The cafés on the Unter den Linden Strasse were too sumptuous for me. The large corseted women with hats and feather boas who stood in doorways calling out *"Liebling"* as I passed by looked like aggressive painted cooks. Men had loud voices and smoked cigars. Cricket and rugby football were unknown so I had no chance to show off my English skills. There was an atmosphere of menace in the headlines of Goebbels's *Völkischer Beobachter* and the hooked cross flags on poles and balconies. The Siegesallee repelled me with its rows of stone heroes. I felt effete, especially as my own university had recently passed a motion deploring the idea of fighting for king and country – an attitude that seemed incredible to my Berlin acquaintances and took a lot of explaining away.

In Eggersdorf, Herr Mark, a kindly Prussian with spiky white hair, put me through a strict disciplinary régime. I had to sit up straight, buy a purse, be punctual for meals and leave nothing on my plate, not even the chopped swedes. I was made to learn the names of flowers, trees and mushrooms. I rode my bicycle (for which I had to buy a bell and a pump), played handball, was treated to beer by local storm troopers who used to drill on the football field and learned their songs. Herr Mark forbade me to speak to girls (the pretty ones, he said, were *"Huren"*, whores).

When Herr Mark gave me German lessons in his little sandy garden at the edge of a pine wood he used to open an atlas and point to the German frontiers. He had been born in Gnesen (Gniezno), which had been incorporated into Poland after Germany's defeat. "One day," he would say, "we will recover our lost territories."

None of these people was evil. It was I, a product of different influences, who was the outsider. I heard after the war that Heinz had been shot dead by a Red Army soldier while trying to stop him stealing a boy's bicycle. Ernst through his wit and intelligence survived the war as a radio engineer. Eggersdorf is now, I believe, a commuter suburb and much of the pine forest has gone.

In 1933 it was still too early to foresee the horrors that were to come. Yet even then Berlin seemed to me to be a city of menace, and it was a pleasant relief to spend the last weeks of the long vacation in the relaxed atmosphere of Vienna, where I stayed with a Hungarian Jewish family. Herr Weiss was a failed businessman without ambition. Artur, the son, was interested only in swimming and the opera. His sister was a charming flirt – *"mollig und frollig (fröhlich)"*. Yet it was among the charming Austrians, the Viennese and the Tirolese, that the Nazis found some of their most vehement support.

When I had last sat here in flannels and a college blazer the future had stretched ahead full of mysteries and untasted experience. Now, fifty years later, I had come back through a hole in a concrete wall. The slogans and street names were changed. The pavements were full of Balkan trippers in sandals. I no longer sprinted for the bus. I was older now than Herr Mark had been, with his spiky white hair and red-veined nose, when we watched the Warsaw express tear past his garden towards the lost provinces of West Prussia.

I bought some apples and ate them on the bench. Then I went back to the Friedrichstrassebahnhof to take the S-Bahn to Wannsee. I had been given a visa to stay in the DDR for a fortnight and if my van was sound enough it would get me to Leipzig.

9
LEIPZIG – BUCHENWALD

HALLE

After being frustrated by the Berlin Wall and constantly reminded of it by peering watch towers and the crosses where
young men had been shot in the back during their desperate
flight to freedom, I was glad to have left it behind. Now I could
drive freely through the East German countryside like any
other law-abiding Socialist citizen. I felt at home. I had lived
with Germans for several years – stayed in their homes, read
their literature, soldiered against them, climbed their mountains and skied with them over the high Alpine glaciers of the
Silvretta and the Ötztal. To be back again in the outlawed
fragment of the old German Reich, in the country of Dresden
and Jena, was a sort of delayed homecoming. The politics had
changed but the old ways of life must surely have survived.

Traffic on the road to Leipzig was not heavy: small east
European cars, trucks with rattling bodies, puttering motor-
cycles – nothing to compare with the swirl and roar of speeding
vehicles on the western *autobahns*. I stopped at a roadside
restaurant but found a long queue waiting for an empty seat.
The lay-bys smelt of urine and litter. One is not encouraged to
dawdle for police cars are always on the prowl.

I turned off for Halle and went into two restaurants but they
too had queues. In a side-street I found an open-air snack bar
with frankfurters and ice cream and a big bowl of mustard with
a spoon. I saw a Russian lieutenant walk in. He was small and
dark with round shoulders and a hooked nose (Armenian Pay
Corps?). He had his little briefcase with him and his peaked
cap was too big. No one took the slightest notice of him.

The East Berlin travel office in Alexanderplatz had given me a voucher naming the camps at which I was authorised to stay. The camp in Leipzig was in a field at the edge of the town. It was unpleasant and noisy, crammed with tourists (many from Hungary and Roumania), more like a fair ground than a camp, with disco music, broken bottles, youths drinking beer at long trestle tables, chaotic family cooking and washing lines. I parked my van out of sight by a brook and slept to the music of the frogs.

On my way to the city centre next day I found myself walking through cobbled streets and rows of blackened buildings that reminded me of Birmingham in the depressed thirties. There was poverty in the rickety old balconies and dirty windows, a smell of sewage, and many shops were closed. As prices were cheap I stocked up with groceries: tinned Russian sardines, Bulgarian plums and Hungarian goulasch, Emmentaler cheese and a salami sausage shaped like a rolling-pin. At street corners posters were proclaiming the Soviet Union's friendship with its East German brothers in the DDR. I joined two pensioners sunning themselves on a bench by a fruit stall. Both had been prisoners-of-war in Russia until they were released in 1948. I asked them why so many of the shops were shut. "*Urlaub*," one of them said ironically, "holidays". "The owners have gone fishing," said the other, smiling. "The DDR is *kaputt*," he went on. "We are all poor. The West gives us some help but the Russians nothing. Whatever jobs we do we're still poor. *Hier ist nichts mehr los*, there's nothing here." A woman who was listening turned to me and said, "Leipzig is the dirtiest city in the whole of the DDR."

Trams, cream-coloured and joined together in three sections, are cheap and give an efficient service. I took one as far as the Merkur hotel. The centre of Leipzig has been levelled and rebuilt in steel and concrete in the familiar Socialist manner round a big open square. Among the few old buildings that have survived are the railway station with its vaulted halls reminiscent of steam trains and travel rugs, and the renamed Georgi Dimitroff museum with a dingy dome and statues. I passed several Russian soldiers in jackboots and belted shirts waiting for an officer who had gone into a station bar. The modern Merkur hotel caters mainly for tourists. It is empty during the day when guests are sightseeing. Opposite the market there is a column with a frieze depicting Leipzig's history. The inscription tells us that the earliest settlers were Poles in the seventh and eighth centuries. This must please the Poles, whose historians make much of their ancient connections, as an Ur-Volk of Saxony, with the historic town and fair (Leipzig) which they call Lipsk. The relief shows a Polish peasant with a hunchback and enormous head, looking like a Neanderthaler, driving a plough yoked to two oxen.

In the market facing the splendidly restored old Town Hall I talked to several Germans. The most interesting of them was a retired school teacher of sixty-eight, a bear-like sweaty man with poor sight, who told me he had been taken prisoner-of-war in the mountains of southern France in the winter of 1944, suffering from severe frost bite ("legs black and swollen"). He had taught German language and literature (Class 9) and praised *Macbeth* as a "highly apposite play – the noble thane turned terrorist and murderer, which is the fate of most political leaders". His students, alas, had not been interested – "these days they want to smoke, drink and fornicate" – and the study of German classics had been largely dropped from school syllabuses in 1972 when classes were ordered to concentrate on Marx, Engels and Lenin. He said the Allies had bombed Leipzig and Dresden with high explosives because the atom bomb wasn't ready, otherwise they would have used it. It was a great pity, he added, that the Americans had not reached Leipzig before the Red Army. But even if they had won the race the politicians would have forced them to withdraw, just as they had been made to abandon Chemnitz and Weimar.

One of the many street posters commemorating the fortieth anniversary of victory over the Fascists and Hitlerites shows a peace dove flying from a five pointed Soviet star and the words "Dank dem Sowjet Volk". Another poster says "We are Lenin's brothers". These exhortations are as cheerless as the attractions – the museums and poor quality shops – that are meant to entice the traveller. Restaurants in East Germany, as I soon discovered, close early, by 6 or 7 p.m. when there is a last rush for a meal. But the Ratskeller was open and I went into a dark downstairs parlour for tepid soup, pork, potatoes and peas. I shared a table with four Germans. One, having gobbled his meal, left a small pea on the table cloth. When one of the others asked for the menu I pointed to the pea and said, "You can have that too". He was not amused. But the man next to me whispered, "Saxons may rule the DDR. But they can't see a joke."

REPAIRS

I bought my first car, a Beetle, in 1960. But I am a poor mechanic, and though I have driven thousands of miles alone in rough country, I have done so in the knowledge that if I break down I must rely on luck or on a good Samaritan. In Turkey it was perhaps a blacksmith, in Africa a villager with a spanner or a good-natured Indian bush-trader who helped me on my way. Diagnosing a straightforward mechanical problem is one thing, repairing it is another. My Bedford van had been due for the scrap heap when I bought it to drive me to Warsaw. Sooner or later it would give trouble.

Within a few minutes of leaving Leipzig city centre for the road to Weimar the engine began to fire unevenly and stopped. Battery, ignition, fuel line, dynamo, distributor? It seemed to be the distributor. The wiring was badly corroded. So I parked on the pavement and walked to the nearest workshop.

The receptionist said he couldn't help. It was a state-run workshop and it was not allowed to handle private repairs. Besides, there were no spare parts in the DDR for an English vehicle.

I was about to leave when the works foreman came in. He had a sympathetic face and I had a word with him. He agreed to look at my van and bring a *Junge* (apprentice) with him. "This is unofficial. Say nothing."

It took an hour to straighten out the corroded mess and secure the distributor. When the engine fired at last I uttered a small prayer to Allah (I don't think the Christian God should be bothered with a man's small private woe) and I was off.

It was bumps and cobblestones that I feared. Constant shaking was bound to disrupt the wiring system again. And so it happened. After forty miles the engine died in a stretch of rolling green country. But I had noticed a small factory and vehicle park in a village, so I walked the two miles back. The works manager was splendid. He towed me to his yard in his own car and handed me over to his "best fitter". Half an hour later I was on the road again. But not for long. There was a bang and the engine stopped. This time I was stranded on the brow of a hill and was conscious of looking absurd. My white van was standing conspicuously against the lonely sky line like an abandoned lighthouse.

I didn't have to wait for long. A man on a motorcycle gave me a lift back to the workshop. The mechanic was amused to see me again. *"Machen Sie sich keine Sorgen,"* he said. "Don't worry, I'll fix it properly this time."

When he had done the job again he banged the distributor hard with his fist and said, "Keep praying and it should get you back to Dover."

WEIMAR

The countryside was opening up into the round green hills of the Harz, and from a crest I saw a long convoy of vehicles climbing up from the vale towards me. I pulled off the road to let them pass and brewed coffee. They were dark-green East German army lorries, blunt-nosed and ponderous, driven slowly, with pilot vehicles and impeccable spacing, loaded with soldiers and stores. The effect was impressive. If these were the enemy, they were obviously well disciplined and equipped. They rumbled past for over half an hour.

A mile farther on I waited at a level crossing while four trains passed. Some Red Army lorries with troops halted behind me. The men jumped out, took off their caps, smoked and urinated. Their officers stayed in the cabs.

It was getting dark when I bowled down a long hill into Weimar. I found an empty space behind a garage and walked into the town. The streets were almost empty. Hotels and bars were closed, the street lighting dim. The effect was beautiful: the peace, the dark old squares and gabled houses, the moonlit church and silent trees reminded me of parts of Oxford, beleaguered but still unscathed behind her college walls.

In the shadows of the Schillerplatz I saw a man in a T-shirt and jeans sitting under a lime tree. He was black. He was delighted when I spoke to him in English and pumped my hand. He was a Zambian. I asked him what he was doing in

Weimar. President Kaunda, he explained, had sent African students to East Germany as part of a deal. In exchange for Zambian copper, the East Germans had agreed to deliver arms to Zambia and to provide educational facilities for black students at their technical colleges. Mlanje (the young man) had been given a bursary. "The scheme is all right on paper," he said, "but Kaunda has been swindled. We learn almost nothing."

Mlanje began to unburden himself. He felt lonely and ostracised. "The Germans ask me rudely what I'm doing here. They stare at me but never invite me to their homes. If only I were in England!"

We talked about the Russians. "They are everywhere," he said, "45,000 soldiers based in Weimar alone and more along the border with West Germany." He though Russia deliberately kept the DDR poor as part of her punishment for the war. "But DDR Germans are less trustworthy than those in the west. They inform on each other and watch you. Many are disguised party members."

"What about girls?"

He made a sad face. "They are racists. And African girls are hard to find – there are very few and they're all booked up."

In the morning I went to Weimar's best café, near the monument to Schiller and Goethe. It was filled with people eating cakes – there were four sorts to choose from, displayed in trays. I sat with two Cubans who seemed to have money to spend and were drinking coffee with vermouth. Both had finished their course in mechanical engineering and had German wives. They liked East Germany. This would normally have surprised me, but these young men were Castro's children and had been indoctrinated.

Two white-haired ladies took their places when they left (there was, as usual, a queue). I find elderly women often easier to talk to than men. They are more personal, less interested in politics, not so gruff. The two women were widows of long standing (forty and twenty-four years) and had pensions of about 150 marks a month. They had witnessed the Allied bombing of Weimar – it had not been severe – and bitterly regretted that the American army which had liberated Weimar in 1945 had been ordered to withdraw after a few weeks to make way for Russian occupation. They thought the destruction of Dresden (*so eine schöne Stadt*) had been a crime, an English act of revenge.

They made ironical jokes about life under the DDR's Socialist regime – about the shoddy consumer goods, idle and inefficient workers, too many officials and regulations. Every shop and business was under state control. I asked them how the Red Army garrison behaved. Russian soldiers, they said, usually came into town under officer escort and were too closely supervised to misbehave. But they drank heavily in their barracks.

During my three days in Weimar I saw many Red Army soldiers in the streets. They gather outside the Russian bookshop and a Russian club, a gloomy place with a broken roof that is under repair. They are typical young conscripts, with shiny faces and red ears. Many are swarthy and black haired. I had seen many like them before, from the Caucasus, Georgia and Tashkent, when the entire Turkoman infantry division fighting with the Wehrmacht was captured by the British army at Ravenna towards the end of 1944. Overnight, as a result of an agreement with Stalin, their German uniforms were thrown away, they were put into British battle dress as "free Soviet citizens", paid according to rank, and after a few weeks of idleness herded like sheep on to ships that took them back to Russia. No force or armed guards were used. I last heard of them as convict labour gangs working in the Donetz coal mines. Italian peasants said that the Turkomans were notorious looters. They organised themselves into clans and once turned loose on the Italian countryside would steal anything from a door lock to a bicycle.

The Russian helicopter base at Weimar is a constant irritant to the people of Weimar. All day long until midnight the helicopters circle over the town on training exercises, the beat and scream of their engines making it impossible to rest. Another sign of the Soviet presence are the street posters. One shows a Red Army soldier-hero holding a child in his left arm and a dripping sword in the other. It bears the word *Druzhba* (Friendship) and commemorates forty years of post-war co-operation between the DDR and the Soviet Union. Another poster reads "Dank Euch Ihr Sowjet Soldaten 1945–85". No one pays the slightest attention to these exhortations. The German finds it galling to be constantly reminded of his catastrophic defeat in war and to be told moreover to be thankful for it.

In the historic park where Goethe used to stroll the Russians have enclosed a military cemetery within a low wall and railings. I counted about 450 graves – roughly half of them dated 1945, the remainder from 1946. There are six separate graves with upright marble slabs and red-painted Soviet stars for Soviet colonels: five dated 1951–52, the other 1982. They are inscribed (in Russian) "Rest in Peace", "Friend and Comrade", "To Father from Son". Despite everything one is told about Russia's callousness and contempt for human life she has been punctilious in honouring her dead on foreign battle fronts. The importance for morale and the propaganda value of maintaining war graves and erecting memorials and statues are known of course to every army commander and government. Without feelings of patriotism there can be no true soldiers – only a conscript rabble that will not stand up under fire. Yet I still think it odd that in the Soviet war cemeteries I have seen only officers are named. Rifleman Ivanov remains nameless.

BUCHENWALD

Despite its elegant cultural past, its museums and Baroque architecture and connections with Bach, Goethe and Schiller, Weimar has a sinister side to its recent history. It was the rail head for the nearby concentration camp of Buchenwald, the point of departure for thousands of wretched slaves who were forced to struggle up the long hill to the cages on Ettersberg four miles away. And Weimar was the collecting point for other doomed men who were routed in cattle trucks to toil in the underground V2 missile factories hidden in the tunnels at Nordhausen not far to the north.

I drove up the hill to Buchenwald on a sunny morning. Its situation is idyllic. The air is sharp and clean. It looks down over woodland and rolling corn fields. The spire and red roof-tiles of Weimar peep out of a green valley like an early etching.

Except for a few preserved buildings and relics the camp where men were flogged, worked and starved to death has been stripped, and the rows of wooden huts in which they were penned demolished. As I stood on the ridge above the entrance

I was struck by the cruel contrast between this civilised land-scape where Goethe used to walk in the woods and the fate of the Nazis' slaves who were driven like vermin into the wired cages among the pines. For the Nazi camp guards, Buchenwald was a sanatorium: they had pets, flower beds and vegetable gardens looked after by the prisoners. The prisoners starved.

Among the relics that have been spared are the crematorium, a brick building with a tall chimney, and the reconstructed execution cell where prisoners were shot by an SS guard through the back of the head (*Genickschuss*): a gallows, a cart (a team of Jews had to load each iron-wheeled cart with five tons of heavy stones from the quarry and sing while they dragged it along – the guards called them "singing horses"); a clothing store that has been converted into a museum; the rail-head ramp and the deserted quarry (both outside the fence). The old administrative buildings near the gate, and the guards' quarters, are still standing.

The museum and of course the crematorium are the main "attractions" for visitors, who wander quietly over the levelled enclave and enter the crematorium in awe and silence. When the SS ran the camp they told the prisoners, "Nobody escapes from here, except those who leave by the chimney". Today the refurbished crematorium has lost even the faintest smell of death. It reminds one less of burning flesh than of a hospital boiler house tidied up for inspection.

The museum exhibits include prisoners' clothing (striped pyjamas), utensils and plank beds, office records – which the SS kept in great detail and are flawlessly typed – and photo-graphs of prison scenes, inmates, SS guards and the rise of Nazism.

The historical record begins with that ominous photograph of Hindenburg, the wooden giant, giving his senile blessing to the new Chancellor, Adolf Hitler. The upstart is shown in profile with a small indrawn mouth and pasty, plebian features – the face that people used to laugh at until the mouth opened and began to rant and deafen Europe with cries for revenge. The record ends with a final shot of a Red Army soldier hoisting the hammer and sickle over the Brandenburg Gate. A separate section is dedicated to German socialist leaders. The place of honour is given to Ernst Thälmann, former head of the German

Communist party, who was shot in the back on 18 August 1944 in the crematorium yard. A memorial stands on this spot.

Among other memorials in the camp there is a stone slab commemorating the British and Canadian servicemen who died here. A fresh wreath had been laid on it with the words "A survivor remembers. Squadron-Leader S.A. Booker (retd)". Until it was destroyed by Allied bombers on 24 April 1944 there was an arms factory (Gastloff works) near the railhead ramp. Nothing is left but traces of the concrete foundations.

The present Buchenwald camp complex is divided into two parts. Half a mile away, on the reverse side of the Ettersberg ridge, the main memorial and mausoleum area has been painstakingly laid out. One descends hundreds of steps to a wall with slabs and tablets overlooking the open cornfields and spinneys that roll gently down to Weimar. The memorial tablets represent eighteen nations whose citizens died in Buchenwald. Great Britain has no tablet, and I saw no reference here to Jews.

The steps are flanked by limestone friezes showing gruesome camp scenes of guards with dogs, clubs and rifle butts beating prisoners, emaciated men dying through exhaustion, corpses. The reliefs are accompanied by verses that are moving but overwritten. At the head of the steps stands a bell tower with mausoleum and a striking bronze group, "The Oath Takers", by Professor Cremer. The eleven figures represent working-class resistance fighters swearing an oath never to submit to Fascism and tyranny.

The memorial project has been splendidly sited and conceived. Alas, it is frankly political in spirit. It is explicitly dedicated to "resistance fighters, socialists, workers and anti-Fascists". Much of the verse written on the friezes is spoilt by kitsch and slogans. The bell tower is hideous – I thought at first it was another Russian watch tower (perhaps it has a double purpose). Among the victims of Buchenwald the Communist Ernst Thälmann has been named the hero, though Dietrich Bonhoeffer, the Protestant theologian, was also murdered here. Hitler's main enemy and scapegoats, the Jews, who were also inmates of Buchenwald, get scarcely a mention, though it is true that this was primarily a transit and work camp, it had no gas chamber, and the Nazis found it more convenient to ship

Jews (and gypsies) from here to be liquidated in specialised extermination centres such as Auschwitz.

I visited Buchenwald twice and saw at least fifty Russian soldiers, all youngsters, in clean walking-out uniforms and shoes (not jackboots). Their peaked hats, mostly with a blue band on them, seemed ill-fitting and uncomfortable: they were constantly fidgeting with them or taking them off, like schoolboys with new caps. They were escorted by officers and like the other tourist parties (Czechs, Jugoslavs and some West Germans) they kept together and looked suitably grave. I wondered what thoughts were passing through their minds as they wandered round the camp and saw the quarry and the traces of mass graves (over 8,000 Russian prisoners-of-war were slaughtered in Buchenwald) and read the Russian language inscriptions that proclaimed the "defeat of German Fascism and the rebirth of freedom". They know, of course, that their own country is covered with guard towers and of its system of slave labour and convict camps. Would the young Russian conscripts who are brought daily to tour Buchenwald make ironical deductions about the Soviet Union's own penal camps?

I put this question to several Germans I talked to among the visitors. They shook their heads. "Such thoughts would never occur to a Russian soldier. He's too thick!"

As a museum show-piece Buchenwald is hygienic, austere and without hysteria. The relics and exhibits, being artefacts, are lifeless. The grisly spectres of the dead have been exorcised. It is clear that as a national memorial the project has been devised and cleverly exploited to make a strong political point. The Russians, it proclaims, liberated the DDR from the Fascists ("You are brothers of Lenin") in the name of international solidarity and *druzhba* (friendship). The liberation of Buchenwald, runs the message, was the result not of the bravery and enterprise of American soldiers who unlocked its gates on 11 April 1945 but of the Communist-inspired resistance elements among the inmates themselves.

When Jean Michel, the Resistance leader who was arrested in Paris in August 1943, was first marched to the quarry he used these words to describe what he saw (*Dora*, 1979):

"We arrive at the quarry. It is open to the sky. There we see a long, long line of prisoners carrying rocks, putting them down, or lifting them up. It snakes and stumbles, an unforgettable sight. SS and Kapos spur the prisoners on: the dogs snap at them: blows rain down on their backs. Sometimes even, for fun, a whim, to speed up the work or for vengeance, an SS or Kapo throws down a prisoner from the top of the quarry. He screams and crashes down several yards below. Dead. 'An accident. He slipped.'"

By the time the package tourists from Prague, Budapest and the Rhineland have made their round of the camp and gone for a meal in the restaurant their thoughts will have reverted to food. Buchenwald, a place of torment, is ticked off as one more *Sehenswürdigkeit* or spectacle to be visited on the way to Wernigerode castle or the galleries of Dresden.

GOTHA

I reached Gotha in the evening, parked in a side-street, and walked to the town centre to look for a meal. The main square and *Rathaus* have been carefully restored but behind them are broken buildings and swathes of waste ground left by wartime bombing. Earlier, passing through Erfurt, I had noticed the same contrast between buildings that have been meticulously restored in the original style and the patched houses and cracked façades in neglected side-streets – evidence that even after forty years the East German authorities have not been able to find the resources to replace the dreadful wreckage left by the war.

As everything else was closed I went straight to the *Rathauskeller*. There were about twenty guests in the stuffy underground parlour, half of them East German soldiers, and a waiter in a dirty white collar and bow tie and a frayed black jacket. I shared a table with a lorry driver and asked for the hot dish. The waiter said it was stew with sausage but it looked like toasted caterpillars and was so hot and gluey that it scalded my mouth. My companion was amused. "They serve it like that so you can't taste what it's made of."

He told me he had spent ten years as a steward on an East German ship that sailed between London and east Mediterranean ports. Now, as a long-distance lorry driver, he worked a sixty-hour week. Lorry driving, he grumbled, was an unhealthy job. The bumping and jarring day after day over roads surfaced with badly fitting concrete panels hurt his back and spine. Russians, he said, were poor drivers except when under convoy discipline. "Never stop to help them on the road when they have a flat tyre or engine trouble. They don't want you to interfere. Russian soldiers have orders to keep away from civilians."

When I asked him why every *Rathaus* serves guests only in the basement he said it was an old German tradition for civic officials to congregate in the *Keller* – "they can booze in the vaults without being observed".

I walked back through the dark alleys of Gotha at 10 p.m. Everything was ill lit and locked up as though the town was being run by Calvinists. No strollers with dogs, no youths with ice-cream cones. Only the hissing of the street cats. I took the wrong turning down a lane of broken walls and when I headed for a light saw that the three figures under the lamp were white-belted Russian military police. We ignored each other. I remember once talking to a Red Army lieutenant in a street in occupied Vienna in 1945 and inviting him in Russian for a drink. We had scarcely sat down in a bar when a Russian military Jeep drew up and took him away. What dislike and suspicion there was between the Russian soldiers and the allied troops at that time! We seemed to have come from different planets. The Red Army officer always carried a parcel, the other ranks broken suitcases or even sacks; their concern was loot; they were never without their weapons.

When I got back to my van it was undisturbed and I slumped on the floor like a worn-out beetle.

EISENACH

My next stop was to be Eisenach in the Thuringian hills. It had occupied a special place in my memory every since that sunny morning in August 1934 when I had wheeled my bicycle into the market square near the Bach statue and watched a rally of Hitler Jugend schoolchildren. Everything at that moment had been golden – the summer corn, the sun shining on old masonry, one's youth and the unknown, adventurous future. It wasn't so much the boys taking part in the rally that I remembered so clearly, those callow, tow-headed youngsters in shorts with half-developed muscles, as the girls in their white blouses, gym skirts and short white socks, with their yellow hair braided in pigtails or rolled into a bun. They stood there in the innocence and vitality of youth unaware – for who could know it at the time? – of the ordeals and misfortunes that Hitler's war machine was to impose on them. They had been marked out for sacrifice: to be processed as helpmates for Nazi bullies or as brides for Germans who would die in the snow at Stalingrad.

At that time I had not made up my mind about Hitler's character and mission. In 1934 most Englishmen were still prepared (like *The Times*) to give him the benefit of the doubt. There was sympathy for the Germans and fear of their hysteria. As a nation the Germans excited but puzzled me. They mixed bourgeois virtues with contradictory passions. They were sentimental yet aggressive, poised it seemed on the brink of an unpredictable crusade.

The schoolchildren drawn up in the market square of Eisenach were innocents. Their idealism and feelings of patriotism could have been moulded in more than one direction. They were ripe for exploitation. It was in the legendary old towns like Eisenach, Urach and Wurzburg, with their painted gables, their beer gardens and pine woods that the fanatics went to work with the hooked cross and flaming torches to harness primitive German emotion and rustic dislike of Jews in the cause of revenge and later of mass murder. The crowds whom I saw bellowing at Saarbrücken after Hitler's plebiscite triumph in January 1935 were shouting for more victories. By the end of 1935 I was convinced that Nazi Germany meant war. That was the end of my love-affair with the Germans.

In Eisenach again I parked my van at the foot of the Wartburg, where I could see a mob of tourists struggling up the steep hill to the castle, and walked past the statue of Bach (born in Eisenach in 1685) to the old market square. After fifty years I still recognised some of the buildings (many had been restored or completely rebuilt after war damage), and I felt the same vivid emotions as I did then of being transported back into Hans Andersen's dream world of marzipan cottages, of scrolls and figurines and crazy chocolate gables. The town hall was carved and painted like a doll's house. The old church was guarded by a knight killing a dragon.

The quaint statue of St George spearing the dragon shows him with a heavy moustache, an O-shaped mouth, drawers, greaves and a plumed helmet. Behind him, as in a child's vision, the glowing colours of the *Rathaus* with tower, clock and weather vane. However, as soon as I stepped into the Georgen-kirche I was brought back to reality with a bump. A set of framed pictures of the new German martyrs has been placed prominently near the door. I recognised the faces of Bonhoeffer and Pastor Paul Schneider, both murdered in Buchenwald. A prayer is written under the pictures:

> *Herr*
> *Du has uns heimgesucht*
> *1933 – 39 – 45*
>
> *Gefallene durch Bomben getötete*
> *Als lebensunwert ausgelöschte*
> *Im Widerstand geopfert*
> *Gemordete Juden*
> *Blutzeugen des Glaubens*
> *Vermisste, Verschleppte, Verzweifelte*
> *Aller Blut*
> *Schreit zu Dir*
> *Herr erbarme Dich*
> *Unserer Not und Schuld*
> *Mach uns zu Boten Deines Friedens.*

Outside the church hangs this poster: "*Unser Sozialistischer Staat Garant für Sozialisicherheit, Geborgenheit and Zukunfts-wissenheit.*" What elephantine language!

The invocations contradict each other, and the second one seems offensively trite. There is the prayer for God's mercy – and the homage to pagan Socialism. Outside in the square are busts of Marx, Engels and Lenin. Only Stalin and Chairman Mao are missing from the *Prominenz*.

People were sunning themselves in the square. I sat down next to a seventy-year-old man who seemed happy to reminisce. He said he was born in Eisenach and had survived the trauma of

war and captivity "through luck and keeping my head down".
He had served in a field ambulance unit on the Russian front,
had been captured in France, sent to Northwich camp in
England, then returned to Germany and suddenly, with thirty
other German medical staff, taken by truck to "an unknown
destination". When the driver stopped they saw armed women
in uniform – Russians. "*Scheisse*! We had been handed over to
the Red Army."

But instead of disappearing he had been released in East
Germany and a year later managed to trace his wife, who was in
Silesia, through the German Red Cross in Hamburg.

He told me of an incident in Northwich camp. There were
two Jewish sergeant interrogators who wanted revenge (*Rache*)
and abused their authority. The prisoners complained and the
sergeants were removed. This may well be true. The British
Army was always short of British-born foreign linguists and in
overseas theatres such as the Middle East, Italy and Austria
it had to recruit Jews from Palestine as interpreters and in
field security units. No one could blame such people for being
strongly biased.

Two elderly women who were sitting with us had their own
memories. One had a brother who returned from captivity in
Russia with *Wasserzucht* (oedema). "His body was swollen and
full of water. His heart gave out and he died." The other
woman's husband had not been heard of since Stalingrad.

The veteran recalled his early days with the Hitler Youth.
"They were fine lads. But our heads had been stuffed with
nonsense (*Blödsinn*). It was one thing to get a heroes' welcome
in Vienna in 1938. Quite another to slog through the mud and
dust of the Ukraine, and later to watch the Allied tanks come
out of the sea on D-Day."

I have heard a good many war stories from Germans. Almost
every man of over sixty-five has his anecdotes and I don't doubt
their truth. But there is another way of looking at them. What
have they expurgated, indeed what has been blotted from their
minds and memories? How much did the amiable veterans now
vegetating on their pensions in small German towns know
about the Nazi atrocities that were committed all round them in
Russian villages, in the Balkans, in the Jewish *shtetls* of the
Pale? And assuming (as one must) that they did know, could

one have expected them to protest and risk being summarily shot? The Wehrmacht condemned itself to a policy of reprisals by fighting its campaigns among hostile populations. The British Army overseas was spared this problem, for it did not have to deal with an enemy behind the lines until the Zionist underground forces, once the danger from Rommel was over, declared war on the British mandate in Palestine and began attacking our men.

I have discussed these questions with Germans over the years – and with their enemies – and I believe that the ordinary Wehrmacht soldier in the field, the *Lanzer*, although he was an aggressor, had much the same standards of honour and integrity as other fighting men. It was the Nazi element, the SS and political troops, *die Anderen*, as Peter Bamm calls them, that were different.

Peter Bamm's *Die Unsichtbare Flagge (The Invisible Flag)*, Fischer Bücherei 1957, is a brave and fair book and in his account of the campaign in Russia, where he served as a surgeon in a German field ambulance unit, he writes of the front-line soldier's courage and decency. Bamm's *bêtes noires* were Hitler and the Nazi leadership (he refers to Hitler as "*der primitive Mann an der Spitze*, the primitive man at the top"), and the Nazi political troops ("*Die Anderen*, The Others") who followed in the wake of the advancing German army to harass and murder the civilian population. The German soldier, he says, knew of their behaviour but he dared not protest.

"*Die Anderen*," he writes in one passage, "rounded up the Jews of Sevastopol and gassed them in a great box-shaped lorry (*Kastenauto*). The driver would wait for a few minutes until the banging ceased from inside, then drive off to tip the corpses into old anti-tank ditches outside the town. We knew of this but we did nothing. How could we? If anyone had protested or tried to stop this mass murder he would have been arrested and would have disappeared within twenty-four hours. And he would have died anonymously. For it is in the nature of the totalitarian state to deny its opponents the dramatic gesture of a martyr's death. Many otherwise might have chosen it. But to sacrifice one's life in vain was useless. I am not saying that such a sacrifice would have had no moral merit. But its practical results would have been nil."

In another passage Bamm writes: "In Nokolajew *die Anderen* murdered the Jews and threw their bodies into anti-tank ditches. At first we couldn't believe this. A staff officer who had photographed the scene was dismissed from the unit. The army was indignant and found it a disgrace that *die Anderen* should exploit the fighting soldier's bravery for their own ends. But there was no burning fury in their indignation. The poison of anti-Semitism had already done its work. And a general protest by the troops against the murders would not have helped. The perpetrators would simply have committed their crimes more secretively. Worse, if a soldier protested he would not only have paid for it with his life. His family too would have been punished."

The dualism in the German character, the nature of their war crimes, have been analysed and debated for decades. Collective guilt? Individual guilt? In considering this problem we cannot overlook Britain's own record of "punitive expeditions" and forays: the deliberate destruction of the Benedictine Abbey at Monte Cassino; the firestorm over Dresden: our failure to help more Jews escape the Holocaust. Thus, by a terrible distortion of the truth, it was the British soldier in Palestine who became, for the Jewish survivors and avengers of Himmler's death camps, the "terrorists".

WARTBURG

The mediaeval castle of Wartburg is a national monument and for Protestants especially a place of pilgrimage. It was here that Martin Luther lived in retreat while translating the New Testament into German. Generations have plodded up the hill from Eisenach to its steep walls and tower and drunk in the inn.

I joined the tourist trek climbing a dirt path through a wood, and was soon lost in the crowd. The place was an ant-hill. Several hundred people had squeezed inside the castle walls and were struggling up and down the narrow stairs leading to the top of the tower. Butting one's way through a scrum of buttocks and breasts was an ordeal not an act of piety. There were long queues waiting to get into the rooms, children arriving on donkeys, parties of Hungarians.

The tower gave a "picturesque" view of the green Harz hills

and valleys beloved by Heine. He had been entranced when standing on the Brocken on a misty day. But his cynical humour got the better of him. He jeered at the naïve romanticism of visitors who, after feasting their eyes on the vista before them, could only express their thoughts in clichés, then unwrapped their sausage, took out their tobacco pipes, and wrote banal tributes in the summit book (*"Was für eine schone Aussicht!* How picturesque it is!").

From the Wartburg I went back to see Luther's house, wrecked in 1944 and, according to a notice, restored by kind permission of the Soviet administration. It is now a museum housing the German Presbyterian archives and exhibits from Luther's life. A display had been arranged in honour of celebrated Germans who had been either clergymen or sons of clergy: among them Bonhoeffer, Mörike, Schweitzer, Burckhardt, Lessing, Weber and Linnaeus. Dean Inge, who warned against pontificating ("Never put a man entirely in the wrong if you can help it") and hubris ("A man usually does his best work just before he is found out") would have made a witty and welcome addition to the gallery. Schweitzer, however, had run off to the Gabon to escape the establishment. Mörike, a true Swabian, stayed on in his parsonage, writing of spires, weather vanes and orchards.

Luther's scowling face and his turbulent obstinacy used to impress me. Nowadays I am inclined to think of him as a peasant bully, a demagogue and inconoclast. He called the Jews "poisonous bitter worms" and was a precursor of the appalling Thirty Years religious wars.

SONDERHAUSEN

From Eisenach I turned north to Mühlhausen, taking a country road that runs along the West German border. The road was deserted and I soon found myself in an extensive Red Army training area. There were artillery ranges, driving schools, troops doing tactical exercises and guns and armour deployed in fields. It took me an hour to get through this frontier sector, and as mine was the only car on the road I had an uneasy feeling of being a trespasser. But the soldiers took no notice of me as I trundled past them at forty miles per hour.

It was dusk when I arrived at Sonderhausen. I was told that as the inns were closed I would have to ask for a meal at the Kali (potash) Club. This was a cheerful eating place with a bar. I walked in, sat in the only vacant seat, and realised when I saw people looking at me that I had committed a gaffe. I had sat down at the *Stammtisch*.

In a German inn the *Stammtisch* is reserved for the local *Prominenz*. I was about to leave when a red-faced man at the table said, "Stay! You are welcome", and poured me a drink. He introduced himself as the saw-mill manager. A young man sitting next to me whispered in my ear, "*Sie haben Mut*", – "Don't worry, you are forgiven." They were both talkative. The saw-mill manager, who was tight and short of breath, insisted that I ought not to be travelling alone. "When you are in trouble who is there to help you?" He warned me not to fall foul of the police. "One mistake and they will take away your driving licence in a flash." Talking of Poland he said, "The Poles are poor workmen. They make their women do the work, just like the Russians."

Hans, the young man at the table, said he was finishing his apprenticeship as a heavy-duty lorry driver. He also warned me about the police. "One beer is enough – they'll make you walk home. I'll give you a bed tonight at my step-parents."

Hans roused his step-parents from bed. His step-father was an engineer in the local Kali works, an enormous concern based on potash deposits, employing an army of workers housed in a massive concentration of housing blocks. They persuaded their daughter – aged fourteen – to appear in her nightdress and show me her English grammar books. She had chosen English as her main foreign language (Russian was in any case compulsory). They had a cosy flat but so cramped that everything from a coat hanger to a clock had to be put away in a special place.

"The Russians won't bother you unless you provoke them," said the step-father when I told him of my trip through their training area. "Just drive past as though you aren't looking. But they have no road discipline, they drive like bulls."

"The Russians keep to themselves and are bored," he went on. "They have no money. If they had cash (he grinned) they'd defect. You can see the young soldiers eyeing the girls at bus stops as though they were fresh sausage meat."

We watched Heinrich Böll on television – pouchy-eyed, tired, rather pedantic and very sane. I think it must have been one of his last talks before he died. I slept on a sofa and was woken by the phone announcing that it was 5.30 and time for the Socialist working masses to arise and go about their business. The family was already dressed and had prepared breakfast – coffee, tomatoes and rye bread. Before I left Hans made a touching little speech. "My dream is to visit England." He hoped for peace but he didn't mention freedom.

I had half a mind to turn off at Nordhausen and visit the former site of Hitler's V2 plant. But I was anxious to be back in Brunswick to follow up my Polish re–entry request. I drove slowly through the Harz towards Magdeburg, and made my last stop under the castle at Wernigerode.

WERNIGERODE

In the warm afternoon sunshine the half-timbered houses of Wernigerode looked like a film-set crowded with extras – tourists, bands of schoolchildren, young couples and pensioners, all trooping up and down the hill to the castle, sucking ice-cream cornets, happy, sun-tanned and relaxed in sandals and summer clothes. The crooked alleys were a puzzle, losing themselves in the shade of churches, spires and chiming clocks and big dark doorways. Among the steep-pitched roofs and painted *Fachwerk* there was a hubbub of voices talking rustic German, Polish, Hungarian and Czech. I left my van at the edge of a fairground and went into a café which had an ugly poster in the window: "For International Solidarity, Peace and Brotherhood"; but it had a carved front and flower boxes and smelled of frankfurters and cakes.

A thin-faced man with glasses made room for me at his table and we began to talk about the war. His unit, he told me, had been given barely twenty-four hours' notice before marching from Soviet-occupied Poland across the border into Russia. "We received a warm welcome, people were happy to provide us with billets, our soldiers were well disciplined and correct. Then the SS special troops (*Einsatzgruppen*) came and spoiled everything. I saw two SS clubbing a Jew outside a ghetto and was going to stop them but my comrade said, 'Don't interfere –

you could lose your life.' The SS units behind the front were politically trained, not real soldiers; they operated independently of the Wehrmacht." The name "Katyn" meant nothing to him. But in a forest near the Polish–Russian border his unit had come across mass graves of Poles. "The graves were rotten and swampy. Two of our men fell in. Partisans were firing at us in the woods." He said he was wounded three times – shoulder, arm and neck.

After dark everything closed and the little streets emptied except for a few youths standing outside the *Rathaus* necking girls. Three young blacks were standing at the edge of the group. They told me they were technical students from Halle spending the vacation on factory jobs.

Turning north-east I left the Harz behind and drove through yellow corn fields and cobbled villages. Approaching Magdeburg I had to slow down for a long Russian convoy of army supply vehicles. One lorry had broken down and was picketed by Mongol military police with batons. I overtook a Russian Black Maria truck and saw a doleful face looking through the grille. In Magdeburg I avoided the centre and drove along streets lined with unbroken rows of twelve-storey apartment blocks painted blue and white. The pattern was so uniform they looked like prefabricated army barracks or prisons: startlingly ugly after the golden corn fields a mile or two away. Soon I was on the Berlin road. The East German frontier officials at Marienborn let me through without a search and I spent the night near Helmstedt next to a small convoy of American army lorries.

There was no letter waiting for me in Brunswick from the Polish Consulate in Cologne. I rang up the consulate and was told to inquire again in a fortnight. To fill in the time I decided to go to Dresden.

---

* NOTE: The myth of Buchenwald's liberation by its prisoners is disproved by witnesses. The first Americans entered the camp within three hours of the SS guards departing. Just before they arrived, when the coast was clear, "daring" prisoners took hidden weapons from the secret dump and marched about "looking childish", as though they had defeated the entire German *Wehrmacht*. Cited by Bruno Bettelhim, *Surviving*, 1979.

10
DRESDEN – NORDHAUSEN

I was used by now to the Marienborn border crossing into East Germany. I was not smuggling anything and the police seemed unconcerned about the mechanical state of my van with its worn fittings and ugly rust stains. But the Iron Curtain isn't to be treated lightly. You must follow the right arrows, get into the right lane of cars, be prepared to start, switch off, restart half a dozen times, move a few feet, push if your battery is weak, and look on patiently if everything you are carrying is taken out and searched by a brusque customs official. Then, when all is over, you can sit back behind the steering wheel to enjoy the rush of landscape, the fields of rye and the dark green forests and the grey ribbon of road sweeping you on to Berlin.

I slept in a coppice near the Kohlhasbrücke not far from Wannsee. Just before midnight a gruff voice called through the window and a bearded young man asked if he could park his Peugeot next to me. He was an Australian. "I'm tired of being told by people to bugger off," he said. "In Belgium whenever I found a good place to kip the police moved me on. In Papua there were no problems." I asked him why he was travelling alone. "Because I don't like quarrelling," he said.

I collected my East German visa from the Alexanderplatz in the morning and returned to the crossing point at Checkpoint Charlie. The guards at the Wall told me to go back and re-enter at the Friedrichstrassebahnhof where I had come in. There is much war damage and some rebuilding in the wrecked streets behind Checkpoint Charlie. A building engineer whom I met in a café told me that some of the key construction work was being done by Swedes. He complained about the economy. "Everyone by law must have a job, which means chronic overemployment. It's a great waste of resources and enterprises lose money through it." He had two teenage sons at school. "The school smothers them in anti-West propaganda and when they come home they say 'I hope this will soon end.'"

In the public lavatory at the Friedrichstrassebahnhof I made a poor joke. A man had just dropped his spectacles into the urinal and cursed loudly as he fished them out. "You're lucky it wasn't your gold watch," I said. My remark was received by the other urinators in deadly silence.

The crowded pen at the crossing point was filled with women loaded with heavy shopping bags and food. "They treat us like camels," a woman said to me gasping under her bundles. As a West German she would have to wait some time before being cleared. I was through in five minutes. As I waited on the platform for the S-Bahn I looked up at the roof. The caged apes were still there, watching from the girders. The train took me past the gaps in Berlin's shattered jaw. In the morning I would be on my way to Dresden.

MEISSEN

As it was the peak of the holiday season the lay-bys on the Dresden road were full of picnicking families with little over-crowded Trabant, Wartburg and Fiat cars. Twenty miles from Meissen I stopped at Grossenhain *Ratskeller* for an evening meal where food was served between 6 and 7 p.m. I had a piece of beef, tough cucumber and weak beer. One of the guests, who was drunk, insisted that I should give him a lift to Meissen. He was uncouth and dribbling so I refused (cleaning up vomit from the passenger seat is a nasty job). In the little square there were ten youths, four with light motorcycles, who gave me a push start.

As darkness fell lightning flickered on the horizon and the wind increased to a gale. Before the storm broke I pulled off the road on to a steep bank looking straight down into the Elbe, and while I was battening down a man came out of a cottage and asked if I needed help. "There are no hotels here," he said. The war had brought no one any profit – "only death and injury and power to the few, blast their souls!"

It was a tremendous storm with deafening thunder and un-interrupted lightning that lit up the grey river as though it were day. Hailstones hit the roof like grape-shot. When the storm blew over a few stars appeared and I rolled on to my awful bed.

It took me more than an hour the next morning to thread my way over cobblestones and tram lines through the shabby suburbs of Dresden to the city centre. Luckily I found an excellent parking place – the forecourt of a splendid new hotel, the Belle Vue, looking straight across the Elbe to Dresden's famous "picture postcard panorama" of palaces and churches, which I could see were horribly battered. The parking place was meant for hotel guests and government officials. I had no right to be there. But having found a space I drew the curtains and determined to stay. I intended to stop in Dresden for four days. I noticed that my van had left a trail of rust on the clean white concrete, so I slipped away into the town hoping I had not been observed.

The knowledge that the RAF, with American daylight support, had destroyed the heart of Dresden in two days of fire-storm raids gives an Englishman a gruesome interest in the city. Its wonderful array of spires, domes and towers clustered round the Zwinger palace and the gutted *Schloss* resembles now a row of battered and broken stumps in a diseased mouth. I felt dismay as I walked over the restored Dimitroff bridge and saw for the first time the blackened, twisted remains of the *Schloss* and the *Frauenkirche* and the incinerated wasteland between them. The brutal crushing of Dresden from the air gives no cause for English pride and patriotism. As a military and strategic objective there was no purpose in destroying it and our work of aerial vandalism dragged us down to the same level as the barbarians who sacked Rome. No doubt the effects of the bombing on German morale were significant. Yet the result of the war had already been decided at the time of the raids. The lesson of the Dresden operations for the British is painfully clear. It is that war, even between angels or God-fearing clergymen, cannot be fought by humanitarian means. To argue otherwise is hypocrisy. Victory is only won by hard men.[1]

[1] In the allied air attack on the undefended city of Dresden (13–14 Feb. 1945) 2,000 bombers dropped 3,000 tons of bombs (including 650,000 incendiaries) on the centre of the city. This terrifying blow and the resulting fire-storm killed 135,000 people. Dresden at the time had been

ZWINGER PALACE

I went first to the old masters' gallery in the rebuilt Zwinger.
The Canalettos were on the ground floor and I walked upstairs
to see Rafael's "Madonna di San Sisto". A print of the picture
used to be familiar in English middle-class homes. Because of
her beauty she has never been left alone, and here in the
Zwinger she attracts a day-long throng of gazers: a young
woman stepping gracefully over a carpet of heavenly clouds as
though on a stage. One notices the sensuous curve of her left
thigh and leg outlined under her blue gown. Above the two
little winged urchins the Christ-child gazes back at the world
on his mother's arm as though they have been posed for the
camera. The picture is elegant, flattering and uncontroversial,
with a southern sensual beauty alien to the solemn visions of
northern painters and eastern craftsmen.

Many of the visitors to the art gallery were tourist parties. A
group of fifteen Russians was being conducted by a guide from
one recommended picture to another like a flock of penguins.
The guide had a Russian cassette that recited boring details.
They were not interested in Rubens's "Leda and the Swan" –
a creature with a beak and bony wings snuggling against a
voluptuous woman.

Both the Protestant *Kreuzkirche* (which was almost empty)
and the Roman Catholic *Hofkirche* (full of Poles) are still
being restored after hideous war damage. The *Kreuzkirche* has
posters appealing for money to pay for repairs and has, I was

swelled to twice its normal size by a massive influx of refugees from the
east, Allied and Russian prisoners-of-war, and foreign labourers. Air
Marshal Sir Robert Saundby wrote in his foreword to David Irving's *The
Destruction of Dresden* (1963): "That the bombing of Dresden was a great
tragedy none can deny. That it was really a military necessity few, after
reading this book, will believe. It was one of those terrible things that
sometimes happen in wartime ... " and yet "Those who approved it
were neither wicked nor cruel." He notes that an air attack on Tokyo
by American bombers (9–10 March 1945) killed 83,793 people. The
Hiroshima atom-bomb killed 71,379. The attack on Dresden devastated
over 1,600 acres of the city in one night compared with the 600 acres
destroyed in London during the whole war.

told, fewer resources than the Roman Catholic church where restoration work has been more rapid though with less of the customary extravagance on gilt and decoration.

Back at the car park a middle-aged German looked at my van and said, "I envy you. Here in the DDR we are imprisoned. A man has to wait till he's old or a pensioner before he can get permission to travel abroad and enjoy himself. We are stuck with this terrible inhumane system." Later two Germans poked their heads through the side-window and offered to buy sterling from me – at 10–12 DDR marks to the pound (twice the official rate).

The raised right bank of the Elbe at Dresden with its Baroque palaces and domes, despite war damage and unfinished repairs, is still an authentic survival of old Germany. But behind it the heart of the old city has been torn out and replaced by a socialist-style central square with a Centrum – a great concrete space from which motor traffic is banned. The square is dominated by massive blocks with thousands of small windows and is almost treeless, with uncomfortable benches, fountains and slogans. Shoppers, tourists and strollers collect here. The goods on sale are shoddy. There is no litter, no take-away junk food in paper bags. Everything is clean, stereotyped and soulless. But the wide spaces have a certain grandeur.

Getting service in a restaurant was a problem. There were queues for seats and much bad temper as people pushed and grumbled in draughty doorways. When you have found a seat you must hurry over your meal and vacate your place immediately. "No Smoking" notices discourage dawdling. I chose the Prager restaurant: tepid sausage and mash and *kompot*. An Ethiopian student with whom I shared a table told me he was on paid vacation work. "Finding a job is no problem. In fact if you don't work you will be punished."

Among the crowds in the main precincts I have seen Somalis, Koreans, Vietnamese and Africans: no Tamils and no Turks (they flock to West Germany). The Somalis looked wild and poor, shaggy, with bad complexions. Two young Vietnamese were sitting on a bench playing loud disco music on an outsize transistor radio with a crowd round them. A German pointed to them and said to me, "Communist rubbish".

Many young Red Army conscripts visit the Zwinger and the

museums, in groups of twenty to thirty escorted by officers. They wear their walking out uniforms with peaked caps (no jackboots). Among the museums the Transport Museum is their favourite. They have short haircuts and clean necks but show no military pride in their bearing and slouch along swopping fags and fiddling with their new caps as though they're not used to them. They look like young peasants, decent, harmless and shy. I was passing some Russian soldiers sitting bareheaded on the steps of a fountain when I saw a boy of about four run towards them pretending to aim a gun. "I'll shoot," he was saying, "Bang! Bang!" Good for the boy, I thought. No one seemed upset. When the soldiers got up and walked away one of them was limping badly. "He must have broken his leg," I said to a German. He grinned contemptuously. "They won't win a war with that one!"

It can be argued that the world's most hated and feared country is in essence a colossus of peasant power led by highly trained military professionals and by politicians. We in the West have an advanced culture and technology. But do we have the red-necked peasants to supply the essential cannon-fodder?

REVENGE

On Saturday I saw a few noisy drunks with beer bottles in the square. One of them had passed out and a policeman took him away. Off-duty policemen often carry shopping bags and walk arm-in-arm with their girlfriends looking relaxed and friendly. But they have to keep their hair short, unlike the West German police. Among women the fashion for slim figures has at last reached Dresden. It's mothers from the country who are dumpy.

An elderly woman in a queue to whom I mentioned the bombing of Dresden showed no resentment about the raids. "You paid us back in our own medicine." Another woman told me the bombing was a crime. I gave her one of my stock replies. "Hitler went on fighting the war six months after it was lost. The Allies thought that a few mighty blows might bring it quickly to an end." "The war was *Unsinn* (madness)," she said.

Near the car park there is a German–Russian Friendship club with a bar, disco music and dancing. Young people go there in the evenings. It closes early and there are no troublemakers. The police have a patrol car nearby. At the north end of the Dimitroff bridge, the Neustadter Markt with its conspicuous gilded equestrian statue of Augustus the Strong is another modern architectural show-piece. It has been laid out as a tourist trap with travel and cultural agencies, souvenir shops and ice-cream parlours. Soon after 10 p.m. it is dead.

I have been watching a gang of workers who were using a light bulldozer and a roller to lay a small road along the embankment. They work slowly and break off early. This is a trait I have noticed elsewhere in the DDR. Nobody makes the slightest pretence of working briskly – a very unGerman attitude. I once had a slight professional interest in navvying because in 1954 I spent nine months (till frost hardened the ground) working in the Pfalz with a local contractor's gang of labourers. We were building a country road, sewage pipes and water mains in villages, and laying hard standings for army vehicles in the French army barracks at Speyer. My arm muscles swelled up like a boxer's and I was very hungry, but at fifty DM a week I could only afford one good meal a day. The labourers were displaced Germans from East Prussia. Our foreman had lost a leg in the siege of Brest and blew a whistle when he saw anyone slacking. Slacking was forbidden, and to steal a short rest one had to be crafty. "Just hold on to your spade and waggle your trousers (*Lass bloss die Hosen wackeln*)" the men told me. During the midday break I drank water as I had no money for wine. They jeered at me for this. "*Du kriegst eine blaue Darm* (Your gut will turn blue)". We had no mugs of sweet tea or rashers fried on the end of a spade. The working hours were from seven to five. It was a hard but carefree life which I enjoyed. Watching these DDR idlers smoking in the shade I thought they wouldn't have lasted a single day with Herr Baumeister Scherer's road gang in Rülzheim and Speyer.

I was sorry to leave Dresden. Despite the ugly memory of the RAF bombing and fire-storm that left shrunken, charred bodies, people melted into sludge, or suffocated by lack of oxygen or through carbon monoxide poisoning, everyone has been kind and friendly. There was none of the brusqueness of the Berliner. The older natives had been brought up in a beautiful and cultured Baroque town with magnificent

architecture and treasures. As Saxons they have produced
princes and kings, writers and artists. They have the un-
mistakable Saxon humour and accent. Their masterpieces and
buildings have been blown up, the heart of their city incinerated, their relatives scattered. New citizens have flocked in from
the south and east to replace the dead – Germans from Sudeten-
land, Poznan and Silesia. The Red Army keeps a garrison in
the neighbourhood, and instead of a democracy they have a
People's Socialist Republic separated by watch towers from
their kin in the west. They are poor and their goods are shoddy.
Propaganda and slogans constantly remind them of Hitler's war
guilt. They are still being punished for the past.

Revenge has a sour taste and reprisals strike most of all the
innocent. England's role in shattering Dresden in two days of
holocaust, with 135,000 (almost all non-combatants) dead, is a
nasty entry in the record of man's inhumanity to man. It was
this equation – the brutality of the Nazis emulated by the
savagery of the bombing – that accounted for my mixed feelings
during my visit to the Baroque city on the Elbe.

AN ANCHORITE

On the road to Karl-Marx-Stadt (Chemnitz) I stopped at a
village petrol station run by a married couple. The man looked
after the workshop, his wife managed the petrol pump. He took
me aside, gave me a drink of Kornschnapps and began to talk.
He was very scathing. "Communism!" he said with a bitter
laugh. "It's a farce. No one in the DDR does a proper day's
work. People just check in for their wages. No pride in the
job. It's forty years since they started to restore Dresden and
still they haven't finished. As long as the tourists come the
authorities are happy."

"There are too many foreigners in the DDR," he went on.
"Koreans, Vietnamese, Cubans, blacks. We have to feed them,
and when they get into fights the police daren't arrest them.
The Germans have changed," he concluded. "Yet I must stay
here for ever."

In Chemnitz I bought groceries (the milk had gone sour) and
asked a young man with a bicycle where I could find a quiet
spot for the night. He was an art teacher, and asked me to

follow him. We stopped in the yard of a beautiful old church. "You may stay here. No one will disturb you." The yard was covered with brambles and lit by two old-fashioned street lamps with gas mantles. There were signs of builders working: stacked fragments of mediaeval sculpture and stone tablets from the church, cement bags and tools. The wind sighed, chestnut trees rustled. After dark a cold breath rose from the earth and I huddled up in my wrappings. I had found a sanctuary and felt content.

Early in the morning Roman the art teacher returned and asked me to climb up the bell tower to visit a friend who was living there. I gritted my teeth and plodded up 220 steep spiral steps, to be shown into a small furnished room where Werner was waiting for me.

It was a joy to meet these two delightful men. Werner worked in a music shop and had been living in the bell tower for a year. "There are five churches in the DDR that have rooms built in them for bell ringers and firewatchers." he explained. "This is one of them. I light the gas lamps in the yard and keep an eye on the men restoring the church."

The church (it is the historical *Schlosskirche*) was badly damaged in the war and was being restored by part-time specialist stone masons and craftsmen, but there was scarcely any money to pay for the work. The Germans had used the tower as an observation post and American gunners, who were only a few miles away, had shelled it. Later the Americans were ordered to withdraw and the Red Army marched in to capture the town.

I stayed for three days in Karl-Marx-Stadt. The room in the bell tower where I shared meals with Werner would have suited an anchorite. It was an eyrie, safe, privileged and cosy, with a small iron stove, overlooking a lake with willow trees, a park and the Schlossberg. As I looked up at it from the churchyard and at its rusty dead clock I felt almost as though I had found a home, though after climbing the 220 steps several times I realised that I would never have been a success as a *mullah*, condemned for ever to mount his turret five times a day.

The bell tower gave a splendid view of the town. Some of the old smoke stacks are still standing but in the centre a great space has been gouged out and surrounded by high new buildings with flat roofs. "The old city centre has gone," explained Werner. "It's had a heart transplant and a great bust of Karl Marx has been enthroned there."[1]

Werner described how he had visited Irkutsk in the Soviet Union with In-tourist. "The town centre was new but the rest of the place was a slum, dirty and poor. The Russians," he said, "have simply skipped a whole epoch of history and plunged straight into the modern world." He dismissed my pre-war life in Germany as "old history". "The past is dead. Yet in the DDR we are still being punished for Hitler."

KARL-MARX-PLATZ

My first memory of Chemnitz, fifty years earlier, had been brief and unpleasant. As an undergraduate in 1935 I had spent a fortnight tramping through the Böhmer Wald and had walked across the border into Saxony over the Johannestal. I had found the cobbled streets and heavy grim buildings of Chemnitz crowded with SA men marching with banners and shouting slogans. Their aggressive voices and gestures had depressed me. I went to a cinema and left the following day.

This time I wandered through the city with Roman. We stopped to look at the great grey-black bust of Karl Marx in the central square (Karl-Marx-Platz), the huge head brooding, morose and bearded like a dyspeptic old lion. I asked Roman why Marx looked so bad-tempered. He pointed to the Inter-shop stores opposite and laughed. "Can't you see? The capitalist shop where you pay in dollars has been placed right in front of his nose." The Karl-Marx-Platz is an outstanding example of Socialist pomposity. It has a double role. It is a display ground for Socialist achievements recorded in inscriptions and memorials: and it is the administrative centre with Stadthalle, Party and government offices and a multi-storeyed emporium. No doubt it is an efficient arrangement to concentrate the reins of government in a single place, with car parks for officials, an

---

[1] The RAF planned to give Chemnitz the same treatment as Dresden on the night following the Dresden raid. Chemnitz was a legitimate industrial target defended by night fighters. The aircraft set off but thick cloud cover saved the city from sharing Dresden's horrible fate.

elite shopping precinct, and houses of culture presided over by Marx's solemn bust. Architecturally the big steel, glass and concrete arena is clean, cold and repellent. Now that the tourists have left it is lifeless, waiting for the next Party rally or national day to fill it again with parades, soldiers and crowds.

At the far end of the square, among the thousands of windows, stand two lonely relics of the past: the old town hall and the *Jakobskirche*. People were lined up at the restaurants. To smoke one had to find a table out of doors.

We ate a meal which had a soapy taste. Roman was silent for a time, then he looked at me. "Mr Denis, I can see that you don't like this place. What about me? People like myself have simply retired from life. We do what is necessary to earn our wage but we live our real lives privately among friends, among people we can trust. Friendship here is based on keeping confidences. We don't go out at night. East Germans accept the system but hate it. It's an insult to one's self-respect to live in such a regimented and boring society. But one must be careful. The Security Police are perfect, their intelligence service is first class – no other state organisation can compare with it for efficiency."

We discussed the Church and the Russian occupation. Attendance at church, he said, was not encouraged. "If you are a regular church-goer it will be noted in your file and held against you." He agreed that Russian soldiers were "bumpkins". "They aren't allowed out on their own and daren't make trouble. But officers can move about and sometimes have their wives with them. Sex problems, in the Russian army, by the way, don't officially exist. They're not allowed."

Later I had another look at Karl Marx's bust. The sculptor has given him the face of a humourless prophet, as grim and ill-natured as the Socialist regime itself. The head stands in front of a wall inscribed with proletarian catchwords. Even the street pigeons seem to avoid it. At Oxford we would have placed a chamber pot on the sage's bushy head.

I saw three punks. They had long snake-like legs, ankle boots and hair like cockatoos. No one turned to look at them. I thought they deserved a good mark for boldness.

The *Schlosskirche* stands at the edge of a pleasant lake and public gardens near the *Schlossberg*. There are a restaurant, boats and plaques and pensioners sit under the willow trees

looking at the grey water and the ducks. When they were young
there was martial music in the gardens. The stamp of marching
feet sounded in the street. The newspapers had exhortations
in heavy Gothic print – abuse of the Poles, contempt for
Chamberlain. Later came the victories, the Badenweiler march
and the long trek to Moscow. Then the bombing and the defeat,
the hammer and sickle flying from the Brandenburger Tor, the
counting of casualties and loss of homes. Today there are the
memories, the regrets and resignation: a bench in the park near
a broken church in a rebuilt city bearing a hated new name.

JENA

My next stop was at Jena in Thuringia. I remembered Jena
from pre-war days as a beautiful old town filled with painted
Fachwerk houses and inns jostling each other along narrow
cobbled streets. The rye bread, the fresh sausages sold by the
butchers, the *Eisbein* and cold beer were delightful, the large,
clean women looked kind and motherly, even the SA men with
their brown shirts tucked inside breeches over sagging bellies
seemed innocuous – many of them were, after all, only time-
servers: timid officials, postal and railway clerks anxious to keep
in with their Party bosses. They stood me beer ("You look like a
German") and I paid two shillings for bed and breakfast in an
inn with a snow white quilt and a crooked floor.

   Now, when I came to the old town centre, I had a shock. War
has levelled and destroyed it as though a brutal dentist had
wrenched out its teeth by the roots and left an ugly gap. It has
been renamed Platz der Kosmonauten and is dominated by a
huge black and white cylindrical tower block studded with
hundreds of windows. Only the *Rathaus* and the fourteenth-
century St Michael's church and a few *Fachwerk* houses –
which were wrecked by bombs – have been restored. Jena has
Lutheran connections. The pastor at St Michael's, an upright
man with the bearing of a scoutmaster, showed me the brass
tomb panel intended for Luther at Wittenberg (it was installed
in the church in 1551). He agreed that the manner in which the
old square has been redesigned is hideous (*eine Schande*). The
great barrel-shaped steel and concrete tower block dwarfing his
church was "a monstrosity intended to rub in the triumph of

modern technology over bourgeois architecture. There should never again be war." He admitted, though, that the authorities had given generous financial aid to restore his gutted church – "not because they approve of religion but to attract tourist *devisen.*"

Among several plaques hung in the square I saw an inscription in memory of "the victims of Anglo-American bombing raids on Jena in spring 1945", and a pointed tribute to the "Socialist Humanitarianism of the Red Army in saving Jena's art treasures. Let us for ever be grateful to the Soviet peoples". Another plaque praises "the indestructible bond of brotherhood with the Soviet Union as the foundation of our Forward March". The inscriptions make it plain that though the Anglo-Americans had assaulted Jena, the Red Army had repaired the damage. In Hitler's day, I remember, a copy of Streicher's Jew-baiting newspaper *Der Stürmer*, with cartoons of bottle-nosed Jews mauling Aryan German girls, used to hang in a wire frame outside the *Rathaus*.

In the rebuilt *Rathaus* restaurant I shared a table with a man who had children at school. He said he was not happy about their education. He wasn't against discipline, order and cleanliness. "But schools in the DDR are militarised; flag-waving, assemblies and parades, preparing the youngsters for the Volksarmee. Teachers are closely watched; odd-looking dress or behaviour is absolutely discouraged. Children are expected to inform on each other and on their teachers."

I asked him about syllabuses. Philosophy, literature and art, he replied, were taught with a strong Marxist-Socialist bias. "Socialism isn't interested in *real* truth – it considers that to be *quatsch* (twaddle). Too much discipline," he added, "dries up the personality."

I tried to cheer him up by pointing to the dangers facing young people in a permissive society in the West – the thin white arms scarred by needles, the green cockatoo crests of punks. "They copulate in railway carriages" (this made him laugh).

But then, I have been lucky. I was brought up to admire Britain's achievements and her great men, from generals (even Boer war leaders in plumed helmets) to writers and sportsmen. Oxford had been a splendid interlude. It enabled one to reassess one's prejudices. One could listen to H. G. Wells – a reedy voice addressing the Communist Club: to Major Yeats-Brown of the Bengal Lancers at the Fascist Club; to Professor G. D. H. Cole with his red tie lecturing on the planned Socialist economy of the future; one could heckle Michael Foot (an incessant talker) and work out radical ideas.

Walking back to my van I spent my spare East German marks on five pounds of brawn from a butcher's, some apple pie, cranberry jam and a bottle of Kornschnapps.

WEIMAR REVISITED

On my way back to West Germany I stopped again at Weimar to see Lucas Cranach's paintings in the *Residenzschloss* and to find company at an inn. Russian helicopters circled overhead till after midnight and I had just fallen asleep in the car park when I was awoken by a loud bang on the van door. A drunkard? At 7 a.m. I was startled by three more heavy bangs.

"*Was wollen Sie denn?*" I cried angrily.

Looking through the curtains I saw two policemen, one with a pink round face, the other in glasses. When they saw my mad, tousled head poking out like an angry tortoise they burst out laughing and walked away. I know that after a few nights on the road I look rather seedy and my van is too far gone ever to be smartened up. True, some children are impressed by my GB sticker – "*Aus England!*" But behind my drawn curtains I have overheard less complimentary remarks: "*Alter Schrott, vergammelt, beklopft!*" When I unwind myself from my wrappings in the early morning perhaps I look less like a disturbed toad than an ancient mariner creeping out of a damp sail-cloth.

The State Art collections in the *Residenzschloss* are beautifully and elegantly kept. I spoke to a woman cleaner and she was glad to have someone to grumble to. "The Amis were in Weimar first," she said. "Then *our friends* came." She gave a bitter laugh.

"No one wants to work any more," she went on, pointing to rusty scaffolding on the façade and an abandoned wheelbarrow. "The builders left their rubbish months ago and never completed the job. In my apartment the *klo* stinks but the plumbers won't come; and I can't get medicine for my grandchildren."

While I was sitting on a bench near the Schillerplatz looking at some well-kept old houses with groundfloor shops I watched a lorry driver tip a load of lignite coal on to the pavement in front of a ladies' fashion-wear shop with a noise like a small thunder clap. Everyone fled from the filthy cloud of black coal dust. A few minutes later the driver was back again and tipped another load in front of an antique bookshop. "*Unglaublich* (unbelievable)," said a man dusting smuts from his hat. "It's like being in China," I said. Two shopkeepers in white aprons started to shovel the mess into holes in the wall. "Does it always happen like this?" I asked the bookseller. He said yes. "There's a labour shortage and if we complain we get into trouble."

A war veteran of eighty-one with a craggy face joined us. He had been seven years as a captive in Saratov and released after typhus. "My body is iron-hard," he said. I asked him about the Russians. "Ivan is decent enough. But the occupation troops will never leave East Germany. The Soviets want even more land, and England had better watch out!" He confirmed there were a number of Russian refugees in Weimar and they had borne children there.

The Black Bear hotel caters only for prearranged tourist parties and all I could see in the reception lounge was a stack of empty luggage trolleys. But the *Ratskeller* was open, an ancient stuffy vault lit by candles. I sat with three Germans. One of them was in charge of a visiting youth tennis team. He had spent two years as a prisoner in France ("The Amis were not bad"). The other couple were a man and his wife. He was a party member, owned a car and was in a good humour. He described how he had been in command of a landing craft on the Elbe during the 1968 invasion of Czechoslovakia. "The Czechs pelted us with stones – the only time in my life I've ever felt scared." He said that the Polish units who took part in the invasion behaved badly and went looting. "The Poles hate the Czechs," he said. "They are too nationalistic. Education in East Germany has put a stop to such nonsense. At school the history we learn is presented in terms of socialist ideologies. Nothing about the old German *Heldentum* (heroics)."

When Iron Curtain propaganda refers to the past it does not name the Germans as the enemy but Nazi Fascists or Hitlerites (the *Henker*, or hangmen). The implication is that the German

people, the *Volk*, are all right. It was the leaders, the Party and
the ideology that were evil. With the emergence of American
power it is American Imperialism that has become the *Feind*
(enemy) Number One.

The tennis coach drank a good deal of wine and related his
adventures at the Reeperbahn in Hamburg. "There was a peep-
show. People were goggling through the hole with eyes as big as
ash-trays. Yet some of these idiots drove 10,000 DM cars and
had beautiful wives." He turned to me. "You and I have the
distinction of being the oldest people in the restaurant." "They
should give us a free meal," I said.

I left the *Ratskeller* and walked past the Goethe–Schiller
monument to my van. Under the trees there was a scent of
limes. No lights were shining in house windows. The two disco
clubs had closed at ten. Weimar was like a deserted city. In the
morning I would go to Nordhausen before turning towards
Brunswick.

DORA

The Nazi concentration camp at Nordhausen, north-west of
Weimar, where slave labour was worked to death, was known to
the inmates as "Dora". It was a complex of underground V2
factories hidden in an immense network of tunnels and galleries
running through Kohnstein hill where for centuries sodium
sulphate had been excavated. The production of V2 rockets
was transferred to Nordhausen following the disruption of
Peenemünde by the RAF on 13 August 1943. Prisoners were
made to work and live underground till they collapsed. Those
who died were instantly replaced by fresh drafts from labour
camps. It is estimated that of the 60,000 men who were deported to Dora one half perished. The camp had its own
crematorium.

Its site lies a mile off the main Weimar road and I spent a
morning there. It is an oval-shaped arena. The old barracks and
camp buildings have disappeared. Steps lead up to the crematorium and assembly place where inmates were hanged. There
is a memorial with a bas-relief and flower bed, and a museum of
documents, literature and photographs including several of the
V2 designer Wernher von Braun. A single watch-tower and a

punishment cell are still standing. At the entrance is an old V2-transporter with platform for hoisting the rocket into the firing position. The tunnel entrances have been sealed off.

The camp is surrounded by beautiful pine forests and fields. In spite of the extraordinary efforts made by the Germans to build the underground Dora factories, the enormous resources and thousand of lives that the "wonder weapon" programme cost, its results seem, in retrospect, to have been modest. V2 rockets dropped about 3,000 tons of explosive in eight months. American Flying Fortresses dropped the same amount in one day! It is ironic that the enslaved men who were forced to manufacture the rockets that hammered Belgium and England were friends and allies.

Dora was liberated by American soldiers on 11 April 1945 with its plant and design rooms intact and a stock of half-completed V2 rockets. As the Red Army, by previous arrangement, was to take over the whole complex on 1 June the Americans had to work against the clock to salvage as much vital equipment as they could before the Russians got hold of it. In fact, the Russians did not occupy the Nordhausen area till 5 July. But by 31 May the Americans had managed to load components for one hundred V2 rockets for shipment to the USA. These were followed by a contingent of German engineers, on provisional contract, to help with the development of a rocket programme in America ("Stay here and face the Russians or pack up what you can and go with us," the Americans told them). The first rebuilt V2 was successfully launched in the desert of New Mexico in May 1946.

After the Russians occupied Nordhausen it took them just over a year to rebuild thirty rockets. Components and plant were then transferred to sites near Moscow: Zavod 88 in Kaliningrad and Zavod 456 in Khimki. At the same time Red Army soldiers seized 20,000 German engineers and scientists (including families) and packed them off to Russia in ninety-two trains. About 200 of them were rocket experts. A V2 rocket range was opened in Kapustin Yar, seventy-five miles from Stalingrad, and some twenty V2s were successfully launched by the end of 1947. Ten years later the Russians sent the first Sputnik into space.

Once the Russians had picked the brains of the impressed

German experts they gradually, from 1951 onwards, repatriated them. As tutors they had satisfactorily earned their passage
home. Russian scientists outpaced the Americans in rocket and
space research by firing the first unmanned and then manned
spacecraft into orbit. Though the Americans had got Wernher
von Braun and the elite of the Peenemünde rocket specialists
they lost ten years by failing to make full use of them.

I have a special interest in Nordhausen because in 1949–50
when I was with the Control Commission in Germany I spent
some months interviewing former German war prisoners who
had helped the Russians instal the Nordhausen rocket plant and
test beds in Kaliningrad and Khimki and been employed in
labour brigades on the sites. Others had worked in the German
engineer housing compounds. The engineers had been closely
supervised but had enjoyed various privileges – sport (boating),
expeditions to Moscow and theatre tickets. Jean Michel, the
French Resistance leader, who survived the horrors of the Dora
slave camps, writes in his book *Dora* of his disgust that von
Braun and other German rocket specialists, in return for co-
operating with American rocket development, should have been
forgiven for their involvement with the subterranean labour
camps where 30,000 prisoners died through inhuman treatment. In America they were cosseted and praised. However, at
the time of their evacuation from Peenemünde to the USA, the
war with Japan was still on, and the Americans quite naturally
argued that "their future scientific importance outweighs their
present war guilt."[1]

After leaving the camp at Nordhausen I went into a country
inn for a beer. It had a wood panelled parlour, stout farm
furniture, some old prints and a jolly barmaid. The V2 rocket
was the grandfather of all the big rockets in use today. How
ironic it was, I thought, that these flaming dragons of death
should have been spewed out of the idyllic hills of Thuringia in
the heart of Grimm's fairy-tale country.

[1] See Frederick I. Ordway III and Mitchell R. Sharpe (*The Rocket Team*.
1979).

III

RETURN
TO
POLAND (2)

11
WARSAW IN AUTUMN

There was no letter from the Polish Consulate in Cologne waiting for me in Brunswick. I rang them up. A woman speaking German said they had no knowledge of my visa request and she was about to ring off when I addressed her in Polish. She immediately changed her tone, told me to post my passport with a visa application form and wait three weeks. I put down the phone with a slight stirring of hope. Perhaps the Warsaw bureaucratic machine was not very efficient and would overlook my previous expulsion order.

The Polish lady kept her word. The visa was delivered by registered mail on 20 September, I tidied up my van, bought provisions from a supermarket, and was off.

MUSHROOMS

I was elated to be on my way back to Poland. I had been getting into a groove in Brunswick. Café Haertel in the morning, among the silver-haired ladies spooning cream into their coffee, a copy of the *Frankfurter Allgemeine* propped in its wooden frame against the sugar basin: a walk in the Stadtpark after lunch, and evening beer with unkempt Greenpeace youths and artists at the Vier Linden Gasthaus. I had an incontestable three months' Polish visa stamped in my passport. I had also widened my perspective through visiting East Germany. I had seen how two nations were grappling with Marxist Socialism and could compare their response. The East Germans were cowed. They had learned how to idle, an unGerman trait that had made them more amiable. The Poles remained troublesome and truculent. History had taught them how to grumble and survive.

This was to be my seventh crossing of the DDR frontier at Marienborn since I had driven off from Miss Parsons's snug manse in Snitterfield and turned on to the road through Stratford and Bedford to the coast. The van door that had fallen off was holding and the mended roof had stayed water-tight. I had learned now how to squeeze into the column of cars and trucks waiting at the barrier to roar off along the Berlin road, and I was soon through. It was a fine clear day. A few miles on I passed a police car that had stopped an old Benz crammed with Turks. I had seen them at the frontier noisy and laughing as they push-started their old banger through the barrier. They now stood morosely in the road as the police rechecked their papers and baggage.

I reached the Berlin ring in the afternoon. The traffic thinned out between here and the Polish border; mostly snub-nosed East German and Russian trucks, small local Fiats and Trabant and Wartburg cars. I bought Dutch pipe tobacco at an Intourist shop, filled my tank and arrived at Frankfurt-an-der-Oder before dark.

Some forty vehicles were already waiting at the barrier while customs snoopers walked up and down like guard dogs and ransacked their belongings. No banter, no jokes. A tense business for a motorist with a few West German presents tucked away among his underwear or under a seat. I had left most of my books in Brunswick and had nothing to incriminate me except one small paper back (Reiner Kunze's cynical sketches of German life under Ulbricht's DDR regime, *Die Wunderbaren Jahre*) which I hoped no one would notice. The official who climbed into the back of my van turned everything upside down – food tins, letters and books, including Colonel Grainger's *Don't Die in the Bush* (I cherish this manual because it reminds me of the African bush, of snakes and water-holes and naked men with beads). When he spotted Kunze's little volume he grunted. "A bad book, defamatory to the DDR. We shall confiscate it." He gave me a receipt and I moved on to confront the Poles. They made only one comment. "Your car insurance will expire in five days. You must get a new one." I drove off into the shadows.

My headlights were weak and I soon lost my way among the black hedgerows. After a mile or two a red light suddenly shone out of the darkness and a soldier with a lantern challenged me. "This is a military zone," he said. "*Co pan robi tutaj?* What are you doing here?" He called a lieutenant out of a shed. He was sleepy and vague. "Go back and watch for road signs," he said, pointing into the night. "Be careful. You might get arrested."

Twenty miles on I spotted a forest clearing and crawled on to my Heath Robinson bed. The moon was almost full but dimmed by mist. The firs were silent: not a cricket or a falling leaf. There was an ominous nip in the air – the season was getting late. But I had crossed the Iron Curtain again and I was happy. This strange restless country wedged between the Germans and the Russians had taken me back, and I would sleep among the firs.

Mushroom pickers were out in family groups on the road to Poznan. They had parked their little cars and battered buses (some specially chartered) by the wayside and had disappeared into the forest with buckets, bags and sheets which they were filling with mud-coloured fibrous knobs. I looked into a woman's pail of mushrooms. They had an unwholesome green-ish tinge, better suited, one might have thought, for a witch's cauldron, but she told me they tasted delicious.

Passing through the industrial outskirts of Poznan I drove slowly through quarries, mud and dying trees, past factory stacks and workers' compounds. I find it impossible to be inspired by a system that makes men and women work in such hideous industrial plants and sleep like cockroaches in concrete honeycombs. I spent the night in the garden of a small motel. When the bar closed the yard and garden filled with drunks and cursing.

At Konin I bought cheese, bread and a jar of pickled herrings and went into a restaurant for a bowl of vinegary soup. The parlour was occupied by rough-looking men on stools drinking beer or vodka out of bottles. There was a strong smell of unwashed clothes and sour food. The men looked tough. They had lined, bony faces and thin mouths, tousled hair falling over the back of their collars, big hands. I shared a table with two farmers who were drinking in a silent daze. It was too early for customers to be noisily drunk. But one party had lined up fifteen bottles and was emptying them at alarming speed. In an hour or so the hubbub and the thuds would begin. A familiar notice over the bar read, "Alcohol will damage your health and ruin your family life". I didn't use the toilet as I knew it would be an unspeakable bog.

Forty miles from Warsaw I stopped to buy apples and sweet damsons from a farmer's stall and soon after was waved down by a policeman with a red and white wand. He looked at my passport and asked me what foreign currency I was carrying.

"Sterling."

"No dollars? My eldest son collects foreign coins. Can you oblige him?"

I had a florin piece somewhere in my van and climbed into the back to look for it. "Close the door," said the policeman after a few moments. "People will see you."

When I gave him the florin and explained its value the policeman made a sour face. He had expected at least a pound or two. He pointed angrily at my tyres. "They're badly worn," he said. I was afraid he might investigate the van and cover his uniform in rust. But he let me go, and I was not followed.

I found my old Gromada camping place about to close for the year. The tourist season was over, the gypsies had gone, the caravan trailers had been wrapped in tarpaulins. But Andrzej was there. "You came on the first day of the season," he reminded me, "and you have returned on the last." When I had first arrived at the end of April the poplars were naked. In May they had put on leaves. Now they were bare once more and the scented limes stretching between the Soviet war cemetery and the Airman's monument were shedding leaves like yellow snow flakes. In the evening the young lawyer came with his dog. He was startled to see me and thought I had been remarkably cunning or lucky to get back. "Keep away from the Press and embassies," he warned me. "Don't be seen in their offices. Every office has a spy and you will be watched."

EMMA

I went for my first walk along familiar roads. A cold rain was falling and people were scurrying through puddles without umbrellas or coats. The buses were crammed with football fans. A woman at the bus stop pointed to my sandals and advised me to change them for warm shoes. "This is not Italy," she said.

My first call in the morning – it was Sunday – before seeing
Emma was at the red-brick church of St Michael's. Nothing had
changed. The priest was giving his homily on love and charity
and the Holy Mother. "The hanging body of Christ symbolises
the sufferings of the Polish nation. His gaping wounds its
blood." I was delighted when Emma invited me to stay in her
flat in al. Wyzwolenia. After sleeping for weeks in the open,
watching summer turn to autumn and autumn moving slowly
into winter with darkness closing in soon after tea time, I was
certainly going to enjoy a divan bed and the use of a bathroom.

I have been meeting old friends again. Tomasz has shown
me his rhymed translation, in English, of one of Boleslaw
Lesmian's most famous poems, The Girl (*Dziewczyna*). Some
passing travellers – twelve brothers – hear a girl's voice crying
sadly from behind a stone wall. They begin to smash down the
wall with hammers ("We must not allow her to rust to death").
When they give up exhausted the hammers go on pounding the
wall on their own till it is finally crushed. But there was nothing
there. "It was only a voice – and nothing but the sound".
   "They were seeking what is not," explained Tomasz, "an
illusion. Lesmian revelled in despair."
   I showed him the Cohens' book of *Modern Quotations* which
I had brought with me. After a time he said, "The Poles don't
have this sort of wit. We use our language ponderously. Our
aphorisms have no edge, the flowers are swaddled by ivy."
   We discussed my recent impressions of the East Germans –
"a dazed people, assaulted by slogans, constantly reminded of
the sins of their fathers, concealing their true thoughts."
   Tomasz found this hard to believe. "The German never
changes his spots. He is still a potential aggressor. We Poles, on
the other hand, are ungovernable, the Russians too servile."
   Emma's apartment block is shaded by maple trees and chest-
nuts. There is a big grassy square in front, with benches. Rooks
perch on the trees like black rats. Scores of pigeons nestle along
the balconies, waiting for scraps of stale bread. They are unkempt and stain everything and Emma doesn't like them. The
working residents who live in the square leave early in the
morning with a banging of doors. The older people, pensioners
and old ladies, take bags and join shopping queues. The

discomfort and waste of time lining up at counters or on the pavement creases people's faces and gives them a morose look. In some food stores there are not enough metal shopping trays – perhaps only a dozen in a supermarket and a crowd of customers waiting for them. The number of sales girls is always too few.

The main thoroughfare through Warsaw's centre (al. Jerozolimskie) has recently been barricaded for half a mile from the Marszalkowska crossing as far as the Praga end of the Poniatowski bridge. Behind the wooden fences bulldozers and drills are working with a dreadful clatter: traffic has been diverted along side streets. The rebuilding project and bridge repair are scheduled to last from four to five years. This will cause gross inconvenience to shops, businesses and pedestrians. But in a socialist country the comfort of the public is not a top priority.

If the Palace of Culture had a clock it would at least be worth looking at to check the time (many Poles don't possess a watch). As it is, people have grown so accustomed to the monstrosity that they scarcely notice it. The great windy space stretching round the Palace adds hundreds of yards to the distance you have to walk to get round it.

Now that the Poles have put away their summer clothes and are losing their sun tan Warsaw has become drabber and greyer. Men and women have taken to thick anoraks and jumpers, children wear padded suits. Thinning hair exposes ivory-white pates. It is getting too cold to enjoy sitting in the Lazienki Gardens. The black ponds are strewn with ducks' feathers, the paths greasy with fallen maple leaves. I have been to the Praha restaurant for a meal: four *platkis*, red cabbage, mashed potatoes and a rissole made of soggy flour warmed in gravy. The restaurant is always full, however bad the food. One must be careful when carrying a tray. It may crumple, decanting soup over one's shoes.

Barnett has left for England. When I went to the reading room today the customary queue of about twenty people was standing at the issue counter. Is this because the Council is short of staff or has queueing been accepted, even encouraged, as a necessary bureaucratic control? Yet two idle retainers look after the cloakroom, smoking like Turks. It is good to see the Poles' lively interest in English books.

MATEJKO

One of the best known and admired of the pictures in Warsaw's
National Gallery, indeed in Poland – every school child is taken
to see it – is Jan Matejko's 'Battle of Grunwald' (Tannenberg)
painting. It is now on view again after the reopening of part
of the gallery's historical section. At Grunwald the combined
armies of Lithuania and Poland beat the Teutonic Knights on
15 July 1410 in a decisive victory that put an end to the Knights'
power. Matejko paints huge men slashing and stabbing each
other with swords, pikes, daggers and battle axes, the Knights
mounted on heavy chargers, the Lithuanians and Poles fighting
on foot except for Witold, Prince of Lithuania, a magnificent
figure with shield and heavy sword and carmine surcoat over his
armour.

What bone-crushing blows and splitting of German skulls!
The Grand Master is shown at the moment of being slain by
two soldiers, one wielding a pike, the other, wearing short
breeches, an axe. The horse of Markward, the Brandenburg
knight, is already down and he is about to be speared through
the neck. Jan Zyska, enormously strong, one-eyed, bareheaded, is slashing away at the knights like a man felling trees.
One can almost hear the panting, the clank of cold steel, the
screaming of wounded men and horses. Yet a self-portrait of the
artist hanging next to the scene of slaughter shows him to be a
gentle-looking man in rimless glasses looking like a retired
librarian.

In the mediaeval Christian art section I looked again at the
figures and paintings of the dead Christ. They show him horri-
fyingly wounded with thorn and scourge marks on his body and
dried blood caking deep gashes. In the Pietà representations the
gaunt grey hand hangs limply. This is no place for a handsome
shepherd knocking gently at the door with crook and lantern.
We are left with a tortured scarecrow.

Among the riffraff who baited and taunted Christ at the
crucifixion the early artists have drawn men with big hooked
noses – obviously Jews. Such caricatures are disturbing. They
reflect the historic antipathy between Christ-worshippers and
the Jews in Poland. Seen in this light, Zionism and the birth of
Israel are merely the belated recognition by Jews of the futility,

especially after the holocaust, of staying in their old homeland in eastern Europe and of trying to rebuild a new life there. After centuries of residence that ended almost with their extinction, age old prejudices have driven them into a new diaspora.

I noted that a significant number of the religious exhibits originate from areas such as Silesia where German craftsmanship and religious fervour were high.

Later, at a friend's party, there was much talk of corruption and intrigue among Polish politicians and the boorish behaviour of the police. I would have preferred to hear less about the Polish problem and more about Chekhov ("the good doctor") and his country patients or Rasputin the Siberian monk who seduced respectable court women ("he made love like a horse"). A woman at the party said "I long to live in Greece. Give me olive trees not a pickled cucumber."

The magazines and books which the Polish customs confiscated in July have been returned to me at the request of the British consul. He has not been long in Poland – his previous posts were in Bulgaria and Moscow – and he finds the Poles "very eastern-orientated". The government welcomes Polish visitors from America as they have hard currency to spend. He hears many sad reports of newly arrived Polish travellers from America, people who had been saving up for years to visit relatives and friends, being mugged at railway stations or on main-line trains, especially on the train to Cracow. This in spite of police and plain-clothes men at stations. He had recognised my Bedford van parked outside Emma's in Plac Zbawiciela. "The registration number identifies it as very old." Later I went to the airport customs to retrieve the money I had been made to leave behind at the border. It seemed an extraordinary amount in zlotys. How to spend it? Fur-lined boots, sheepskin jackets, jewellery?

DACHA

Anna, a university colleague, had a rented *dacha* at Podkowa Lesna twelve miles east of Warsaw. I went there with Emma and some of her friends in a rattling electric train (no ticket control) that took us through a ragged suburbia of factories and tenement blocks, torn up land, fields and sand, into wooded country with summer cottages built in little clearings. We walked along a cinder path from the station, our breath smoking in the mist. The *dacha* is a simple wooden house sparsely but adequately furnished. It is screened by birch trees and there was an old horse munching behind a fence. We sat on the verandah until the mist thickened and blotted out the pale sun.

The people who live in this *dacha* colony, I was told, are not intellectuals or artists but mostly professional and private businessmen who have had the luck and initiative to make their own money. Anna's neighbours run a prosperous enterprise which makes toys. Others grow market flowers. One wouldn't expect to see Pasternak's gloomy, equine face emerging through the birch trees.

We had lunch in the local restaurant, quite an elegant establishment with tender black-market cutlets and good wine. Two rough-looking men who had been drinking came in and sat at the next table.

"So you're English," one of them said to me in a thick voice. "I like the English." He asked me if I intended to visit Russia.

"No," I answered. "Russia is *gowno* – a bloody place."

Alas, I had spoken too loudly. The word "*gowno*" rang out above the scrape of cutlery. My companions looked embarrassed and stared at their plates.

"You can't say that sort of thing in public," Anna whispered in my ear. Then we all laughed.

We left in a dark mist, shivering in the rattling train, and waited outside Warsaw central station for a late night bus to take us home. On a fine day it must be delightful to leave one's cares behind and retire for a time to a *dacha* among the silver birches and magpies, to lie in the sun and live on biscuits and vegetables and wild strawberries. But with winter on the way hedges drip, footpaths churn into mud, dogs bark out of the shadows, and the train is like an ice-box.

At a party of teachers last night Felicity, a visiting lecturer in English literature who has spent a year at Sarajevo university in Bosnia and is finishing her tour in Warsaw, asserted that there is no such thing as a "good action". Every act is motivated by self-interest, either deliberate or sub-conscious. Martyrdom, or laying down your life for another, is a disguised form of self-indulgence.

I am startled by such cynicism. As an "old Colonialist" I have admired the altruism that has been shown by many white civil servants, doctors and churchmen in the less comfortable parts of the British empire. The priest and the hospital nun, by opting out of normal society, may have spared themselves a life troubled by erotic lust and ensured a smooth path to heaven. But it seems ungenerous to focus on the element of self-righteousness in the benevolent and often Spartan lives of such people as the Verona Fathers, who are still active in Kenya and Uganda.

Felicity gave an interesting analysis of how state socialism in eastern Europe has replaced the traditional "blood feud" – the inter-clan rivalry, the cut-throat family codes of honour and propriety, the brutal competition to survive against others – which activated life under the old social systems. Yet socialist governments, she said, "have no real consideration for people". Life under socialism is "regulated, dull and predictable". Poles especially resent this sort of arbitrary paternalism. They hate being nagged at and told what to do.

A student at the party complained that "Poles spit a lot". When they sit talking out of doors they leave a ring of spittle around them.

"For reasons of hygiene?" I asked. "Like Turks clearing their mouths during Ramadan?"

"No. Spitting is a way of showing contempt for the world, the way things are run. It's a form of protest."

The tenants who share Emma's staircase and lift rarely greet each other. Each family or couple seems to have retreated into its own shell. One neighbour is a former naval officer, correct and courteous. An elderly couple has a tiny Fiat parked outside the entrance. They rarely drive it, but every morning dust and polish it till it shines like a new shoe. A well-known film actor has a girlfriend on the top floor. Twice, when drunk, he has knocked at Emma's door by mistake. "He was quite charming," said Emma, "but difficult to handle. He wanted to sleep in the kitchen."

There is one splendid old lady with a resonant voice, a heavy walking stick and moth-eaten clothes who looks like a nineteenth century duchess. The arrival of two new tenants – both Arabs – has caused misgiving and the porter watches them closely.

The back of Emma's flat overlooks a school playground. The children arrive soon after 7.a.m. in an explosion of energy, shouts and wrestling. They are let loose again at the morning break and at noon. Only a curmudgeon would resent their high spirits. Yet I remember one crabby fellow, my neighbour in Knightsbridge, who used to lean out of his window when he heard children playing and shout "Bugger off, you brats!"

RUSSIAN FILM WEEK

The Russian film week which has just ended has been a flop. Few people went to see the performances. I saw a Georgian epic and a Cossack spectacular. Only four people were at the Georgian film; myself, Emma, a boy and a man who fell asleep, and a dozen at the other. The cinema operator and attendant would have been justified in cancelling the programmes and going home for an early night. But that would have offended the Russian sponsors.

The Georgian film showed the introduction of collective farming methods in upland farms, a scuffle in a hayfield provoked by obstinate *kulaks* and the triumph of the Soviet plan. It was not an overtly propagandist film. The theme was Caucasian passion: treachery, jealousy, murder. A young husband shot dead in a field; his bride forced to accept the murderer's advances. Magnificent mountain scenery, raven-haired actors, gypsy music.

The Cossack epic glorified the Cossack cavalry commander Budyonny, an early hero of the revolution, leading his Red Cossacks to victory in bloody battle against Denikin's better equipped and more numerous White Russian troops. This was a triumph of Budyonny's revolutionary spirit over the hesitations of his traditionally trained ex-Tsarist staff officers and advisors. Budyonny was shown as a man with a fierce black moustache and eyebrows and a hard eagle face. For an hour horses rolled on the ground and men fell dead. Alas, the Cossack leader was whirling his sabre at a virtually empty house and the message was lost. The film was like a Wild West movie with a cavalry hero played by John Wayne.

The Soviet embassy stands at the end of the fashionable al. Ujazdowskie: a large building in the old Imperial style enclosed by a long white wall like a piece of the Berlin *Mauer*. Its portentous entrance is flanked by great columns. Next to it is a block housing the Soviet Trade Mission. I once stopped for a moment to look at it, while with Emma.

The sight of a Soviet enclave always gives me a queasy feeling. The inmates lock themselves in behind the Cyrillic signs as though afraid of the light. The hammer and sickle flag evokes memories of revolution, of Lenin snarling at a crowd of ragged soldiers and sycophants, of frozen kulak corpses. One knows that Moscow's diplomatic missions conceal unpleasant secrets and nests of highly trained security agents.

"Don't gape," said Emma, "anyone loitering here is under scrutiny."

In Ankara the Soviet Embassy on the Ataturk boulevard was also sealed off behind a high blank wall that made it look like a prison compound. I sometimes saw its staff playing volley ball – their daily exercise – in the garden. They wore sweaty vests and looked bourgeois and ungraceful. In Kampala the Soviet diplomatic wives organised their shopping in droves. One recognised them by their cheap print frocks and thick ankles. Africans didn't consider them proper memsahibs. ("They aren't smart and they haven't been to school – they can't speak English").

I once met a Soviet commercial attaché at the Ankara tennis club who challenged me fifteen times within a month to play him at singles. A nice man but he was determined to win and he brought two Russian colleagues in square coats to give him moral support. I never allowed him to beat me. Wasn't my national honour at stake too in this duel of dwarfs?

The very name – "Iron Curtain" – is to me sinister. Living behind it one feels cut off, vulnerable, even suspect. One's mail is likely to be opened. It is tempting to imagine drama where there is none. The drab people plodding along Warsaw pavements, elbowing each other at the traffic lights and queueing at vegetable stalls, are clearly dull and harmless citizens. And yet how many of them burn with secret fires and are potential

rebels or revolutionaries awaiting their chance to wreck
police stations and march through Victory square with Polish
Freedom banners? How many of them, angered by daily frust-
rations, turn into drunkards or family tyrants? The pale
working-class girls with tight lips shivering at the tram stop will
have secrets too. Perhaps in private they are passionate and
faithless creatures?

ELECTION DAY

Today 13 October is polling day in the national elections. The
mood is one of apathy. For my Polish acquaintances it is a non-
event, and I have heard of no demonstrations or trouble-making
in Warsaw. During the day police in large numbers have been
on duty with parked vans and militia patrol cars. Solidarity has
called the elections a "farce" and has appealed to voters to
boycott them. But even if fifty percent of voters were to stay
away from the polling stations the government wouldn't admit
it. An acceptable minimum of absentee voters has already been
determined and it will be issued as the official figure.

I notice that many of the pensioners who live in Emma's
apartment block or in neighbouring flats have indeed cast their
votes at the polling booth set up in the school behind the
square. I saw the retired senior official who lives next door
walking proudly back from the booth holding up his voter's
badge – a carnation. Many pensioners, I am told, have adjusted
to their present lot: they have, after all, a flat, ration card
and medical care. What they fear is any violent change in the
political scene that might lead to disturbance and disrupt their
ordered existence.

In the evening Emma and I went to look at the polling station
set up in the school. It was neat, clean and well lit, and empty
except for two female polling officers at a table. The voters had
already called during the day. People don't like going out at
night.

We had just walked home from a tea party near Father
Popieluszko's church, St Stanislaw Kostka. It was packed
as usual with worshippers and banners (one of them marked
"Solidarnosc"). But many of the old Solidarity posters have
been removed from the churchyard railings. The wicks were

burning in pots of oil round the priest's grave. Inside the church, with its two rather ugly twin spires, the kitsch and bric-à-brac had been burnished and neatly displayed. Among the worshippers plain clothes policemen were lurking. The crowd was still and quiet. No one spoke and hardly anyone coughed.

THE HEJNAL

for Kyrstyna Nazar

Cracow, St. Mary's Church: from the high tower
  As the clock strikes twelve
    A trumpeter sounds the Hejnal – an alarm
Sounded in earnest when some foreign power
Threatened the city. Once, when Tartars came,
  A marksman shot the trumpeter
    Who fell, leaving the panic-tune unfinished;
Since when, to give the event its proper fame,
The fanfare is shot down in mid-flight
  Each day, as the hour strikes,
    The unfinished call blown to the four winds,
The trumpet but no trumpeter in sight;
A tiny sound is heard by gaping tourists
  In the Square – the horns of Elfland,
    A ghost-voice risen from the dead, which can't
Be exorcised by priests or scientists.
Through centuries such hauntings kept in sight
  Grievances best forgotten,
    Now relished, like the scars of battle wounds
Old soldiers show, as proof they once could fight.

Some day, for a lark, another trumpeter
  Will add the missing notes
    From a neighbouring roof. 'What's that? What's going on?'
People will cry; in the turmoil, the great stir,
They'll hear a shout, 'Let the poor ghost have peace!
  Seven centuries are too long
    Even for a ghost to keep on haunting us'.
But then, with batons flashing, the police
Will put up road blocks, hunt from door to door
  Until they trap the joker,
    Impound the offending instrument, and let
The Hejnal flourish as it did before –
Always unfinished, like a sun half-set
  On the horizon, never
    Setting; never allowing the tired wound
To heal; ensuring no-one shall forget.

                      Edward Lowbury

12

LUBLIN – CRACOW – OSWIECIM

SISTER MARIA

It is time for me to move. I am off to Lublin, Cracow and Oswiecim and will return through Czestochowa. Breeze has booked a room for me in the lecturers' hostel at the Catholic university in Lublin.

I left Warsaw on a bright cold morning. There was little motor traffic on the road but I was slowed up by strings of farm carts loaded with beet, the drivers and their wives, wrapped in warm clothes, leaning over the horses' tails as though they were half asleep. Straggling villages marked by road signs appeared among the fields: wooden cottages, barns with patched roofs, flaking two-storey houses with pretentious wrought-iron gates (a status symbol) and untidy gardens. The air was frosty, the sun cold and brilliant. In the outskirts of Lublin a farmer pulled up his horse and showed me the way to the university. Sister Maria, who runs the lecturers' hostel, was expecting me. She was a smiling fresh-faced woman in a grey habit and had a degree in English from Manchester University. She gave me a corner room at the end of a corridor and demonstrated how to juggle with the light bulb if it failed to work. The hostel had not yet been plastered. Workmen were still busy and my tiny room, though spotless, was unheated. I sat on my divan bed shivering till supper.

Luckily I had arrived on a guest night for visiting foreign priests and a small feast had been prepared for them: white bread, sliced sausage, poppyseed cake and bars of chocolate. My neighbours were a Belgian and a Polish priest. They were stout men with thick white necks. Father Stefan, the Pole, told me he had travelled in Britain, America and Africa. He started straightaway to talk about Polish politics, criticising Urban, the official government spokesman. Urban, he said, had grossly exaggerated the size of the recent turn-out at the national polls ("the government daren't admit there was so much apathy among voters") and the electoral results were faked. He was scathing about Urban – "a lackey with ears like a donkey – they stick out like television aerials". The government, he said as though imparting something new, was waiting for a pretext to tighten the screws on the Church. "It will fail. The Church has centuries of survival experience behind it."

He asked for my impressions of East Germany. "The older people," I said, "seem to have opted for a quiet life. They don't like the regime but accept it. Young Germans are frustrated and may one day cause trouble."

"In Poland," Father Stefan commented, "no one is resigned to Communism. Young people are bitterly opposed to the regime, its message and atheism. They are turning more and more to the Church for spiritual comfort."

I finished my cheese cake and turned to Breeze, who was explaining Benthamism to a credulous girl student.

THE CATHOLIC UNIVERSITY

The Roman Catholic university of Lublin, founded in 1918, has a unique distinction. It is the only private Catholic university in the entire Communist bloc and the only one in the world (it claims) which centres its studies on man. Pope John Paul II was formerly a professor in the ethics department. The university has 3,400 students. It is not subsidised by the state but is entirely maintained by funds collected by parishes and by the generosity of benefactors.

The Linguistics department employs a Swiss lecturer (he had acute laryngitis and wore a muffler indoors), a Viennese, an American couple, Breeze and Doyle. We meet at breakfast and supper in the hostel kitchen over Spartan meals of bread and cheese, jam and hard-boiled eggs which we prepare ourselves. Since Breeze and Doyle are teaching subjects of which I know nothing I treat them with proper awe. One of their Polish students has told me that the Celtic courses are not popular. "We would do better to learn English."

The inauguration ceremony to mark the beginning of a new academic year is to take place tomorrow (20 October). The Primate of Poland, Cardinal Glemp, will be the guest of honour. A concourse of bishops and dignitaries is expected. Students are ironing their suits and borrowing ties. The girls have dressed their hair. For Sister Maria and the nuns it will be their big day. I have spent some hours wandering through the town, exploring the narrow alleys of the old city and visiting churches. The grey light, the drizzle, the shabby people standing in the aisles and the poor shops produce an atmosphere of melancholy. Standing on a mound behind the cathedral I could glimpse the Street of the Tormented (Droga Meczenikow). The doomed wretches who were driven this way to Majdanek death camp (a mile farther on) were watched by the whole town as they trudged along the road with their bundles and their children. The Jews from Lublin ghetto walked past their own familiar houses and yards. Then, like the Pied Piper's flock, they vanished. But they were not sucked up by a magic cloud. They were stripped naked, the women's hair was cut off, they were suffocated in a black tomb, the gold fillings and dentures were wrenched from the mouths of the dead by metal hooks and the bodies were incinerated. The hair was weighed, packed in sacks, invoiced and sold for profit. Their ashes were thrown into fields where Polish peasants now grow vegetables.

I shall stay in Lublin for several days. I find it invigorating to be the guest of a Catholic establishment that is at war with the tenets of government ideology. And I have to visit Majdanek.

At the inauguration ceremony the assembly hall was packed and from the crowded gallery I could see little but rows of clerical profiles and the Rector reading the annual report from a lectern. The report was very long (over two hours): a roll call of names with titles and academic honours and a list of scholastic achievements and projects. The reception for dignitaries, however, made up for the ordeal. Borsch with *pierogi*, sliced veal, ham and pâtés, macaroni puddings, salads, cream cakes and cheese – but no alcohol or smoking. Bishops with waist-sashes pulled tight round large firm bellies. Senior clerics, balding and pink with heavy peasant shoulders. Champing jaws and an array of velvet caps and birettas. They were a splendid advertisement for the pleasures of ecclesiastical privilege. Only one guest misbehaved. The young Viennese lecturer was not wearing a tie ("I cut myself while shaving") and he smoked.

Cardinal Glemp is a small sturdy man looking like a tough little terrier. The Americans, having withdrawn their ambassador at the time of martial law, were represented by a deputy. When the Rector announced the benefices made by foreign governments to the university the American contribution was loudly applauded. The reference to British aid met with formal claps. I recognised Kevin Ruane among the guests. "I never thought to see you with the prelates," he said.

I did feel a little out of place among the *Prominenz*. They were fine mediaeval specimens and hair shirts are not their style. They live well, are adulated, and hand on their privileges from one generation of the religious hierarchy to another. Under a Polish Pope they can claim to be the court favourites.

MAJDANEK

In Buchenwald genocide was committed on our own western doorstep in a bucolic landscape where Goethe and Schiller had taken country walks. The camp was within range of the RAF, who could have dropped some of their surplus bombs on the SS barracks and exterminated a few of these monsters even though they might have killed inmates too. But Majdanek was a faraway place lost in a Slavonic bog.

Poles have long memories. Wherever they have settled they have built monuments to their heroes and to tragic events. Lublin's street names reflect Poland's chequered modern history. There is a Heroes of Monte Cassino street, a Lenin avenue (named under duress) and a Red Army street leading through Majdan Tatarski (ominous reminder of Tartary) to the Street of the Tormented, the Via Dolorosa along which Jews and Christians were marched to the furnaces.

I took a municipal bus to Majdanek – a mundane way of arriving at a death camp – and got out at a great block of concrete raised as a memorial stone on a platform near the entrance. The block has been shaped like a huge rotten cheese,

cracked and pitted in symbolism of death and hopelessness and
the chaos of evil. In the distance I could see a dome – the
mausoleum – and walked towards it. It was a cold misty morning. Rooks and magpies were flying over the flat grassy arena of
the camp. Only a few of the old prison barracks have been left
standing. But the barbed wire fences, the sentry towers and
gates are intact. Along the perimeter I saw some peasants
working in a field.

The dome is suspended over a circular pit filled with com-
pacted human ash. Next to it is a crematorium with a stout
brick chimney. I went inside. As a protected monument the
crematorium is kept very tidy. The furnaces are swept and
labelled, the cement floor, showers and fittings are in good
order. The atmosphere is antiseptic. At first sight one might
have taken the building for a bath and disinfestation unit.

A Polish attendant in a blue uniform came up. He told me he
was a retired army sergeant. "Do you get many visitors?" I
asked him. "Only in summer. They are mostly tourists, some
American Jews."

"Does anyone make trouble?"

"Some visitors get upset but the guides know their job." He
pointed to the showers. "The heat was so intense that the men
working the furnaces constantly had to cool off."

"What happened to the ash after the bodies had been burned?"

"It was packed in bags or thrown on the SS vegetable
gardens."

I looked at the peasants working in the beet field near the
fence. The soil must have been well fertilised.

I walked across the empty camp to a row of barracks standing
near the lower end. There were twenty numbered huts housing
the "museum", filled with grisly mementoes. One shed was
crammed with mouldy prison shoes (they had a bad smell),
another with prison uniforms – striped jackets and trousers,
washed and threadbare. There was a hut with nothing in it but
piles of prison caps. In some of the huts the bed boards had
been left. They were built in tiers, with wooden frames. Other
exhibits were a pile of human bones with a skull on top, countless bundles of thick human hair and sets of cyclone gas containers with poison crystals.

Wall photographs illustrated the insane perfectionism and

methodical callousness of the Nazi extermination machine. There were copies of prison records, clearly typed and stamped, medical returns and disciplinary reports, personal documents. Enlarged pictures of execution scenes. Corpses being thrown on a pyre, gallows with meat hooks, armed guards herding women and children. Outside one of the huts a cart, like a tumbril, for carrying the dead, and a heavy concrete roller.

When I had seen the "exhibits" and visited the smaller crematorium and gas chamber at the end of the block I sat on a stone in the drizzling rain. I had been in the camp all morning and had seen only three other visitors. I felt the banality of my position. For the years had swept away the stench of burning flesh and, as was inevitable, left only relics that had been turned into a show-piece. All that remained of the 350,000 people who had perished here were some old clothes, hair and bones, and a mound of human ash. I would now give the attendant a few coins and catch the local bus back to town.

It was when I went to the office building to see the film of Majdanek that the horror hit me with dramatic force. The film has been pieced together from photographs taken by the Germans and later, at the liberation on 24 July 1944, by the Russians. Here on the screen are people, not their shades. Emaciated ribs and staring eyes, families trudging through mud and snow, mothers shielding their babies from blows, frost-bitten Russian prisoners with ragged ear-flaps. The *Sonderkommandos* stoke a pyre with bodies, men are lining up to be gassed, shot or hanged from meat-hooks. The SS guards look like a different sort of animal, warmly clad, straight-backed, armed and peremptory. Himmler is there in shiny boots and spectacles walking along a gravel path with his staff. When at the end of the film Red Army soldiers arrive, mud-covered corpses are dragged from a mass grave.

What sort of Germans did these things? Who were the SS men who carried out the orders? The question has been asked ever since the world learned of Hitler's death camps. Germans have told me that the key to Nazi sadism was indoctrination. Young men were recruited, specially trained and conditioned to run the camps. It was impressed on them that they had been chosen to wage a crusade, a sanitary campaign to destroy the parasites which were poisoning the German blood stream.

They were the anti-vermin squad. Jews were bacilli, cockroaches: and prisoners had to be humiliated deliberately till
they lost all human likeness. Clean soldiers hate bed bugs.
When British soldiers found them in their mattresses in Cairo
barracks they burned them out with candles and blow lamps.

In a way I regretted coming to Majdanek – even its name,
which in Arabic means "open space or parade ground", has an
ominous quality. I didn't want to stir up old aversions that I
thought I had long exorcised. I had gone to Germany (after
army service) in 1951 as a university teacher to help young
Germans to prepare themselves for the future, not to remind
them of the past. The sins of their fathers were taboo. Nevertheless I still had to visit Auschwitz and Treblinka.

A PAINTER

Doyle is shy, clean and feels rather lost in this remote provincial
town far from Cork. Breeze is a conundrum, an expounder.
One has to dig beneath his pulpit manner. With them I have
been to the home of Wranja, an artist who paints water colours,
and her husband Boris. The yard was a patch of mud and we
had to take off our shoes and put on wooden pattens before we
could enter. Wranja's studio looks out over the debris of half-
completed building sites dominated by a huge empty hospital.
She sells her pictures through an agent in Hamburg for hard
currency. With his wife's earnings her husband has added a
third storey to their house and a rickety flight of stairs.

Wranja has worked in England and one of her canvases filled
me with longing when I saw it on the wall. It showed a lane in
Kenilworth tucked away among old cottages, and as a boy I
must surely have passed it. It was like discovering an old letter
or a faded school cap. I used to go blackberrying in the fields
near Kenilworth. The ruined castle walls on a grassy mound
had fired my imagination. Cromwell's Ironsides had shot cannon balls into the keep and Royalist cavalry galloped through
the hawthorn buses and over the black ditches.

A Pole will never disappoint a guest. We were given mushroom soup, Russian sardines and rich Hungarian *goulasch* with
Bulgarian wine. Neither Breeze nor Doyle had visited Majdanek
so I asked our hosts to talk about the Jews. Lublin, they said,

had a large Jewish population before the war. The Jews lived in their own ghetto and the narrow streets in the Old City were crammed with them. The majority were strictly orthodox and many wore the kaftan. They were preoccupied with their own affairs and kept to themselves.

The apathy of the Jews at that time of crisis on the eve of the Holocaust has always surprised me. I remember the composure of those I met in Bucharest in early 1940 – the absence of alarm and panic despite the omens from Hitler's Germany.

"The Jews," I remarked, "should have cleared out when there was still time."

"No other country wanted them," said Boris. "Besides, there were too many."

"A man fleeing for his life will always find a bolt-hole."

This was unfair. Over three million Polish Jews could not have struck their tents and vanished overnight to safety, like an army of gypsies. But where was the animal instinct for danger that should have warned them of their likely fate? Why did the Jewish oracles stay silent?

Nor have I understood why such an exceptionally gifted people, blessed with Oriental brains and shrewdness, could have wasted their lives for centuries as petty hucksters, traders and scholars in the mud and cold of eastern Europe. It seems the Jewish leaders themselves, the elders and rabbis, encouraged the fatalism, patience and endurance that despite the constant danger of pogroms glued them to their crowded *shtetls* and insanitary slums, from Grodno to Czernowitz.

"The Jews," I argued, "should have tried to assimilate more, to keep up with the times, instead of lingering on as unwelcome strangers in an adopted country whose people gave them little love and received from them little love in return."

"The Jews," said Boris, "felt that they had created the Kingdom of God in their own midst. The *shtetl* was their earthly kingdom."

It's easy to say rash things in discussion. Yet one has to face the brutal truth that torpor, fatalism and religious obstinacy, an unwillingness to foresee the worst (as well as a lack of the resources to make escape easy) produced a mentality that led in the end to millions of Jews being deceived, trapped, rounded up and driven, with little resistance, to Hitler's gas chambers.

Penned in the market places and alleys of one of the most unstable political areas of Europe, the Jews trusted in illusions though the bells were tolling across the Elbe and the Oder.

THE POPE

I have been lunching at the university canteen. The meal is usually soup with noodles or a small sausage and an apple served on a table cloth. As a Catholic establishment that prepares many of its students, including numerous nuns, for a teaching career, Lublin's university enjoys the special concern of the Polish pope who spent some of his formative years on its academic staff. In a green quadrangle behind the building there is a dramatic statue of the newly elected Pope embracing his old master, the late Primate Cardinal Wysinski. The Cardinal had bowed to the Pope in obeisance, and the artist has portrayed him pulling the Cardinal to his feet and warmly embracing him in brotherhood and respect. The gesture has been memorably sculpted and is very much in character with the Pope's spontaneous nature.

In the morning there was snow on my van. I spent my last day in Lublin wandering through slush and ice-covered puddles. From the hostel I walked past the grand new hospital – after four years it has still not opened because of lack of equipment – and a modern church built with a curious white concrete roof shaped like a pair of wings or sails. The main street is wide, in the old Russian style, with solid buildings. Mud-stained articulated buses, lorries carrying coal, sand, bricks and vegetables splashed the wet crowds. There were many soldiers from the garrison walking about, students, and dog lovers in a park. The victory monument (with Polish and Russian inscriptions) shows a soldier holding a flag and a Kalashnikov.

To escape the rain I went into an old-fashioned café with a yellow carpet and heavy curtains. Four women were in charge. One stood at the counter, handing out glasses of tea and sweet cakes to the waitress. Another woman sat in the cloak room and made every guest take off his coat. A fourth woman was knitting at a small table outside the toilets (five zlotys a time). The guests were sober and quiet, the men reading newspapers. The café was warm, stuffy and Victorian, the world seen through the window wet and unfriendly. When the street lights came on I did my last shopping. There was no bread.

A new guest arrived at the hostel late in the evening. He introduced himself as Hubert Lowenstein. He has a fluffy yellow beard, prominent blue eyes and an ivory-white unlined face. His clothes were crumpled after the train journey from London. He was carrying a heavy orange frame-pack. I boiled some eggs for him in the kitchen.

Lowenstein is a comprehensive school teacher in north London, visiting Poland to write articles about the church for Catholic newspapers. He has been to Poland before and has the addresses of several priests to call on. I have agreed to give him a lift in the morning to Cracow where he is to stay with the Dominican Friars.

TO CRACOW

Sister Maria gave us sandwiches, cake and a cucumber for the journey and we took the road through the fortified old town of Sandomierz on the left bank of the Vistula. Destroyed by the Tatars, ravaged by plague and by Swedish invasion in the seventeenth century, damaged in two world wars, its record of sieges typifies the history of Poland. Lowenstein told me he dislikes teaching – "I'm allergic to chalk dust. I once sneezed twenty times in class and the pupils laughed at me." He said that Mrs Thatcher was mean and tyrannical – "teachers are scandalously under-paid". His heavy pack, he explained, was filled with gifts of medicated bandages for the church. I wondered about this. He has an unusual appearance but doesn't strike me as being a hippie. Perhaps he is a kind of courier.

It was a clear frosty day. The breath of horses pulling farm carts smoked in the cold air, my tyres hummed, the van rattled merrily over village cobblestones. The endless fields were broken up by little groups of cottages, church towers and rows of leafless poplars. As we neared Cracow the clarity of the landscape began to fade. Then the sun disappeared behind a lurid haze and we were passing through the smoke and yellow air of Nowa Huta.

Nowa Huta is the huge industrial project, centred on the

Lenin Steel Works, which has been developed just outside
Cracow as part of Poland's post-war economic planning. For
several miles we drove through a smoky inferno of steel plants,
stacks, cooling towers and power stations. The pollution is
notorious. Smog and acid discolours, taints and erodes the
historic buildings of Cracow and poisons lungs. Acknowledged
as one of the most heavily polluted spots in Europe, Nowa Huta
is a prime instance of ruthless Socialist planning that shows no
consideration for history or people.

I wiped the dirt off my windscreen, followed the tram lines to
Cracow city centre and parked in a side street. Lowenstein had
offered to direct me to the university building where I was to
visit a teaching colleague. But he was late and wanted to hurry
so I quickly checked (or thought I checked) the door locks of
my van and followed him. I remembered a few moments later
that I hadn't drawn the curtains to keep prying eyes away from
my travel kit. But there was no time to turn back. When I
returned an hour later my van had been broken into.

The windows had not been touched. But the passenger door
was open – evidently Lowenstein had not locked it – and my
belongings were strewn about. My packed suitcase, spare clothes,
my irreplaceable vest and pyjamas of pure New Zealand wool,
my toilet things and the radio were gone.

I blamed myself. I know the rules of travel and I had broken
them: for the slightest lapse of attention in safeguarding one's
property will sooner or later be punished, which gives point to
the advice, "always travel light". I have had a good deal of
experience of this. I had seen the thieving street boys of Cairo
and Naples at work, untying the spare wheel from a moving
army lorry, snatching handbags from tram passengers with
lengths of hooked wire. I knew about the "pole fishers" of
Kampala (they trawl through windows) and the pickpockets
outside Nairobi hotels who are in league with the shoe-shine
boys and lottery ticket sellers. In the African bush, miles from
anywhere, agile phantoms watch you from behind an ant-hill
waiting to dart off with your laundry or binoculars. I once
caught a bogus porter in Cairo railway station sprinting down a
subway with a lieutenant's bedroll and kicked him so hard that I
sprained a toe. In a world of wealth, hunger and survivors it's
cunning and boldness that count.

A woman street cleaner with a broom came to help me, shining her torch into dark yards and corners where the thief might have dumped his loot. Nothing but cats and rubbish, and an irritable concierge's wife in hair-curlers who said "Cracow is overrun with thieves and scoundrels (*lobuzy, zlodzei*)" and banged the door. Then a man got out of a car, showed me his card and said with an air of importance, "I work for the police. Car theft is a serious crime. You must report it."

He guided me to a police station which had a row of basement rooms along a silent corridor leading from the charge office. A thick-set policeman with a heavy moustache put on his jacket and got out some blank forms. "Your statement, please."

By the time the officer had inquired about the source of my income, my parents' origin and religion, and my *bona fides* as a "*turysta*" (tourist) I could see that it was going to be a long business. The officer must have felt the same and evidently wanted his supper for he suddenly closed his pad and said, "The procedure is long. There will be no time to finish your case now. Come tomorrow." As soon as I was outside I decided not to return.

DOMINICANS

Lowenstein was staying at the Dominican Brothers' hostel in a wing of their thirteenth century church. He was not there when I called for him but a handsome young priest radiating energy and humour took me immediately into the refectory for supper. When I told him about the theft he said, "Forget it. You might of course spot your clothes being hawked in the old clothes market but you'd have to be very lucky. Whatever you do, keep away from the police. They won't find your property. All they will do is pester you with a lot of personal questions."

In the big vaulted refectory about fifty Dominican Brothers were seated at long wooden tables eating hot potato pancakes, cottage cheese and stewed plums washed down with glasses of boiling tea. They made splendid figures in their long white belted robes and cowls. Despite my crumpled appearance they treated me with great courtesy. Yet I felt the paradox of my position. Here was I, a Protestant reprobate among these clean, handsome monks whom childhood stories had led me to associate with the Spanish Inquisition and heretic burning. For centuries England had banned the Pope from setting foot on its shores. I had no theology, no toothbrush or pyjamas, yet I was being fed like a fighting-cock – and being offered a bed for the night.

My host, Brother Michal, told me in almost perfect English that he had been educated at a Roman Catholic college in England. "I have happy memories of England and many friends there," he said. He made no bones about his hostility to the Polish government. "No one believes their lies. The whole nation, body and soul, is with the Church. Our work flourishes." He approved of my visiting Poland. "Poland needs friends." But he was not interested in my projected trip to Oswiecim. For him, it seemed, the Oswiecim/Auschwitz death camp was an incident of German-Jewish rather than Polish history.

Brother Michal led me upstairs to an attic adjoining an extension to the hostel under the curve of a great stained dome. "We built this annexe," he explained, "without government planning permission. It can't be seen from the outside and people don't know about it." He gave me blankets to make up a bed on the sofa, a new bar of soap and a towel. "The secretary uses the room as an office. So you must be away by 7 a.m. Good night to you." He left me a candle, and I slept in my clothes cursing the thief who would be using my razor in the morning.

The secretary, presumably an immaculate friar with a clean morning face smelling of carbolic soap, might be embarrassed to find a tramp sleeping on his couch and I was up early. The Brothers were already astir, pink with health, hurrying on errands through the great vaulted chamber next to the aisle, tidying the altar and chapels, preparing for instruction, the young novices as brisk and energetic as school prefects. The older monks in their long white habits secured at the waist by a cord and the cowl round their shoulders had the dignity of senators. They are formidable people. No godless bureaucrats will tame them. When they step out of their dark weather-stained church into the mediaeval alleys of Cracow and walk in their white habits past the towered square of the old market place they remind me of Crusaders.

SEAN MALLOY

I have spoken to Sean Malloy on the telephone and he has invited me to meet him at his morning lecture. "The subject will be Commonwealth literature. As an old Africa hand it may interest you." I looked forward to seeing a British Council pundit in action.

I identified the linguistics building through a statue of Paderewski in the garden. The ground floor is occupied by the Russian and Soviet studies department and is plastered with wall posters of the Kremlin and of black-haired Georgian maidens picking grapes. Sean is an Irishman from Sligo. He has a good-humoured, battered face and untidy greying beard. His last teaching post was in the Sudan. There were fifteen students at his lecture and I joined them.

I was disappointed in the lecture, because I disagreed with much of what he said. Sean dictated the names of some thirty Commonwealth authors listed in the British Council pamphlet he had on his desk, made a brief comment on each, a discussion followed and the lecture was over. It was the comments I found debatable. The writers he praised were those who had attacked the old colonial system and the Empire. Rudyard Kipling, he admitted, was a border-line case – indeed the stuffier sahibs had found his fondness for the British private soldier a vulgar affectation. But Sean thought E.M. Forster's *A Passage to India* completely admirable – in fact the awful white sahibs sailing back to tiffin in India had found the book so painful that they had thrown their copies overboard. Listening to Sean's homage to Forster I couldn't help thinking how this muddled-up old bachelor used to demean himself waiting for hours at a tram stop in Alexandria for the young Egyptian ticket collector who (for an emolument) served him as catamite.

Sean commended Paul Scott – he had exposed the "unacceptable face of the British in India" during the collapse of the Raj: Jean Rhys, for her version of Rochester's cruel marriage to the West Indian Creole which ends in her going mad;[1] and Doris Lessing whose account in *The Grass is Singing* of a white

---

[1] 'The reason she sets fire to Rochester's house is simple,' Jean Rhys wrote in one of her letters (1931–66). 'She is cold – and fire is the only warmth she knows in England.'

farming couple in Rhodesia who maltreated their native servants has stuck in the throat of any white Rhodesian settler who
may have read it. Other Commonwealth writers whom Sean
praised where Chinua Achebe and Ngugi (strong critics of
British colonialism in Africa), Nadine Gordimer (an author of
Lithuanian origin), Fugard and Patrick White (a cynic and
sexual oddity). Sean passed over Alan Paton, Van der Post and
Narayan. Karen Blixen was disqualified as a "foreigner".

The students were attentive and wrote notes. But I felt like
grimacing at the lecturer's back when he turned to the blackboard. I don't like books that set out to belittle people one was
brought up to admire; books that debunk Nelson as a bungler
and immoral rake, Gordon (a hypocritical dypsomaniac),
Tennyson (an unspeakable bore with a foul-smelling pipe),
John Buchan (Fascist!), Montgomery (a cad).

Sean didn't mention (perhaps the British Council pamphlet
was to blame for this) the mass of fascinating writing to be
found in the memoirs of the old colonial servants and diplomats, of explorers, missionaries, doctors and soldiers; of William
Hickey, seeking a quick fortune in Calcutta; Captain Burton,
Dr Cook of Mengo, Meinertzhagen, the scourge of unruly
African tribesmen; Leonard Woolf (Ceylon), Corbett, who
saved Indian peasants from man-eating tigers and lions,
Thesiger. Knocking the imperial tradition has grown into a
literary imperative. But I can't forgive George Orwell for ranting
(in *The Road to Wigan Pier*) against the "evil despotism" of
Empire. After several years in the Burma Police Force doing
"the dirty work" for white masters he resigned because his
conscience troubled him. Why then did he stay for so long
serving "an oppressive system" that he hated? Why, if he
punched coolies and bullied old men and prisoners, did he not
worry about it till it was too late? Did he find nothing good
about British rule?

Sean's remarks on Commonwealth writing would have been
entirely acceptable to his British Council sponsors. His point of
view – which would have appalled Lord Lloyd, the Council's
first director – is now the standard one. It is I who am the
Blimp.

However, when I had lunch with Sean who ordered pork and
spaghetti and a Serbian wine I found him an excellent fellow.

He admitted that he hadn't read all the books he had quoted in his lecture. But his anti-colonialist feelings are sincere. "You can't wave the flag of empire in a Communist country. You are," he added, "a bit of a fossil if you don't mind my saying so."

Sean likes food and ordered more. Shreds of macaroni were sticking to his untidy beard as he talked. He is writing a novel and praised Polish women. "They are pretty and captivating – even on the phone they manage to sound like actresses. And they are *available*."

After another day strolling round Cracow I changed in my van and met Sean for dinner at the Francuski Hotel. In the ill-lit alleys it was hard to find. Sean had two friends with him, Raymond and Neinstein, both English language teachers at the university. As there were not enough tables and waiters we had to wait an hour for a place. The meal, steak and a dollop of mushrooms in sour sauce, with Bulgarian wine, was lukewarm and expensive. We must have looked an odd bunch. Myself in clothes that I had been wearing every day since March. Sean with his battered bearded head sticking out of a rumpled pull-over. Raymond, thin as a wireworm with a gaunt rabbinical face and two dark eyes framed in a mass of black hair. Neinstein, Fulbright scholar from America, small, bright, birdlike.

I found I had something in common with Raymond. He had lived for a year as a Russian language student in Erivan, Armenia, within sight of Ararat; and he liked cricket. I have a special feeling for Ararat as I climbed it three times in the 1950s and from the ice-cap I had looked down on Erivan, a black blob on the other side of the Soviet watch towers. "Seen from Erivan," said Raymond, "Ararat soared out of the plain like a geological freak. The Armenians are still upset that the mountain – their holy mountain – is no longer in their homeland."

Talking to him brought back memories of the black felt tents of Kurdish herdsmen pitched halfway up the mountain below the snow line, the wolves that howled at night and stampeded the horses, the glittering ice-cap with its bonnet of cloud. On my second climb I had hired a Kurd to carry my tent and baggage on a donkey as far as the herdsmen's *yayla* camp and set off alone. When I got back from the top five days later I found the donkey had been killed by a wolf and I had to buy the Kurd a new one.

On my last visit Muzaffer and I had walked along the line of Russian watch towers to a point where the frontiers of three countries – Turkey, Persia and Russia – converge. I was wearing at the time a red and white British Embassy football shirt. We had stared back through Muzaffer's field glasses at the nearest Russian guard post only 150 yards away. It was a sad, lonely place, a no-man's land where the Free World came to a sudden end in sedge and wild grass.

The Kurds sitting round their dung-cake fires used to joke about the frontier fence and the guards peering through field glasses over the empty Aras plain, "The Russians," they said, "have locked themselves up in their own prison walls." From the peak of Ararat I had picked out the long shadow of the Caucasus to the north and of Hakkari mountains to the south.

Raymond, however, thought Erivan a rather dull place. "The best thing about it was the wine."

Raymond must have been a useful cricketer for he has had a county trial with Essex ground staff and knows Gooch – "an excellent man, thoroughly professional, all he wants to do is to pile up the runs and collect the cash."

We mixed our drinks, ran up a heavy bill (in zlotys) and were the last to leave the restaurant. Sean tried unsuccessfully to date the cloak-room attendant, a stout, formidable woman of about forty. Our boots clattered loudly in the dark, stony alleys. I spent the night on a couch in Sean's flat. There were empty bottles and crusts on the table, the toilet didn't flush and the light bulb flickered. But it was a great deal snugger than my cold, damp van. Indeed I envied Sean his Bohemian life. Enough money to live on, Bulgarian wine, a mediaeval city almost as magical, in parts, as Oxford, friends, and congenial work.

ROOKS

A Polish woman teacher I have met at Raymond's flat tells me that her students are only concerned with getting a working knowledge of English. "With this they feel they have made contact with the west, they feel less culturally isolated. They haven't the slightest interest in Russian."

Raymond had a fifth-floor flat in the linguistics building. From the balcony I looked down on the grey rusting roof-tops of Cracow. It was Sunday, a hazy day, with little street traffic. The smog blown in from Nowa Huta was lying over the city like a miasma. It was yellowish, as though tinted with sulphur fumes. As I watched the sun dip in a lurid ball the sky suddenly filled with black shapes. They were rooks – a few at first, then an endless stream flying back like kites or bats in Africa to their roosting places. I pointed to the birds but Raymond and his guests said they'd not noticed their daily procession. For me this turbulence of dark wings against the radiance of a dying sun has always been a moment of drama.

Motor traffic is not allowed within the main square area of Cracow. I was using a parking place not far away. The nights were cold. I slept in all the clothes I had and woke up with hair tousled like wild grass, odious socks, crumpled trousers. Cracow's historic ambience reminds me of Prague and Vienna. The three cities were part of the melting-pot of the Austro-Hungarian Empire. They are far away from the sea and the Protestant north. People of many nations have migrated to them, from the Balkans, from the south and from the Jewish *shtetls*. The atmosphere is Catholic and Baroque. Lublin smells of Russia, Cracow of Franz Josef; it has no massive Palace of Culture to perpetuate the memory of Stalin and Muscovite Communism.

Like the Piazza Venezia the great market place is overrun in summer by tourists and pigeons. Bus parties of American Poles cram the souvenir shops in the old Cloth Hall, schoolchildren are marched into the museums. But it was mid-October now. The visitors had gone, leaving empty café tables in the square. A cold gritty wind blew across the grey stones, driving people indoors. In the vast empty space the bugle call from the clock tower of St Mary's sounded every hour with a beautiful and thrilling clarity far more startling and evocative than any chime or muezzin's cry. Poles say the call originates in the thirteenth century legend of a Polish watchmen who sounded the alarm when he glimpsed a Tatar horde approaching the battlement. He was shot by an arrow that made the call die in his throat. But the alarm had been heard and the city was saved.

The clear notes of the bugle echoing like bird song over the

stony square and the vespers that I attended in the Dominican
basilica on my last evening are memories that will stay with me.
When the service was over the lights went on and a choir of
twenty Brothers rose to sing. Their voices haunt me – sonorous,
melodious, perfectly drilled, a product of labour, faith and
creation. The old church shone and sparkled in its armour of
stained glass. The holy figures gleamed with gilt. The carved
woodwork, the paintings, the white vaulted roof reflecting the
glow of candelabra and flaming candles transformed what a
moment before had been a shadowy cavern into a glittering
palace.

Or was I being decieved? Was this only a magician's grotto
decked out with kitsch? Witchcraft – with incense and tinkling
bells? Medicine men in white sheets? A masquerade with paid
players? Or was it the expression of man's immortality, of his
faith? There is a choice of visions and in a Communist country
the choice is a vital one. The Christian execution stake? Shiva?
The rattling gourds and monkey tail in a Congo sorcerer's hut?
A five-pointed star? Poles have chosen the litany and the sacred
chants.

OSWIECIM-BRZEZINKA CAMP

I took the new autobahn from Cracow to Oswiecim-Brzezinka
(Auschwitz-Birkenau), twenty-five miles of almost empty highway (six vehicles and some mushroom pickers) to Chrzanow,
then thirteen miles of winding country roads to the camp. The
camp area is divided into two sections. The smaller compound
(Oswiecim proper) comprises a group of former Polish army
brick-built barracks which the Nazis used as an administrative
centre for the whole concentration camp complex. Just over a
mile away is the much bigger Brzezinka section which the Nazis
added later. The barracks at Oswiecim house the camp museum
and exhibits. This is the tourist centre with bus park, reception
office, cinema and restaurant. The town itself has developed
into an industrial centre with a modern railway station and
extensive sidings.

I walked through the massive iron gate. It is in itself macabre,
for stamped over it in metal letters is the greeting *Arbeit Macht
Frei* – Work Makes You Free – a sick joke to find at the entrance

to hell. The insulting words of welcome must have been photographed many thousands of times and found their way into albums all over the world.

As in Majdanek the barracks are crammed with the debris of death. Piles of worn shoes, prison uniforms, suitcases (many carefully marked with the owners' names and addresses in ink), twisted spectacle frames, dentures, shaving brushes, mirrors, enamel bowls and mugs, kitchen utensils, a huge hoard of human hair and a heap of artificial limbs and trusses. The walls are hung with copies of prison records and blown-up photographs of prison scenes. The death and torture cells and the yard with its execution wall have been neatly preserved. Medical wards and orderly rooms are sign-posted.

This is the place people flock to see first. No matter how solemn our thoughts we are the rubberneckers, the ghouls and we have only a short time to complete our sightseeing schedules. Here are the garrulous guides, heads craning at imagined horrors, a few Jews from America in round caps, children pestering their parents for fizzy drinks. A culture that was brutally extinguished by poison gas and fire has left, as in Buchenwald and Majdanek, nothing but relics, trinkets, pitiful rubbish and documented mementoes. There are no blackened mummies, no mud-covered bones, no tape recordings of screams. The barbed wire fences and sentry towers, the execution yard and gallows ought to be haunted by angry spirits. But spirits didn't breed in plague pits.

I walked over to the gallows where Rudolf Hoess, the former commandant of Auschwitz, was hanged from a heavy iron hook. His camp memoirs, which he wrote in a Polish prison awaiting trial, show the smugness of a loyal SS man who felt he had done his duty well to Führer and fatherland. "I too had a heart and I was not evil," he said. This didn't stop him from gassing his "best-loved prisoners," the gypsies. (They were "undisciplined" and some fought like wild cats to avoid being driven into the black chambers.)

A few steps away from the gallows is a crematorium and gas chamber with gas vents, control room and spy holes for the SS, furnaces and trolleys. The guides marshal their clients inside the thick brick walls and recite a script with statistics. Then

back through the massive iron gate to the adjacent camp of
Brzezinka (Birkenau).

The entrance to Brzezinka is through an archway with the
former control room and a tower above it and a railway track
running underneath. From the world of the living the rusty
rails brought the death waggons direct to the gas chambers and
crematoria at the far end of the camp. The camp today is a
desolate expanse of grass and mud. Before the SS withdrew,
with the Red Army at their heels, they hurriedly set fire to the
hundreds of barrack huts and kitchens, leaving only a few low
wooden sheds and a rash of brick chimneys which stick up like
posts in a graveyard.

Today only one of the crematoria and gas chambers that
stood at the end of the off-loading ramp is still identifiable, and
demolition has levelled it into a heap of rubble with a collapsed
roof. Of the other extermination buildings nothing is left but
foundations and broken walls. The debris is overgrown with
brambles, thistles and stinging nettles. Nearby are stagnant
pools where human ash was tipped. Behind the ruins is the
memorial, a row of inscribed stone tablets. The inscriptions
remind us that Brzezinka was not only a place of death for Jews
from Poland. Brzezinka was an international murder factory
and victims were sent there from all points of the compass, from
Athens and Amsterdam, Paris, Budapest and Prague. Families
were packed into sealed freight trains without food or water.
Many had been lured into the Nazi trap by promises of work.
Even when they saw the smoke and glow from the crematoria
and smelt the stench they were slow to realise what was awaiting
them. Within minutes of being dragged out of the waggons they
were segregated. Those whom the SS rejected as "rubbish"
(disposable) were, if women, shorn of their hair, they were
blinded by lights, stripped and pushed naked into the gas
chambers where they died in agony, smeared with vomit and
excrement and menstrual blood, trampling, as they struggled
for air, on their own children.

The *Sonderkommando* prisoners who were given the heavy
work of handling and clearing the corpses had to be exceptionally tough. After a time it was their turn too to be liquidated
(a few have survived to tell their story). The proximity of
factories and town buildings within sight of the camp must have

heightened the grim contrast between the prisoners' tormented lives and imminence of death and the ordinary world outside the wire where people went about their daily tasks.

Before I left the camp I walked round the outer perimeter past the watch towers into a coppice that encircles the far end behind the wrecked crematoria and memorial. This was the spot where Soviet prisoners-of-war were executed and shovelled into mass graves. Firs and birches have grown over the ground, damp and dripping, the birches shedding yellow leaves, the turf boggy, the place empty and silent. I thought I was alone as I picked my way among the depressions left by old graves. Then I saw a woman with thick legs grazing a cow, and a man came from behind the trees holding a child by the hand. He was looking for berries. "There are many mass graves among the trees," he told me. "Russians and children were thrown into separate pits. They are not marked – you may be standing on one." He was a local man, a water engineer. I asked him what he felt about the camp. "The Germans," he replied, "were *bestia* (beasts) – *nienormalny*. But it was long ago and I don't think about it any more.

"And the church?"

"The local priest remembers the camp in his prayers and there are memorial services."

Over the graves the new trees are greedy and flourishing. On my way back past the memorial tablets I caught up with a small procession of church-goers led by a priest, singing a hymn. The mist had thickened, turning the camp into a wasteland dotted with forlorn barrack chimneys and a few weather-blackened sheds. It was no more than a relic, artificially preserved, cut off from the world by barbed wire and ditches. The place was almost boring.

The documentary film shown at the camp cinema revives, however, the appalling shock of Auschwitz. The film puts the living ghouls back into the empty cages. We see the prison transports arriving at the ramp, bewildered people worrying about their luggage, many of them handsome and well dressed. Those who escape immediate death turn quickly into shaven-headed witches, emaciated men with large heads, stumbling "Mussulmans". Towards the end of the film Red Army soldiers and commissars appear. In carefully selected shots we see them helping crippled inmates to stagger out of their huts to freedom. Children are photographed with toes and feet a spongy mass of gangrene; others lifting up their arms to show the prison numbers tattooed on them. There are pictures of an international commission of doctors examining skeleton-like patients, of naked corpses dumped on the ground by the Germans because they had no time to burn them. We watch a Russian officer slit open a sack stuffed with human hair.

What a day it must have been when the liberating Russian army marched into Cracow in 1944. Prince Michael Radziwill has left us a graphic description (*One of the Radziwills,* 1971). The first troops, he says, "were magnificently equipped". On the third day "to our astonishment, across the frozen river, a trek of animals was taking place. We saw with apprehension the innumerable camels led by their nose-rings, a contingent of yaks with their shaggy coats sweeping the ice, cattle, goats, followed by carts drawn by the traditional Russian team of three horses, full of soldiers, with others hanging on to the horses' traces. It all looked like a mediaeval picture of an invasion of the West by barbaric hordes. The picture was augmented by the fact that the hordes were supplemented by cannon and camp followers, women, cooks, etc. quite unlike an organised Western army. This went on for hours and was watched from the river bank by probably the whole population of Cracow."

Roman Polanski, who came out of hiding on the arrival of the Russians and joined a gang of scavengers, had a street urchin's view of the liberation. "Poles," he wrote in his autobiography *Roman* "defiled German corpses left behind in the streets by excreting on them and propping empty vodka bottles between their legs." The Russians were "a desperately poor army, not averse to rape, with a passion for wrist-watches and any loot they could take back with them ... I have a vivid recollection of Zim trucks piled high with wardrobes, sideboards, closets, carpets and mirrors and of fat, ill-favoured female soldiers perched on top, stolidly guarding their loot."

The misery of Oswiecim-Brzezinka has long been docketed and reduced to statistics, to memoirs and sad, angry books. The artefacts are displayed for excursionists to gaze at. After the film I went into the restaurant. I had to wait while a party of schoolchildren shouted and shoved for attention. The kiosks were closed and the cold mist had blotted out the camp when I drove off to look for petrol.

KATOWICE

The light was fading when I drove to Katowice on my way to Czestochowa. The birch trees were losing the last of their leaves. The bare trunks lined the road like white bones scarred with black marks. It was going to be a cold night and I was anxious to find a parking place. It was dark when I came to Katowice. The town was badly lit, with awkward tram lines and, as far as I could make out in the night mist, monstrously ugly. Near a level crossing I spotted an empty yard and stopped.

At 7 a.m. I was roused by a thump on the window and saw two policemen looking at me with open mouths. My appearance must have shocked them for they both burst out laughing and walked away. Getting two Iron Curtain policemen to laugh was at least some sort of achievement. I wiped the filth and smog from my windscreen (it was black) and set off for Czestochowa. I stopped once, to visit a large wayside cemetery where the bright fresh flowers caught my eye. About a dozen mourners were tidying up the graves; they were women, old and wrapped in thick clothes. Some had come on bicycles. Most of the dead, I noticed, had died before their sixties. A few (usually men) had their pictures set in the gravestones. It must be comforting for a Pole to know that his next-of-kin will remember him and tend his grave. Flowers are the way of expressing this feeling. Polish flower shops are never closed. On holidays and on Sundays more flowers are sold than on any other day.

JASNA GORA CHURCH

The church and Pauline monastery of Jasna Gora at Czestochowa stands prominently on a hill overlooking the shabby provincial town. Countless Polish pilgrims have wended their way to it during the centuries, on foot, on horseback, in carts and carriages, by train and car and in coaches, hoping perhaps for a miracle to bless their lives and their country in its struggle for freedom. Mecca has its black stone, the Kabaa. Jasna Gora has a black ikon, Matka Boska the Mother of God, the miracle-working Black Madonna. The jewel-encrusted ikon is the focus of the Marian cult, the centre-piece of Polish national feeling and patriotism.

Seen from the outside the church looks old and weather-beaten. It has a high bell-tower with a faded clock (which was working) and a long low roof and is surrounded by a monastic wall. Within is a group of grey cloister buildings and draughty passages. No attempt has been made to smarten the church's outward appearance. The copper roofing is stained a sickly green and is dark with grime. But the interior is a sumptuous treasure house of decorated carvings, sculptures, pictures, trinkets and holy relics, crosses, tablets and chandeliers, huge yellow candles and Oriental carpets. All this has been brought together and bequeathed over the centuries in homage to the black ikon which was to be unveiled at 3.30 p.m.

I sat in a pew a little before the ceremony began. The ikon was covered by a screen in a recess behind the altar in the Matka Boska chapel. I looked at the ornamental eagles, the richly painted ceilings and memorial tablets and noticed that the tablet immediately behind me had been presented by the Polish Carpathian Lancers in 1980. The battle honours were listed: Tobruk, Monte Cassino, Ancona and Bologna. The shield was embossed with two palm trees and a crescent moon. In front of me was another tablet in memory of the Armia Krajowa (the Home Army) and the words "In your name, O Mother of God, we went to war." An engraved map of Poland shows the battlefields.

When I saw the Polish Lancers' memorial and read the names Monte Cassino and Ancona I felt that I had as much right as a Pole to be sitting in this place. For I had been present at those battles and though I rarely think about those long-ago days I have never forgotten the courage and aggression of the Polish soldiers in Italy and the panache of their armoured car reconnaissance units. Rotmistrz Emil Mentel, who had been my host on his farm in Rhodesia during the terrorist war, was one of their officers. "It was like horse-racing," he used to tell me. "Our motto was to get there first."

Those were the days when the Poles were chasing the German army up the Adriatic coast, of set battles, river crossings and pursuit. But the Cassino battle a few weeks earlier, the Poles' biggest test since their long Odyssey from Europe to the Middle East, had been a different matter with its close-quarter fighting, murderous fire and heavy casualties. I recall the night when Polish infantry of the 6th Lwowska Brigade took over the rocky shelters and holes occupied by the Inniskilling forward positions in preparation for the final assault on the monastery. The enemy were so close that for months the dead had been left to rot and mummify in the stony gullies. We came immediately under heavy harassing fire. Though many of the Polish soldiers had scarcely been tested in action before, they immediately impressed with their bearing and coolness. Some weeks later, despite a tremendous opening barrage by massed Allied and Polish artillery the first attack on the German positions failed. It took a few days for the Poles to regroup. They then pushed on to plant the Polish flag on the rubble of the Benedictine abbey, broke through the Adolf Hitler line at Piedimonte and opened the road to Rome. To the Poles' chagrin they were taken out of the line to re-equip and it was the Americans – in Jeeps – who motored into Rome first.

UNVEILING OF THE IKON

By 3.30 the Matka Boska chapel was packed with people, many of them elderly. Women with wrinkled stockings, thick skirts and head-scarves. Thick-set men. They stood on the cold floor motionless in front of the altar. A fanfare sounded, the ikon was uncovered and the service began. I looked closely at the *Czarna Madonna*. She is not, in fact, black (like an African Nilotic) but chocolate-brown. She has a long straight nose, a thin set mouth, an ascetic face and gashes on her cheek.[1] The gravity of her

---

[1] The book (*Z dziejow Jasnej Gory*) issued by the Pauline order that administers the church says that the icon was slashed by a band of church robbers (Czechs, Moravians and Silesians) in 1430. This account quotes the legend that when the robbers loaded the stolen church treasure and the ikon on a cart, they were unable to move it. In their rage they threw the picture on the ground and one of them stabbed its right cheek with a double-edged sword – hence the two scars. Tears immediately sprang from the wounded face and washed it clean.

expression, the solemn features and swarthy skin are in the Byzantine style. She looks very different from the pretty and sometimes simpering Virgins painted in the more modern tradition and preferred by Italians.

The ikon is encrusted with precious stones. The head and shoulders may be decked in various garbs – wearing a golden crown, an Ethiopian headdress or an intricately patterned gown in which holes have been left for the Christ child's dark head, hands and feet. During the singing and prayers an expression of mesmerised devotion came over the congregation. I was conscious of being an intruder, prying into the secret thoughts of hearts and minds. The myth of the Madonna has not entered into my own upbringing and life. Yet I could respect, and envy, the congregation's faith and devotion and understand the promises, vows and expectations associated with the cult of Matka Boska. As the symbolic saviour and guardian of Poland's freedom against Tatar, Turk, Swede, Russian and German, the Black Madonna has the role of a quasi-political figure, a war goddess. For among the Poles sacred love and war and the struggle to be free are indivisible. It is not to be wondered at that the Tsars, faced with the obduracy of this troublesome

Then in 1655 the monastery was besieged by a Swedish army under General Müller but repelled it. According to the chronicles, "Jasna Gora was not saved by men but was preserved by God, and more by miracles than by the sword." The besieging force was paralysed by frost and General Müller struck by a cannon ball on Christmas Day. The Swedes had to abandon the siege in shame.

Miracles and their legends share, of course, common ground and there is a parallel with Moscow's wonder-working Iberian Mother ikon which J.G. Kohl, a German traveller, describes in *Russia: 1842*. "Like all Russian saints she has a dark-brown, almost black complexion." She wears jewels and a crown and "her hand and the foot of the child are covered with dirt from the abundant kissing: it sits like a crust in little raised points, so that long since it has not been hand and foot that have been kissed but the concrete breath of pious lips." The ikon attracted great crowds of all classes. Kohl adds that "there is a very little scratch in the right cheek, that distils blood. This wound was inflicted, nobody knows when or how, by Turks or Circassians, and exactly this it is by which the miraculous powers of the picture were proved; for scarcely had the steel pierced the canvas, than the blood trickled from the painted cheek." See Laurence Kelly's *Moscow*, 1983.

nation, gave up any hopes of compromise and sent in the police, Cossacks and censors to suppress it.

A COLD NIGHT

I left the church, passing a row of empty confessional boxes (in one of which the duty priest seemed to have dropped off to sleep), and looked at the harvest festival offerings which were on display on a raised platform inside the wall. Here were holy figures ingeniously fashioned out of corn and maize grains, straw, leaves and flowers: models of farm tools; wreaths, rosaries and immortelles, and a memorial to the murdered Father Popieluszko showing a great blood-tipped sword.

I could find only one restaurant near the church, a shabby place with a tray of frayed meat balls on the counter and dirty tables. Some of the guests looked like tramps trying to keep warm against the hot-water pipes. One man looked so sorry for himself that I gave him a glass of tea and a roll. A young man came and sat with me. He told me quite seriously that according to the Pope the world would come to an end in 1988. It would then be reborn and everyone would be happy.

"You mean Poland will be free?"

"Of course."

I ate two bowls of soup and went shivering into the night. The church was silent and everyone had gone home. I backed my van into a space near the monastery gate, turned on the BBC world news and swaddled myself in my clothes. I still had my duffle coat, which I used as a blanket, and wrapped my towel and wind-jacket round my feet. The floor of my van was damp from condensation. Then I blew out the candle and returned to the tomb of sleep: solitary, tousled, content. No one was bothering me. I had a visa, two spare wheels and camping gas. In England I might have been taken for a hippy. Here in provincial Poland I did not have to feel embarrassed.

When I went back to the restaurant early next morning – it was the only warm place – men were already drinking their first beer. The Veritas souvenir and book shop was open and people were lining up to buy trinkets from a nun in the kiosk outside the church entrance. I was disappointed to find that all traces of the thanksgiving festival had been removed overnight. The ingeniously fashioned offerings had been thrown over a wall, like a load of trash, into a dirty yard. A gardener was raking wreaths and crosses, the poster to Father Popieluszko and the holy figures into a heap and was about to burn them. Jesus lay on the ground like a broken scarecrow. Virgin Marys sprawled among scattered rosaries, pigeons were stripping the yellow corn grains from votive objects. I thought this rather shocking and spoke to two men who were looking over the wall at the pile of shattered exhibits. One of the Poles agreed that it was *przykro* (painful). His friend smiled. "It's the same in the theatre. When the performance is over the props are thrown away."

I had plenty of time to reach Warsaw before dusk and near Piotrkow Tryb. where the road forks to Lodz, I stopped at the Partisan Museum. There had been severe war-time partisan fighting in the neighbourhood, and the museum is well cared for. It has a collection of partisan uniforms, equipment (including crude medical supplies), weapons (some home-made), documents and operation orders, medals and photographs. The museum is marked by an obelisk where commemorative services and parades are held.

In grey light and under a grey sky I reached Warsaw and carried my depleted belongings to Emma's. In two days' time it would be All Saints' Day. To see Treblinka and Bialystok I would have to hurry before the snow set in.

13
TREBLINKA – BIALYSTOK – KRYNKI

YOUNG FOGIES

There's no pleasure in dining out in Socialist Poland. The state-run restaurant has no patron, the food is messy. It is better to stick to pickles, stewed fruit, ice cream and a bottle of Balkan plonk. Two of Breeze's old Cambridge friends have arrived from London by train for a week-end visit and I have dined with them and Emma at the Hungarian restaurant in Marszal-kowska. We had rubbery duck on a dirty table cloth with wilted flowers, and the young waitress upset the vinegar carafe. Still, it was an occasion. The three Britons carried on an extraordinary conversation about art and aesthetics using vogue words that I did not know. Emma whispered that the two visitors belonged to a new breed which I would not have heard about. They were Young Fogies. We didn't visit the cabaret. A security agent stood on guard at the door and people were arguing about tickets. Two touts badgered the Young Fogies for dollars.

On the way home I called with Emma at the Forum hotel. In the lounge nothing had changed. Turks pacing up and down, Arabs in soft armchairs. Whores in short tight skirts and fish net stockings, with thin, hard faces; noisy blondes being chatted up by huge old Arabs in baggy suits who stroked their prayer beads and stared at the girls' legs. Why are prosperous oriental effendis so fascinated by *white* legs? Don't they have their own luscious, brown-skinned *houris*, depilated and complacent, waiting for them on the cushioned ottomans of Gezira and Fez? What can a northern harpy with a smoker's cough offer a *bey*?

Hotel Polonia on the other side of Marsalkowska is another haunt of Arabs, Turks, gypsies, black marketeers and whores. The hotel's hard currency shop (Intershop) draws them like fly-paper. The men have crooked faces. The whores are noisy and quarrelsome when drunk and when asked to leave shout obscenities. Before the war Warsaw's *kurwy* (prostitutes) were part of the city scene. The better sort frequented the night bars. The streetwalkers were ready to oblige at a moment's notice in a dark doorway – a mounting exercise known as the *periskop*, the man craning his head and wagging it from side to side while he kept a lookout for a *glina* (policeman). The girls had an arrangement with droshky drivers. The less favoured had short muscular legs and thick hips. Cabaret girls and hostesses were elegant, often educated but more mercenary and less good-natured than those who prowled on foot and were happy to be treated to a bowl of hot cabbage soup and a *bomba* (beer).

"Nice" girls were elusive and operated in a different league. The Polish male has always been jealous of his women. A Frenchman was acceptable as a rival. But not an Anglo-Saxon grocer.

Now that the old gay night life of Warsaw is dead prostitution is much less evident than it used to be. Police patrols have scared the girls away, and a permissive society where sex is free has robbed them of customers. You can still find them at the hotels, around the main railway station and in Praga where the factories and big tenement blocks are. But the type of sex-starved cleric in mufti, the military officer on leave from some frightful rural barracks, is dying out.

All Saints' Day is a public holiday. It is the day when Poles visit family graves. I accompanied Emma in the evening to the great municipal cemetery, said to be one of the biggest in Europe. Thousands of visitors with children had been flocking there since early morning. They had done a vast amount of tidying up: sweeping leaves and rubbish from the graves and burning them in bonfires, laying fresh flowers, especially chrysanthemums, and lighting candles. People were in holiday spirit. Guttering candles lit up the night, the cold damp air was hazy with smoke and the smell of melting wax. We walked for a mile through the shadows of tombs and crucifixes. The graves are crammed together in family groups, the newly interred, for reasons of space, placed in layers over the old. Many graves have photographs of the dead inserted in the tombstones. Almost all have good Slav names: -off, -ov, -ski, -icz. This vast field of death mantled by twinkling lights, flames and smoke reminded me of a shanty town in Africa: the glow of fires against a black sky encrusted with stars. Or of Greece, where the faces of the dead impressed on the steles give them an eerie life. Emma told me that gypsy mourners make a great noise at their family graves on All Saints' Day. We looked for gypsies but they must have left for home.

HEINE'S POLAND

In a day or two I would be setting off for Treblinka. In the meantime I have been reading Heine's *Über Polen* (1823), an account of his journey through the old Prussian parts of Poland. His observations are curiously dated but are a key to familiar things. Here are some of his impressions:

Heine notes the flat landscape and poor mud villages. Peasants wear their hair long and matted in elflocks (*Weichselzopf*). They dress in national costume on feast days, go to town on Sundays to be shaved, attend mass and get dead drunk. They are obsequious towards the nobility and prostrate themselves ("I kiss your feet"). "I can't bear seeing men bow low to each other," he writes. Yet he believes emancipation would be fatal to the Polish peasant. "He is so improvident that he would fritter away and lose everything he possessed". At present the nobles succour and nourish the peasants when they are in need and treat them with kindness. Not having been softened by comforts, the peasant doesn't yearn for them.

Heine points out that there are different grades of noble. There are those who are as poor as peasants; and there are the wealthy ones and magnates. But they all share the same pride and self-respect. It is only the scions of the most famous families – the Czartoryskis, Radziwills, Zamoyskis, Sapiehas, Poniatowksis, Potockis and so on – who have higher pretensions.

"It is almost laughable," Heine says, "to see how the Poles honour everything that has to do with the fatherland. 'Fatherland' is their first word, 'freedom' only the second. They speak like Christians of love; yet they have failed to emancipate their own peasantry. Indeed the nobility used its own 'freedom' simply to cut down the king's powers."

Polish women, he observes, are "coquettish, attractive and

handsome. They differ in character from the German wife with her thoroughness, pious modesty and quiet virtues."

Poles, Heine says, are famous drinkers and if a peasant falls flat after three jugs of *schnapps* his friends gather round him and jeer, saying he has a weak head. He writes of the martial Polish character. Every nobleman was a soldier and Poland used to be a great military school. But he found that far fewer young Poles were now volunteering for an army career. They were finding other interests, especially in learning and scientific studies in which they showed exceptional talent, and they had great poetic gifts (*"Der Pole wird die Feder ebensogut führen wie die Lanze"*).

Sandwiched between the noblemen and the peasants are the Jews, Poland's Third Estate, comprising a quarter of the population. They are versatile craftsmen but averse to farming, fearing to share the Polish farmer's poverty. Every inn belongs to a Jew, and Jews also run the distilleries. Every noble has his Jewish factor to run his business affairs (estate management). The Jews live poorly in miserable dwellings and speak their own jargon. And yet, says Heine (himself a Jew), "the Polish Jew in his dirty furs, with his verminous beard and stench of garlic and his broken tongue attracts me more than many people of distinguished rank."

Heine says the Prussian officials transferred to posts in Prussian Poland were disgruntled. The idle ones liked the life, those whose philosophy was based on a good meal. But as they sat over their jug of bad beer they complained about the Polish squires who drank Hungarian wine and never had to open a file. The Prussian garrisons quartered in Poland, says Heine, were composed of decent, honourable soldiers. The Poles respected them. But there was no intimacy between the Poles and the German military.

Heine makes much of the Poles' insatiable longing for freedom. He admires the tenacity of the peasants, and the versatility of the Jews and the wit of the growing intelligentsia. But it is a curiously unbalanced picture that he presents, almost feudal in its age-old social pattern: peasants, Jews and nobles locked in their separate categories waiting for a new catalyst to break the mould.

In fact, the peasant has outlived them all. Rooted in his

family plot, eating potatoes, black bread and cabbage, toiling, quarrelling, drinking and praying, the Polish *chlop* has proved as indestructible as the soil. These days he drives a tractor and wears shoes from a cooperative store. But he has survived, a rough-looking man in a green landscape of corn, vegetables and orchards, plodding about his acres with a bag of seed, loading beet on to a cart, tethering his half-dozen cows to a patch of grass, crouched with a bottle of vodka in the inn, badly shaved, in thick clothes, with a chapped face and large, dirt-ingrained hands − the *chlop*, Russia's historic antagonist. In the muddy lane he and his neighbours will have erected a small painted shrine with a crucifix, and somewhere, behind a line of poplars, there is the tower of a church.

TREBLINKA

I drove across the Vistula on a cold wet morning and took the Bialystok road. Forty miles on at Ostrow Mazowiecki I turned off for Treblinka. The road was partly under water, the verges broken and muddy and I kept well clear of them as my tyres were worn. I noticed that the end of my exhaust pipe was hanging by a few threads and wrenched it off.

While I was waiting at a level crossing a farmer came up on a bicycle. He was wrapped in a padded jacket and gum boots.

"So you're going to Treblinka. Are you a Jew? Are your parents Polish? No Polish blood? What do you want in Treblinka?"

I said I was interested in history. He grinned. "There's no history here. Anyone who was sent to Treblinka went up in smoke."

He began to talk about the government. "General Jaruzelski tells us he wants to be our father − the father of the nation. Some father! He doesn't even go to church."

He wanted his children to learn English. "If one of my sons could emigrate the whole family would benefit."

I left him pushing his bicycle through the black mud. Just before Treblinka village I turned off at another level crossing and passed a goods siding with rows of box cars. They were so stained and decrepit they reminded me of the death transports packed with staring eyes that used to be shunted here.

The camp reception office was locked but there were some posters and a map of the lay-out which I copied, pinned up in the lodge. The original camp gate has been replaced by concrete pillars with an inscription: "Here stood a Nazi extermination camp (*obuz zaglady*). Between July 1942 and August 1943 more than 800,000 were murdered here. On 2 August 1943 prisoners organised an armed resistance which was crushed in blood by the Nazi hangmen. In a prison labour camp 2 km. from here the Nazis murdered about 10,000 Poles between 1941 and 1944."

From the entrance I followed the old railway track (the rails have been removed) through a coppice. It ended at a stone ramp where the newly arrived box cars crammed with Jewish families were unlocked and unloaded. From the ramp a grassy slope led to a green hill two hundred yards away framed by fir trees and birches. When I walked up I found I had come to the place of death.

It is a big green arena, quiet and beautiful, covered with an extraordinary mass of pointed grey stones shining like dragons' teeth. The stones are roughly chiselled. This is the symbolic cemetery. In the centre a memorial marks the site of the vanished gas chamber. It is a plain concrete block split down the middle in two sections with a candelabrum design. A small wreath of plastic flowers lay at the foot.

I could only guess at the meaning of its design. Perhaps it was a gate. But what gate? The gate to heaven or to agonising death? To God or to suffering?

Many of the pointed stones have been inscribed with the names of towns and *shtetls* from which the victims were uprooted – Lodz, Czestochowa, Bialystok, Warsaw.

The barbed wire and sentry towers have gone but the perimeter has been replaced by stone markers and I followed them to a line of young trees. I thought I was alone in this beautiful ghoulish place. But I heard voices among the trees and came across two peasant women picking mushrooms. They were shy and didn't greet me. But they told me there were two cemeteries, one for Jews – they pointed to the field of dragons' teeth – and another for Poles. "The crosses," they explained, "are beyond the quarry."

The quarry was at the end of a sandy track (known as the old *czarna droga* or "black road"). Here the ground falls suddenly away into an enormous gravel pit gouged out of the earth by thousands of doomed Polish prisoners: treeless, empty, furrowed with old workings, abandoned. Facing the quarry, at the end of a forest path, I came to the site of the old Polish work camp – a big open clearing watched by a ring of silent firs. No buildings or barrack huts have survived but patches of rubble mark the old foundations. A notice states that the site is under a preservation order. An eagle flew overhead, I could hear sparrows and there were a few red berries. This is one of those places of mass doom – like Katyn, Buchenwald and Vorkuta and Babi Yar – that stain Europe's past. If one were to try to list them, from the Inca to the Armenian massacre sites, the counting would never end.

In the fading light the leafless birch trees glimmered like bleached bones, leprous and skeletal. A farmer came out of them wheeling a bicycle loaded with firewood and carrying a bucket of mushrooms. The Polish cemetery, he told me, was half a mile further on. A trail of old hoof marks and tractor tyres took me to it. It is a small and private place hidden by trees marked by a memorial stone with an inscription "Murdered (*zameczony*) by Hitlerites". I counted eight simple crosses. One of the graves was named. "Anna Zaleska. Shot 1.8.44 aged 14". Her photograph is set in the stele. It shows a smiling, fair-haired girl. Someone had left fresh flowers.

I had been alone all day among these desolate scenes. In the chill wind and under a stormy sky Treblinka seemed forgotten and faraway, a remote hamlet lost in the marshy reaches of the Bug. The place has a special quality of despair and secrecy. The Nazis had good reason to set up their murder machine here. Treblinka was off the beaten track yet not far from the Warsaw-Bialystok railway. It was in the heart of the Jewish settled Pale. And it was so far to the east that rumours and reports of the crimes being perpetrated in this clearing among the woods would not easily reach the west and the outside world. The Nazis, rather than boasting about them, kept good care to keep their slaughter-houses secret. It was not until late in the war that the Allies finally believed that the dreadful reports were true. Treblinka with its lonely woods, its mist and swamps and watery sunsets, has a deceptive idyllism.

On the way back I took a last look at the Jewish cemetery. As Treblinka was an out-and-out death (not a labour) camp the Nazis wasted no time on new arrivals. It took less than an hour to coax, cudgel and whip the convoys of Jewish families from the box cars into the gas chamber. A tunnel (*Slauch*) covered by leaves and branches led straight from the ramp to the vents. It was known as the Path to Heaven. Through this the victims marched blindly, many still ignorant of what was awaiting them. Within minutes they were stripped naked, the women had their heads shaved, they were dazzled by great lights and thrown into the black tombs where they died in agony, vomiting, screaming and trampling each other in the dark as they reached upward for air. Special squads (*Sonderkommandos*) searched the discarded clothing and luggage for money and jewellery, wrenched gold fillings and dentures from the mouths of corpses, collected the luxuriant hair of Jewesses to be stuffed into bags, weighed, recorded and sold – and took away the excrement-covered bodies to be buried or burned. The disposal squads were made to work at great speed, for the murderers wanted to leave no clues behind.

Having seen Treblinka one can more easily understand the unquenchable desire of Jewish Zionists to build Israel. Treblinka is only a mute witness to the past; but its offspring is the state of Israel. Among the Poles too generations of dead souls march with the living in the nation's determination to honour its memories and to survive. Both people have, in their faith, the sense of Judaic mission.

BIALYSTOK

The light was fading as I drove from Treblinka past the rotting freight cars in the sidings and splashed through the waterlogged road to Malkinia. I slept in a lay-by near Ostrow Mazowiecki, huddling in my blanket till the early morning sun came out. Some commercial travellers were already in the bar drinking glasses of scalding tea and eating bread crusts with sliced sausage. Soon after I had started for Bialystok a police car caught me up. The policeman wanted to see all my documents but didn't press me with questions. Later I came to a windmill-shaped building at the edge of a wood called Minaretski Bar and climbed the steps. It was run by a fat matronly woman and a young blonde. They had company – a raffish man with long hair who had bought a crate of beer, and a farmer. The man gave me a bottle.

I told them I had been visiting Treblinka. "The place was quite empty."

This didn't surprise them: Poles never went to Treblinka. "Why should we? It's no concern of ours."

The subject of the Germans cropped up. "They are," said the farmer, "a dangerous nation (*niebezpieczny narod*). With them *Befehl* is *Befehl* (an order is an order). They are not to be trusted."

"Surely there were two sorts of Germans," I said for the sake of argument, "the swine who gave the orders and the ordinary decent soldier in the Wehrmacht."

The man laughed. "The swine gave the orders to murder all right. But who carried them out? It was the ordinary soldier."

At midday Warsaw radio time-signal sounded the bugle call from Cracow market square. I asked my acquaintances if they knew the army reveille call and hummed it with the words fitted to it by Polish soldiers:

> "Get up, get up, you sons of whores!
> I've been blowing my trumpet for half an hour
> And you're still asleep, you sons of bitches.
> Get up, get up, you sons of whores!"

The man with the beer liked this and treated me to another bottle.

About twenty miles from Bialystok I saw a man waiting at a bus stop and gave him a lift. He was a tiny, ugly dwarf. He wore an eye-shade and leggings, carried a haversack, and had a big discoloured nose. He was talkative and well informed. He lived in a nearby village. Because of his bad sight he had been excused army service and received a disability pension. The farmers in the district, he said when I questioned him, were quite comfortably off. "Peasants live well. But the government interferes too much, which is why everyone uses the black market. Without the black market there would be no economy."

The big two to three-storey houses we passed from time to

time among the small cottages and shacks had been built, he
said, by Poles who had been abroad and had brought back
dollars. The older generation of emigrants never returned.
As for ex-servicemen who had fought with the western allies in
the war, everyone knew that they had been treated as Fascists
when they came back to Poland and this had discouraged the
vast majority from joining them. "But things have changed
since then," he added. "There must be many a senior official
today with a foreign medal ribbon pinned under his jacket!"

I asked him about the Jews and said I would be visiting some
of their cemeteries. What did he think about Jews?

He was not at a loss for an answer. "The Jews were not Poles.
They refused to integrate with us. They preferred international
interests and connections, and they were mean and grasping,
great savers, keeping everything for themselves. A Jew was not
one of us." He illustrated his point with an anecdote. "A four-
year-old Jewish child was riding with his father in a bus and
said, 'Look, father, there's the flag'. The father rebuked him.
'That, my child, is not *our* flag. Our flag bears the star of
David.'"

Jews, said the dwarf, had never felt part of the Polish nation.
"Poland is better off without them."

The ruin of Poland, he remarked, was drink. "Poles don't
know how to drink. We don't understand moderation. No cock-
tail's – just straight alcohol, the stronger the better, and getting
drunk, that's what we like. Young people are drunkards too."

I dropped him at an antiquarian's shop in Bialystok. He
offered to pay me twenty zlotys for the lift.

A VETERINARY CLINIC

One of Emma's friends had given me the address of a Polish
doctor and his wife who run a veterinary clinic in Bialystok.
Before calling on them I stopped at a restaurant opposite a
modern church with a tall tower on a mound (St Roch) and ate
borsch. The two waiters were young men in black suits and
bow-ties learning the hotel trade as apprentices. They wished
they knew English – the little Russian they had been made to
learn at school was of no use or interest to them. They were

proud of Poland's several victories over English football teams since the war.

Bialystok has wide Russian-type streets, one way traffic, many detours for repair works, and the house numbers are erratic. It wasn't easy to find the doctor and his wife. Their clinic stood in a yard which could only be reached through a factory gate. They were charming and friendly. I sat in the waiting room till they had attended to the customers' dogs and cats and was then taken up for supper. They had a twenty-five-year old son who was studying pharmacy, a daughter, a granny, a small television set with a blurred picture, and the doctor's Fiat car.

As a vet he saw a good deal of the local farmers. "They have tractors, some have cars, the penury of the old days has vanished." They gave him perks, especially pork, for looking after their animals. But a weak point in the Polish economy was the discrepancy in earnings. "A bad lazy workman can earn as much as or even more than an educated man." The doctor's son, Stefan, was aggrieved about this. He expected to be poor for years, and when he qualified would not be much better off than a plumber.

The doctor and his wife had spent an Intourist holiday in Georgia. He described the Georgians as "handsome rogues." "They love wine and are all black market specialists." The Russian, he thought, was a good fellow and not to blame for the Soviet system. He admired German efficiency but resented the way Germans looked down on Poles as an inferior nation.

The doctor's wife made up a bed for me in a small room adjoining the clinic where I had the porter as neighbour. I planned to see the town and then to visit the Jewish cemetery in Tykocin.

ORTHODOX SERVICE

I parked outside the Krystal, Bialystok's best hotel. It was Sunday morning and in the restaurant Poles were eating breakfasts of fried eggs and sliced salami. They seemed to have hangovers. The women were pretty and dark-eyed with full faces. They wore small fur hats and fur-lined boots. I was admiring the waitresses when a drunk came in and caused some confusion. He wore a scarf, clean clothes and had shaved. I watched him hide his vodka bottle under a chair, then he started to harangue everybody. The waitresses ignored him. So he stood up and shouted "*Chuj!*" (the vulgar word for "penis"). The senior waitress spoke sharply to him. "You are a nuisance. Go home!" This angered him. "*Pierdolic!*" he shouted ("Fuck you!") and started to ramble. Oddly enough he kept a straight face. Only his eyes were glazed and his brain must have been pounding with hammers and crazy lights. After a time he picked up his bottle and left.

Through the window I watched a police car draw up. One of the crew got out and had a close look at my van. There were many disturbing items that might have worried them: the tyres, the broken exhaust pipe, the rusty doors, the flaking paint and general appearance of dereliction. It occurred to me that I had better check all my lights and use my seat belt in future.

From the restaurant I walked over to the Orthodox cathedral whose double-barred cross was shining over a yellow dome against a frosty sky. About fifty worshippers had gathered there, many of them grey-haired women. I stood at the back, adjusting myself to the form and drama of the ancient Byzantine rite, to the rich display of candles, ikons and murals and the priestly robes. This was an eastern not a western occasion. The choir, which stood in a gallery apart from the congregation, sang without instruments (they are not used in the Orthodox service), their voices blending in the deep, sonorous harmony one associates with Russian singing. The congregation remained standing throughout, facing the *iconostas*, the great painted screen that shuts off the altar (the sanctuary) from the rest of the church. A rosy light shone through the screen. It was covered with ikons of the Holy Family, the evangelists and saints, including a replica of the Black Madonna of Czestochowa. A stranger seeing the profusion of gilt, the many paintings and icons, might have thought he was in a picture gallery. The grave, bearded saints, the priest's long white hair and globular crown had an Old Testament flavour. The flickering tapers, the tinkling silver bell, the incense pot shaken by the deacon, were pagan.

I liked the flaming wicks. They warmed the chill nave. Every worshipper had bought a taper for a few coins from the verger, who stood at the back of the congregation. The tapers were placed in burning rings on round silver trays and when they melted and drooped someone immediately straightened or replaced them. There was a continual bustle as people walked up to the ikons, kissed them and prayed before them. Hands were never still as they made the sign of the cross.

I stayed for half an hour till my legs stiffened. Cramp is an essential part of the Byzantine ordeal. The Orthodox service is very long, two hours or more, yet one must remain standing as there are no pews! When I went out into the street, leaving the warmth of the tapers and the cadences of the choir, a cold wind pierced through my clothes and I felt how drab, poor and lonely is the urban world. And yet, if one cannot enter into the spirit of such worship, its panoply must be foreign and bewildering and the ritual objects stacked under the dome little more than fetishes. Seeking reassurance among the bric-à-brac it is the cross that I first look for on entering a church: it may be the heavy timber cross in a poor mountain church, or the simple piece of wood in a Low Church chapel. The cross should be conspicuous. I recall how disappointed I was when I went into St Paul's and could scarcely make out the tiny symbol at the end of the long nave. I spoke to a clergyman about it (he was escorting some nuns) and he was quite offended. "The cross may seem small and inconspicuous to you," he said, "but Wren made it exactly in proportion to its setting – in fact it's over nine feet high." This may be so. But if the cross is not a dominant part of the furniture I feel the religious aura is less. Where else should one focus one's thoughts and prayers? On the man's neck in front of you?

It can be argued that symbols, like idols or graven images, turn worship into a masque. There are so many hallowed objects and secular mementoes. The town regimental colours that hang in a Protestant church belong rightly to a military museum or cenotaph. Frescoes of battle that commemorate naval engagements and heroes pay honour to slaughter and ambition. The Poles have no Aboukir or Trafalgar. But they too hang flags in their churches: the Polish crowned eagle gazing westward towards freedom; the cult of the Black Madonna which transforms her into a queen of battles against foreign invaders.

The images of Christ himself are bewilderingly varied. As a

child succoured by plump arms; as Holman Hunt's 'Good
Shepherd' knocking gently at a locked door; crucified, bleeding
and grey with agony in primitive Catholic art. There is the
gimmickry of relics and trinkets left by pilgrims, the resplen-
dent iconostas screens that open and shut like a conjuror's box
while the priest and his officers come and go during the performance of the liturgy. There are the gargoyles and pealing
bells that are meant to scare off the devil, the evil eye: the
incense pot to keep away plague and smells. Distracted by the
confusion one looks for two simple crossed beams. They concentrate the mind.[1]

JEWISH CEMETERY

In the afternoon I looked for the Jewish cemetery. No one
could tell me where it was until I found an elderly woman who
spoke like a lady to direct me. The burial ground was near the
municipal cemetery. "But it's a ruin."

It was a two-mile walk. On the way I stepped into a red-brick
church under repair. Two chapels had been left open and
there was a gallery of photographs of Father Popieluszko with
tributes. I asked an old man with glasses and a limp if I was on
the right way to the cemetery. "Are you a Jew?" he asked. "An
English Jew? Why do you want to see Jewish tombs?"

We talked about the Jews. "They let themselves be slaughtered like lambs," he said. "Incomprehensible. They had
money, they could have bought arms. There were plenty to be
had, but they seemed to be in a state of hypnosis. Hypnotised
by some deadly snake or animal."

"The Jews in Israel," I commented, "are a different breed.
They will fight to the death."

---

[1] Many people have written with scorn of the pageantry of the Orthodox
mass. Alexander Nikitenko (*The Diary of a Russian Censor*, 1864) said
that its dramatic grandeur became monotonous. "Endless liturgical prayers
... Oh, servile Byzantium! You have given us a religion of slaves! Damn
you! Indeed, the best of Christianity drowns in this gilded rubbish of
ritual which despots have invented to keep the prayer itself from reaching
God ... Yes, there is everything here except simple Christian simplicity
and humanity."

He agreed. "They have a homeland to fight for now. Poland was not their country."

A flower-seller also asked me if I was a Jew. "Have you no Jewish blood? What brings you here?"

I found the cemetery along a muddy lane. It is a melancholy, scruffy field with gravestones lying in disarray among brambles, wild grass, weeds and bushes. The tombs are blackened and eroding as though they had been tossed about by a strong wind. There is a memorial stone on a concrete pedestal with inscriptions and a single domed tomb with a broken roof which has been vandalised and is being used as a latrine. I noticed only three inscribed graves. One bore the name Rebecca Rotblatt who died in 1924. She at any rate had not lived to see her people murdered.

The effect of this grey, untidy field hidden away among broken walls and tangled wire is of total abandonment, oblivion: the end of a culture, the climax to a unique and rich historical process. As a traveller I have seen many examples of this process of decay or violent extinction. In Turkey the toppled marble columns of Greece and Rome, defaced by shepherd boys, lie among flowering capers and wild herbs on her Mediterranean and Aegean coasts. Carved Byzantine masonry holds up the walls of Ottoman strongholds and peasants' orchards. The wild Pontic valleys behind Trebizond hide skeletons of Greek churches. Moslem villagers are using eleventh-century Georgian churches as granaries. The wreckage of extinction is everywhere: Armenian churches converted into warehouses or cinemas or simply abandoned; Nestorian churches like tiny stone mountain forts smashed by the Kurds in Hakkari; glazed cones, blind arches, frescoes and reliefs of fabulous animals.

There are parallels between the fate of Turkey's Armenians and of the Jews of eastern Europe. The Armenians, whom the Turks accused of being Christian allies of the Tsar, a fifth column waiting to welcome the Russian invader, had for long experienced sporadic harassment from mobs of Turkish villagers led on by mullahs. In 1915 the community was dispersed at one blow by wholesale expulsion into the wintry mountains of eastern Anatolia; the survivors fled abroad. Since then the Armenians (apart from their republic in the USSR) have had no homeland. To publicise their cause they carry out from time

to time acts of terrorism. Under the Ottomans the Armenians
had prospered for centuries as skilled artisans and craftsmen,
farmers and merchants. The Turk envied them for their gifts
and despised them. They were Giaours. What more fitting prey
for the predator could there have been?

In a similar sense the Jews of eastern Europe remained out-
siders in religion, dress, customs and occupations. In Polish
eyes many had compromised themselves by identifying with
Communist doctrines. They were not accepted as "true Poles".

Anatolian Greeks were deported to Greece in exchange for
Turks after World War I. The Armenian diaspora continues
while their hereditary enemies, the Kurds, survive to graze
their livestock in the highland pastures of Van and Ararat. The
Jewish response to the holocaust has been to collect their scattered people from the shambles of Oswiecim and Theresienstadt
and resettle in Israel or America. Like the Armenian, the Jew
too (in Palestine and the Lebanon) has used methods of terrorism to further his cause. It is logical that the modern Jew,
victim of the world's apathy and left to die alone under the
Nazis, should have chosen to turn himself into a soldier settler,
heavily armed, ready to defend his kibbutzim to the death.

It is certain that Hitler's death camps, the world's indifference or refusal to intervene more actively to save Jewish lives,
the terrible reward for centuries of peaceful work and life in
Poland, broke the Jew's heart. Nothing can efface the memory
of the gas chambers and furnaces. The last straw must have
been the post-war pogroms in Kielce. They seem to have convinced the Jew once and for all that he was not wanted in
Poland. So the Jews have gone, and founded their own armed
base with commando troops and young women with automatic
rifles in Zionist Israel.

I sat on a fallen stele. It started to rain which worsened the
desolation. Here was nothing but a jumble of neglected stones.
The only sizeable tomb was being used as a latrine. New cottages were already encroaching on one side of the burial ground.
An Alsatian dog barked fiercely at me from behind a fence.

As I got up to walk through the broken wall to the neighbouring Christian enclave I heard singing and followed it. A funeral
procession came out of the trees moving along a muddy path. I
joined them till they stopped at an open grave.

FUNERAL

There were about thirty mourners, a sister of the woman being buried, a priest, and four strong men to handle the coffin. Everyone had brought flowers. The heavy wooden coffin was laid on a heap of spoil while the priest prayed. The four men then lowered the coffin into the grave with straps. They were quick and professional. After another prayer the priest threw the first handful of soil on the coffin. At this moment the dead woman's sister began to sob, for the first grains of earth tossed on the bier were a sign that the deceased had disappeared for ever from the human eye. She had been delivered to the worms that live underground and would become their food. The four men worked silently, shovelling back the earth till they began to sweat and the veins stood out on their foreheads. The contrast between these ceremonial rites and the abandoned Jewish stones a few hundred yards away was painful. Yet in a special way the Jewish dead had been lucky. They had died in peace before the crematoria furnaces were lit. They had not been thumped, crushed, stripped and suffocated by demons.

The bus back to town was crowded with mourners, lively and relaxed as though they had been to a party, wearing their best clothes. A handsome woman of about sixty beckoned to me to share her seat. "You're no longer a young man." I refused her offer. "I may look *stary*," I said, "but in a cemetery one is expected to look old." "You are right, age is only what you feel." She started on a rambling tale about her sister. "Almost overnight her hair turned quite white. Now look at me – I never asked God to keep my natural hair colour but it's not even gone grey!"

She was impressed that "the English still take an interest in our country". When I remarked that all the Polish cemeteries I had seen were excellently kept she agreed they were "better looked after than in the old days. People have more money to spend. Before the war we were poorer but people were nicer then, they had better characters. Now we are better off but not so nice (*grzeczny*)."

She waved when I got out of the bus. Catching sight of myself in a shop window I saw a wild figure with tousled hair wearing a jumble of old clothes. Did I look like a madman?

As darkness fell I retraced my way to the Orthodox cathedral. The flaming tapers on silver dishes would keep me warm. I was in time to take my place at two consecutive weddings. The brides were in white and must have been shivering as they waited in the vestibule. The best men held crowns over the brides' heads while the priest read the service. As the minutes passed I wondered at the stength of their arms. Towards the end of the ceremony the couples disappeared behind the ikonostas. The guests were all young, some with full blond moustaches (which are in fashion).

TYKOCIN

In the morning I drove to Tykocin to look at the Jewish synagogue and school which were founded in 1642 and which used to be widely reputed. The Nazis soon settled their hash. On 25/26 August 1941 German police and guards drove the Jewish community – about 2,300 people – in lorries to a forest and executed them (about 150 escaped). The Jewish quarter, synagogue and school were destroyed. Restoration of the synagogue and school was started in 1976 with the object of conserving them as historic buildings. Some foreign assistance has been given for the work.

The synagogue is now a brand-new building handsomely equipped and furnished as a show-piece with candelabra, crystal, prayer shawl, sacred writings, lectern and priest's chair (*bimah*) and other beautifully made objects, and with an embroidered cloth (*parochet*) in memory of the Jews murdered in the forest which, according to a notice, was presented by Stanley and Rhoda Proesser and their children of New York (1981).

The Poles deserve praise for encouraging the restoration. It has been done in excellent taste. But it is a publicity exercise too and is designed, I think, less to remind people of the Jewish tragedy that occurred in their midst than to attract Jewish and American tourism. There was a caretaker and two young men on the building work but I saw no other visitors.

The restored Jewish school has been converted into a museum of local history with paintings by Bujnowski and examples of peasant crafts. What caught my interest were the

mementoes of a local man Wladyslaw Maliszewski who had
served in General Anders's army overseas and had later died in
England. His documents showed that he had been a sergeant in
the 24th Rifle Battalion of 5 Kresowa Infantry Division. His
campaign medals were displayed together with his flashes – an
8th Army crusader's shield and a Polish bison (*zubr* – the
emblem of his division). I had worn the same patches of cloth
myself and had been proud of the dark-brown prancing bison
on my sleeve. Among the sergeant's mementoes were a certifi-
cate that he had taken part in the battle for Monte Cassino
(honoured by Poles of all persuasions as a famous victory)
and his demobilisation address in England (Polish Hostel,
Melton Mowbray). The photograph showed a stocky bald man
in Polish uniform and later in English battledress.

I remember the battalion and brigade (Lwowska) well. I had
followed their fortunes from the moment they had left Russia
(they were ferried by tanker across the Caspian) and stumbled
out of open army trucks into a desert camp in Irak until the
closing stages of the war when they were battering the German
lines in the foothills outside Bologna. Their division had arrived
(1942) in Khanaquin as an unsoldierly mob, bewildered, suffering from heat exhaustion and the after effects of malaria and
typhus, many with shaved heads, clad in ill-fitting shorts, careless of hygiene, and with no equipment. They were accompanied by a party of tough young girls who were immediately
recruited into the Polish WAS or used as nurses. As part of the
newly formed 2 Polish Corps the division was reorganised,
trained and equipped, was moved to Palestine, and within
a little over a year had gone eagerly into battle against the
Tedeschi.

Sergeant Maliszewski was one of those men. But it must have
been a great sorrow to him that he was never able to take a
soldier's revenge against Poland's enemy number one – the
Russians, who came not so much to liberate the Poles as to
partition and reoccupy their country. It must have been another
bitter moment when he had to refuse repatriation to Poland. He
had fought with the wrong army (the western allies). If he had
returned home the post-war Polish authorities would have
humiliated or punished him as a Fascist.

The woman in charge of the museum was intelligent and

friendly and gave me tea. She was touched when I told her
of my old connection with Sergeant Maliszewski's infantry
brigade. I asked her how the massacre of the Jews in Tykocin
had occurred. They were driven off in trucks to the forest to be
executed, she said. The Germans had also shot many local
Poles. The men had been boasting beforehand that they would
never be led like lambs to the slaughter. But what happened?
The Germans ordered them to assemble one day in the square.
They obeyed the order, and were immediately seized and taken
away. Those who resisted were shot on the spot. There was no
choice, she said. The Poles were just as helpless as the Jews
when the moment came.

SHARDS

The Jewish cemetery in Tykocin lies at the edge of the little
town. I walked there through cobbled lanes between rows of
small cottages and farm houses built of brick, breeze blocks or
wood. The dwellings looked warm and water-tight, the barns
and stables patched and muddy. Villagers were plodding about
in padded jackets and fur hats. I stopped to talk to a woman
who was digging a vegetable patch. "We are glad to see an
Englishman," she said. When I told her I was looking for the
Jewish cemetery she asked, "Are you a Jew? A half-Jew? No
Jewish blood?" She called to two small girls to guide me.

They led me to a big bare field sprayed with chunks of broken
tombstones which lay at drunken angles. The inscriptions were
no longer legible. Only one wall was standing. The grass was
tufted and coarse and littered with cow pats. A single cow was
tethered to a tomb. As I bent over the graves the cold wind tore
at my face and throat and made my eyes water. I wondered
what I was looking for. An artefact, a shard with words written
on it? A message in a bottle? A sign from the dead?

I looked at the bare field, the few scraggy little trees, the
broken fence and the low dish-cloth clouds. The two little girls
were sheltering from the wind against the wall, watching me.
Without my old van, my magic carpet, I might have felt lonely
and lost. True, I was only a tourist. But behind the Iron
Curtain one travels on sufferance. No Communist police officer
is going to believe that a foreigner will come all the way from

the West, at considerable expense, merely to bend over an old Jewish grave on a hill. Beyond the Oder to travel is to pry and the pose of innocence is laughable. But what had I seen in Tykocin? A repaired synagogue, without worshippers, decked out as a museum to attract the curious or the scholar. An old Jewish school and study centre turned into an exhibition of local Polish history, with a tiny shrine to a native son who had fought at Cassino and died in Melton Mowbray.

As for the scattered Jewish tombstones they were so abandoned, so eroded, so alien to the Polish Christian tradition that I could not imagine them surviving for very long. The dead had died peacefully before the Holocaust was let loose. But the very existence of their tombs is an unpleasant reminder to Poles of what happened to the others. Perhaps the mud and tufted grass should be allowed to swallow them up.

When I asked for a bar a boy pointed to a shed tucked away behind a big lime tree. It had a rough parlour and tiny kitchen, wooden chairs and tables, and a girl in an apron. A dozen peasants were sitting in a cloud of tobacco smoke. I joined a farmer and asked for tea. "What brings you here?" he asked.

He was a wiry man in his forties with a prominent bony nose, small wrinkled eyes, missing and broken teeth, and large brown hands twisted and swollen by work. He was wearing a woollen cap with ear flaps, a padded coat and gum boots. He took a bottle out of his pocket and filled a glass with spirits under cover of the table. I had to drink it. It tasted of burning metal.

After a time I asked him about the Jews of Tykocin. "The Germans," he said, "got rid of them within a few hours."

"Did no one try to help them?"

He made a grimace. "People were too scared, and it was no business of ours. Besides, the Jews were not Poles."

"Did the Jews try to resist?"

"No, they behaved like sheep." It was, he added, "devil's work. The Germans showed no pity."

Another man joined us. He had a red face, small grey eyes and thick shoulders. "I respect England," he said. "I hear Poles live well there." He claimed there were over three million Poles living abroad. "Some come back with dollars and build three-storey houses."

I went to the toilet which opened off the parlour. It had no seat, the floor was covered in excrement and a man was standing there with his trousers down. So I urinated against a birch tree.

KRYNKI

I turned back to Bialystok and spent the night in a gap off the road. I found that in my strange assortment of clothes and wrappings I could keep warm despite the frost, but I was woken several times by cramp. My next stop was to be at Krynki, a small town a mile or two from the Soviet border. It had an old Jewish cemetery of which I had seen a photograph in an art book.

In the morning the road was icy. The pine and fir forests were dark and silent in a grey mist, the grass shone with hoar-frost, the little wooden cottages looked lifeless, the fields a sea of muddy earth. There was no road traffic.

I got out at a small square with a public garden in the middle of Krynki and walked along a lane to find someone to talk to. Three men were loading sacks of grain in a yard. They looked at me in surprise when I asked them the way to the Jewish cemetery. "I am not a Jew," I said, wishing to forestall a string of questions about my origins and religion.

One of the Poles – an oldish man with thick grey eyebrows and furrowed cheeks – took me by the arm and led me aside. He seemed upset.

"I didn't ask you who you were and I don't care if you are a Jew or not." Then he said slowly and with emphasis, "You are a *czlowiek* (human being). I am a *czlowiek*. A Jew is a *czlowiek*. Let the dead sleep in peace." There was a whiff of vodka in his breath but he was not drunk.

I told him who I was and that I had been a friend of the Poles since before the war.

"*Doskonale*. But you must understand that we don't want people coming here to disturb the graves. There was one visitor who tried to remove things from the cemetery. We sent him away. Let the Jews," he repeated, "sleep in peace. Jews are humans." He took my hand and his eyes were wet.

A villager in gum boots guided me to the cemetery, past a row of small cottages and outbuildings, some in poor shape with heavy farm carts parked in the muddy yards and strong brown

horses. I turned past a saw-mill and building site, plodded up a
green hill and as the sun came out arrived at the cemetery. It is
a large, rough field littered with grey-black weathered tombstones — about 700 of them — some erect with rounded tops or
shaped like arks, others leaning crazily, many toppled over or
cracked into jagged lumps. Few of the inscriptions are legible.
There is no official memorial. But a freshly chiselled slab with
epitaph stands near the entrance. A brown horse was tethered
to one of the gravestones. The low cemetery wall is broken in
many places.

The air was fresh in the wintry sunshine, the graveyard
scoured by forest winds, with a view across a glade of a Christian
cemetery a few hundred yards away. I walked through a muddy
field towards it but the gate was padlocked. The crosses and
Cyrillic lettering showed that it was an Orthodox cemetery.
There were fresh flowers on the graves. The crosses, some of
burnished wrought iron, shone cheerfully in the sunlight.

Krynki, Bialystok, Kielce, Treblinka were once part of the
Jewish Pale. What were the Jews seeking when they settled — or
were driven — to this neighbourhood from the Rhineland or
arrived as exiles from the interior of Tsarist Russia? The bustle
of small town life, country markets and peasant trading? Peace,
privacy and freedom to pray? They had halted in a land of
forests and lakes, of marshland, rivers, roads and tracks that
were snow-covered in winter, boggy in spring and hard as iron
in summer. They found drab birds, fish, frogs that barked and
bellowed in the ditches.

Above all the Jews had come to the edge of the world. The
present Soviet border is only two miles away. The Tsars once
ruled here. The Jews had been confronted not by Roman
Catholicism but Russian Orthodoxy. The enemy was not a
Polish squire but the Tsar's police and mounted regiments.
Caught between two conflicting cultures and part of neither,
the Jews were in a vulnerable position.[1] The time would

[1] Further south were Galicia and the Ukraine. As a result of Chmielnicki's
Cossack rising of 1648 100,000 Jews perished. After this episode (the Jews
had been butchered not so much for being non-Christians but as servants
of Polish landlords) they became apprehensive about their future and the
old *Drang nach Osten* was reversed into a westward trek across the Oder.
Vienna became a great centre of Jewish influence.

inevitably come when they would have to leave. The more
enterprising began to move away at the end of the last century,
and the first "Litvaks" sailed to Johannesburg, New York and
Whitechapel.

The Ottoman Turks were too idle to blow up Christian
churches. They converted them for their own use or stripped
them stone by stone for building their own houses. In Poland
the legacy of the Jews is represented by scattered gravestones
that will soon collapse into the earth or be built on. Even to be
reminded of their lost love affair with Poland and their final
torments must be a memory too painful for them to bear.

RETURN TO BIALYSTOK

There was a restaurant in the main square of Krynki. The
parlour was full of rough peasants who looked as though (like
me) they had slept in their clothes. The woman in charge
shooed me out and made me sit in the dining room which had
table cloths. I was given some rubbery food and asked the
waitress if it was chopped mushrooms. She pointed to her
mouth. "Tongue". I lapped up the mashed potatoes and gravy
with a tin spoon.

From Krynki I had been planning to turn south off the main
road and go to the village of Kruszyniany about twelve miles
away where a small community of Tatar Moslems is still living.
But the sky had been clouding over and it began to snow – a
steady white fall which blew hard against my face when I went
out to my van. With my decrepit vehicle it would have been
foolish to get stuck in a snow drift on a dirt road. I turned back
for Bialystok.

I stopped briefly at Suprasl, eight miles from Bialystok, to
visit its three churches (one is Orthodox) and a large cemetery
of mixed Polish and Orthodox graves with Polish and Cyrillic
inscriptions. Some of the Latin crosses have a smaller Orthodox
cross engraved in the centre. The chapel has a Latin cross on
the roof and an Orthodox one over the door.

The night in Bialystok was cold with several degrees of frost.
The fields were white. It was 10 November. I had a feeling that
this was the onset of winter.

I spent my last day browsing in bookshops – there were books

on Majdanek and Oswiecim but nothing on Treblinka —
and keeping warm in bars. In the evening, to get away from
the slush, I went back to the Orthodox cathedral. A special
service was being held and there must have been over 300
people, about two-thirds of them women, pressed round the
ikons and crowding the entrance. The priest's reedy old
voice was drowned by the responses and hymns. The children
were enjoying themselves. Parents lifted them up to kiss the
ikons. They straightened and replaced the burning tapers
on their shining stands and gazed at them as though they
were looking at a lighted Christmas tree in a toy shop. The
painted Madonnas with olive skins and gilded crowns and
gowns like embroidered *saris* watched them with black, sad
eyes.

The press of the crowd and the burning candles made
me sweat. This was theatre, quite unlike an Anglican church
gathering with its crusading hymns and pulpit homilies. Was I a
hypocrite, squashed there among the burly, warm bodies and
the work-worn hands crossing their breasts? Did I feel superior
to these ikon-kissing East Europeans with their deep, throaty
voices? No. I envied their faith, its discipline, the artistry and
music of their service, their togetherness as a crowd. What
about the three officiating priests? I had doubts about them.
Perhaps the two junior men with their thick glossy curls and
well-fed faces were private lechers or gluttons. Would that
matter? There came the splendid moment when the bread and
wine were brought in solemn procession from the northern door
of the ikonostas and back through the Royal Doors, with the
choir up in the gallery singing the Cherubic hymn. This was
more than acting. The robes, the perfumed censer, the hot
yellow tapers, the painted prophets and ikons, the gilt and
glittering screen across the altar had the sensuous beauty of the
Orient. And there was the ritualised masque of humility: the
passionate surrender of clerks, peasants and housewives to the
Theokotos, the God-bearer in her purity.

The words of the old Slavonic litany followed me into the
churchyard as I left. I stayed a few minutes longer till I began
to shiver. Then I drove into the night to curl up like a mole in
my wrappings.

A FARMER

In the morning, on the road to Warsaw, I gave a lift to a farmer
who was standing by the wayside. He was in his forties with a
lean healthy face, wearing a fur cap. He didn't smoke and he
spoke bluntly and to the point. I asked him about local farming
conditions. He said he and his family lived mostly on their own
produce – he made his own butter and cheese and when he had
spare meat he concealed it from the government. The economy,
he went on, had been more active in the earlier post-war years
because of reconstruction work and the many rebuilding projects. Things had now slowed down and prices had soared. He
laughed when I asked him if he had a car. "I would have to be
ten years on a waiting list to get one."

He was happy with the village school where he had sent his
children. But like all Poles he knew that by western standards
Poland was a poor country. "In my lifetime Poland will never
be rich. We are poor in possessions but rich in religion." Poles
who went abroad seldom returned. Those who did had made
money and could live in style with "a big house and German
car".

We discussed the Germans. "A dangerous people," he said.
"With them everything must be done at the double
(*Im Laufschritt*). If they'd won the war they would have used us
as slaves. The Russians are worse. They stick like glue. They
take everything and they will never go away."

He was astonished when I told him I had no *renta* (pension).
"A man of your age ought to have one." I explained that as I
had always been employed abroad I wasn't entitled to a pension. But I could claim supplementary benefit. He found this
too complicated to grasp. "A man has either a pension or
savings," he insisted.

When he got out he offered to pay for the ride.

A little later I called again at the Minaretski Bar. The wavy-
haired man was there, a young ex-soldier and three tipsy men.
They were grumbling. "Poland," they complained, "is shame-
fully poor. Bad shops, shortages and queues, and everything is
getting dearer."

"It's the fault of the Russians," said one of the men. "They
take our best products and all we get in return is petrol." They

could scarcely believe that my van was eighteen years old. A
Polish car, they said, lasts four years. The motor is sound but
the chassis shakes itself to pieces.

I could have stayed longer and got drunk. But Warsaw was
not far now and I wanted to change my clothes.

Warsaw had turned into a grey city with snow and ribbons of
black slush. I joined the queue at a food shop in Zbawiciela
square to find something for supper. It was 5 p.m. and everyone was in a hurry. Only a few stale fragments of brown bread
were left. But there was cheese, butter, milk and gherkins. The
old tramp was sitting on the hot-water pipes and champing like
a squirrel at a lump of cheese. Muddy trams clanged along the
gutters, crammed tight with passengers like pilchards in a tin. A
line of about forty people were standing on the pavement outside the fish stall. The street lights were so dim one might have
suspected a power failure.

Emma was at home. Something fragrant was simmering on
the stove and guests were expected.

14
POLICE INTERROGATION

A gusty east wind is upsetting the rooks and pigeons, scattering them amongst the skeletal trees whose nakedness reveals the bleak apartment blocks enclosing the square, the rows of double-glazed windows sealed for the winter, the dingy curtains. A few old people, warmly wrapped up, shuffle along with their dogs over frozen paths – the old ladies in heavy coats, high boots and hats, their dogs panting and fat. It is too chilly and windy to enjoy the Lazienki Gardens. One has prepared oneself for increasingly colder days as winter sharpens and turns to snow and icicles. In the apartment buildings it is warm, with powerful central heating that brings out the fug of bodies, hidden rubbish and cockroaches. When a door opens one smells boiled cabbage, onions, vodka and tobacco. This is the inimitable Slav world battening down for winter: virile, shabby, enduring, poor, cheerless and quarrelsome. The Iron Curtain hangs heavier in winter. The cold brings shortages and physical discomfort. Summer hopes have come and gone – and still no Freedom! But churches are always open and worshippers never cease to call – dropping in from the street when the spirit moves them, genuflecting, brooding, boots echoing on stony floors. There is much parochial activity and pastoral work: vestibules hung with posters, appeals for charity, notices of functions, weddings, funerals and reunions, concerts and religious lectures. Pedestrians – usually older men – remove their hats when they pass the church doors. To save current the churches are dimly lit.

To avoid draughts one sits away from the swinging double doors in cafés and bars. Sugar has just been derationed so there is more to go round (three instead of two lumps with a glass of tea). Anchored in our dull lives we stay warm and keep out of trouble.

UNIVERSITY

My university contacts have again been helpful. I have been asked to take part in a course of BBC English script readings to be broadcast by Warsaw radio to English language classes. The action is rather trifling – an adventure in shoe salesmanship. I am a sales manager with ideas, Emma is the firm's representative, a British-born Polish girl with faultless English has the other part. I enjoy the sessions. We giggle at the dialogue, though we sit in discomfort drinking glasses of tea in a cold corridor during breaks (no smoking in the studio). Emma has done English language broadcasting before and is expert. Transmuted by the machine my voice sounds different: not exactly fruity but like an ageing school prefect or failed don. The Polish producer and technicians are friendly and helpful, and I am being paid a fee.

The African department has also asked me to give a talk on English literature and writing in East Africa. "Chopin lived here," a student told me as we ducked under some scaffolding and crept up narrow stairs to reach the African department. A dozen Polish lecturers and an African from Addis Ababa were waiting for me.

I didn't want to hurt anyone's feelings. I started with the 1960s, immediately after Uhuru, when a new generation of African writers emerged in an exciting break-through to attack western colonialism, its seizure of land, its exploitation of black labour and resources and its disapproval of "primitive" customs. Later writers shifted their attention to the internal problems of a traditional African society adapting to Western ideas and technology and the resulting alienation of educated Africans from their own native communities and villages. Then, in the seventies, African writers grew disillusioned with the corruption and violence practised by their own black governments – "the betrayal of Uhuru". Finally there was a lull in literary activity when the earlier writers dried up and were not replaced, though this has been partly compensated for by the emergence of new African writers from Moslem or Arab backgrounds.

The few lecturers present who had been to Africa had visited Angola, Mozambique, Ethiopia and Zambia but not Nairobi or Lagos. During the discussion I realised that they had only a fragmentary view of African writing in English. Their interest was focused on socialist and anti-apartheid literature and on protest verse, which they had been trained to admire. This had distorted their picture of the rich variety of African writing which ranges from erotic Swahili verse to novels about the Mau Mau fighters of Kenya or plays on witchcraft. The lecturers knew of Soyinka, Ngugi and Achebe but not Senghor, Camara Laye and Oyono who wrote in French. They hadn't heard of Bitek. Ali Mazrui was no more than a name to them. They were familiar with some of the anti-apartheid South African writers. Vernacular tongues were not their field.

I was asked to read aloud some of my Uganda students' poems from my book *Man With a Lobelia Flute*. The poems went down well ("His gun on his shoulder, A hat pulled like a basin over his head, The white pumpkin came over a hill"). The chairman took away my copy and said it should be translated. My final advice to the lecturers was to press for more tours of duty in Africa and to travel in the non-socialist black countries.

I have been shown a copy of the university students' English literature magazine (June 1985) which has an interview with Professor Barry O'Connell, an American, late of the *Anglistyka* department. Here is an excerpt:

Q. What was this stay in Poland for you?

A. I've learned a little about what it is like to live in a society in which you always have to be apprehensive. Wherever I go in Poland and whatever I do in Poland, I'm always slightly apprehensive, and in two different ways.

One of these would be true in any foreign culture I lived in. I do not know what to expect because I do not know the culture. So every day even if I take my sheets to the laundry I do not know whether there would be *Remont, Closed for Personal Reasons*, or they will not take the things I need to wash, or they will take them and I will not see them again, or if the person will be horrible to me or wonderful, or would not care. So at the most practical level there is that kind of apprehension. But there is another one.

I've learned to live in a society in which there is no established set of practices which hold people in power accountable. Part of my apprehension in Poland is realising that almost in any circumstances, if people who have the power, from people in shops on up, choose not to do something they probably ought to do, I may be completely helpless. So I have learned what it is to live in a society in which one must be apprehensive all the time. Nothing is predictable or dependable, nothing can really be made accountable. Those who have power must be held accountable. There must be independent judges, free and critical press. The US is a freer place than Poland. But those freedoms are in danger.

Professor O'Connell's point is that in an authoritarian society power corrupts, whether in the person of the shop assistant in charge of the bread counter or of a higher official with a formidable right of decision vested in his rubber stamp.

POLICE INTERROGATION

I am to take part in another English language programme in a Warsaw radio studio. The script has been prepared by the enterprising author Pan Szkutnik (I call him "Sputnik") whose books are used throughout the country and according to Poles have made him into a rich man with a hoard of zlotys. We are to work in a team – six of us including three Warsaw-based English teachers, a Polish woman, Emma and myself.

Meanwhile it is time for me to pay another instalment of visa fees in sterling. The visitor's fee for every day I stay in Poland is £8 which is returned to me in zlotys which are not negotiable outside Poland. As I earn Polish currency for radio work, and in addition have been offered a contract to help with the translation of a Polish history book, I feel I have a good case to ask the visa department to waive the visa charges. I'm earning enough Polish money to live on and as I don't buy fur-lined clothes or jewellery I don't want any more zlotys. They are an incubus.

My work contracts, I hope, imply that I've been accepted as a useful person.

I waited in the corridor of the visa department in Praga while a Lebanese was attended to. The blonde female director remembered me. "So you're back again," she said smiling. She listened to my request, kept my papers and told me to return in two days. The Lebanese gentlemen, she told me, had given her a present, which she showed me. It was an illustrated book on flowers. An unseasonable gift, I thought, looking at the pictures of lilac blossom and summer roses.

Alas, when I called back two days later I had an unpleasant shock. Two men were waiting for me in Pani Dyrektor's office, sitting at separate tables with the lady at her desk in the middle. I recognise the unsmiling suet-faced man who interrogated me at the end of June. His colleague is younger, with a policeman's moustache. They have ball point pens and paper and are ready for action. The lady avoided my eye.

For fifteen minutes I was formally questioned – coldly, with insolent curiosity. Some of the questions were these:

You have been here before. Why have you returned to Poland and how did you get your new visa?

You have changed your address – who is your landlady? Where did you meet her?

You have been in East Germany since you were last in Poland. Why?

The lard-faced man looked at the history translation contract. Have you studied history? Where and when? Who are your university contacts in Warsaw?

So far so good. Then the interrogator put a sheet of duplicated paper in front of me and asked me to read it. It was a BBC news items of 15 June 1985 in Polish translation, and I read it with growing shock. When the word *wywiad* stared back at me I felt as though I had been struck in the eye.

The gist of the BBC item was that I was (or had been) an employee of the British security service (*wywiad*): I had helped Russian refugees to escape repatriation to the USSR and I had been named in the Soviet press as a "Fascist agent"; I had fallen foul of Idi Amin who wanted to shoot me; and I had come to Poland to write an anti-Communist book.

"This is nonsense (*nonsens*)," I said immediately. "*Klamstwo* (lies), *sensacja* (cheap journalism)."

The heat was now turned on. The lard-faced man focused on the *wywiad* charge. He showed less interest in the other items but like a dog worrying a bone kept coming back to the *wywiad* phrase, pointing to it with a plump white finger. With a part of my mind I was wondering who could be the source of this untimely snippet of news. Someone had been telling tales and elaborating on them in a mischievous way. Perhaps some Polish western news agency had picked up this bit of gossip. Radio Free Europe had then broadcast it and it had been monitored by the BBC at Caversham. But would the BBC stoop to such a base trick? I felt as though I had been shot in the back by one of my own side.

And the source itself? The item was dated 15 June 1985. I could see now that it was the cause of my original expulsion order at the end of June – I could think of no other reason for it – and it would account for the visa department's suspicion of me at the time. I had spoken to only one person in Poland about my war experiences and involvement with Russian prisoners: I had joked with him about the Soviet press's "Fascist Major" sneer. But he was a colleague and a compatriot, a rather muddle-headed academic. Perhaps, in an ingenuous way, he was also a fool?

Meanwhile lard-face went on prodding. "Where did you learn foreign languages? What was your army service? Who were your commanding officers? Why did you help Russian refugees? Why did you anger Amin? If the British government was so anxious to rescue you, you must be an important person. What were the circumstances? What connections have you with the British Embassy? Whom do you know there?"

And then: "How have you spent your time in Warsaw? What is this book you are writing? You are rich – who is paying you? Where have you travelled in Poland? Why did you visit Bialystok? What are your views on Poland?"

Over an hour had passed. "The evidence is bad," said the interrogator, "very bad indeed. You are of course an intelligence agent. Your own BBC says so."

"The news item," I retorted, "is *gowno*! Shit!"

He toyed with the word for a moment. "*Gowno*," he repeated, "*gowno.*" I was hoping he might smile but his cold dead-pan expression didn't change. The *wywiad* charge was certainly worrying. Yet I was never employed on wartime intelligence work. I had no intelligence training. I have attended no intelligence courses. In fact I had always looked down on army intelligence officers as pansies. When hostilities were over I had handled prisoners of various nationalities, notably Russians. These duties were carried out under "A" branch. They were not intelligence operations. It was only towards the end of my army service (1948–49) that I had been transferred to intelligence work. This was in Austria when I had to trace and question former prisoners-of-war on their special war experiences and their activities in Soviet captivity: the role of Field Marshal Paulus's Freedom Army, for instance; battle plans, and battle conditions in winter; the efficiency of Germany's A/A defences of the Ploesti oilfields against allied bombing; the restoration of flooded Donetz coal mines; road, bridge and factory building. Later, with the Control Commission in Germany, I had done similar work with German prisoners recently released by Stalin. Some briefs were more specific. They had to do with the reinstalling (using German labour and expertise) of captured German industrial plant in Russia and the development of the V2 missile in test beds under impressed German scientists and engineers – the Russians exploited their skills till they had no further use for them and after several years sent them home.

But the slightest suspicion that a man has had anything to do with intelligence work (or "spying") is fatal in a Socialist country. The very mention of the word sends a cold shiver down the back. As the interrogator pestered me with his *wywiad* nonsense I felt very angry with the BBC for its treachery. Trying to convince this hard-headed official was a waste of breath. Explanations would be too complicated for him to understand. He had his brief, and that was the end of the matter.

Just before the session ended he put me a last question. "As a writer," he asked, "what will you say about this interview? Will you attack us for it?"

"According to this evidence," I said, indicating the BBC news report, "you are doing your duty. I understand that. But I

deny your charge." I didn't like lard-face. Yet I had no ran-
corous feelings about him. It is the system he represents that
is infuriating – its obsessive mistrust, its suspicion and its
paranoia, as though it prided itself on its own unpleasantness.

To my surprise they didn't stamp my passport with another
expulsion order and I had a momentary feeling of relief when
Pani Dyrektor returned my papers. She told me to apply for a
visa extension shortly before my current permit expired (24
Dec. 1985) and to bring receipts for my earnings from radio and
translation work. I left the building in a slight daze. I had been
reprieved. Yet I had an unpleasant feeling that in time the axe
was bound to fall. I had at any rate solved the mystery of my
apparently groundless expulsion in June. Why, though, had the
police left me alone until today's confrontation? Clearly their
security machine doesn't work very well.

I took a tram back to the city centre and telephoned Kevin
Ruane. He could not believe that the BBC had originated the
report about me. "It sounds like Russian dirty tricks". He
promised to check the story with the BBC files in London.

I shan't bother to trace the "informant". My friends say he is
a "gas bag" and would have enjoyed tipping off the media in
London with an "amusing" piece of gossip. In the meantime I
have plenty to do in Warsaw: films, concerts, lectures, wine
parties, and battening down for the winter.

PAN SZKUTNIK

We report to Warsaw Radio in the evenings, bumping in a
tram through banks of snow. Pan Szkutnik watches us with an
inscrutable smile as we read our parts and seems pleased with
our efforts. He is a balding man of fifty with a dark, scowling
face and bushy eyebrows, and a delightful manner. He has a
reputation too for being reliable and there is no doubt that at
the end of our sessions he will pay us promptly and in full and
with a large chocolate cake into the bargain.

I talk to him as we huddle in a tram: I am wearing a frayed
balaclava, for as a "professional" performer I daren't catch
laryngitis. His mother, to whom he is devoted, is recovering
from a broken hip. He complains about crowded hospitals –
casualty wards, he says, are filled with people who have broken

limbs falling on the icy roads and pavements – and the difficulty of getting good nursing. There are no old folks' homes and the economy could not in any case afford such luxuries. "It is not our practice, as in your country, to send away our aged parents and relatives to end their lives among strangers. If you have no relatives you die on your own."

I have noticed that several of my Polish acquaintances look after an aged parent in their tiny flats. It can be a thankless task. But caring has not been rationalised in terms of cost-effectiveness and convenience as in much of Britain's differently orientated society. Yet in England there is the paradox of countless houses being inhabited by a single aged person, a widower perhaps or an unmarried aunt, causing envy and frustration to those with families who have no roof of their own.

Pan Szkutnik says he will write no more language books. "I want to devote my time to reading good literature." Everything in Poland, he adds, "is out of focus. Too many regulations, shortages and unhelpful bureaucrats – and the Polish weather!"

BOULEVARDS

Over the months I have walked many miles in Warsaw. I have seen a few scuffles, and recently I intervened to stop a house porter from beating a youth with a wooden sign-post. The youth, some sort of hooligan, had fallen in the snow and was lying like a foetus with his arms protecting his head. There is always something to look at. The changing colour of trees as winter grips them, faces in the crowd, strange hats, women's coats, dogs, military police patrolling in threes, glimpses of courtyards where cobblers and watchmakers bend over little tables in basements, food stalls and bookshops.

Strolling back from the city centre to Emma's flat in Plac Zbawiciela I usually take the al. Ujazdowskie, which is wide and elegant and is not railed off by tram lines. The alternative route, Marszalkowska, is a busy street of shops, offices, rattling trams and crowds. From Plac Trzech Krzyzy I pass the Mongolian Embassy, a modest villa with posters of dancers, camels, a slant-eyed child ("The Future of our People") and a factory belching smoke in the steppe. Next door is a second-hand bookshop where the window display has not been changed for months. I can see a Japanese dictionary, histories of Polish revolutionary incidents, some English and German magazines including early copies of Petermanns. The little kiosk at the park entrance where a man stands in summer with a pair of scales inviting people to check their weight (they ought to weigh their dogs too) is closed for the winter. The benches are deserted, the ground soft and slippery with decay and fallen maple leaves. Chopin sits sad and alone on his dark throne.

Embassies line one side of the boulevard. The American building is new and utilitarian and has a special police guard in a sentry-box. At the entrance hang pictures of black American champion athletes, the Grand Canyon and Reagan making a joke. The Bulgarian Embassy displays tourist views of Black Sea summer beaches, roses and women in peasant costumes. The British Embassy is being repainted and is stained and patched. The fine chestnut tree in the garden has lost its leaves. Half a dozen Morris and Volkswagen cars are parked outside. In the old days droshkies would have been clopping past. They were much used by military officers, priests, Jews in black felt hats and smart women. Most people travel nowadays by tram or bus.

At Plac Zbawiciela one can cut across to the Marszalkowska and walk back to the city centre through the shopping crowds. Neither of the two restaurants, the Bucarest and Szangai, looks attractive with its dirty curtains and table cloths. I was looking for camping gas and tried the Scouts and Sports department store. They had blankets, rucksacks and plastic toys but no gas. About ninety percent of people who enter department stores and clothing shops don't buy anything. They look for some object that isn't there, crane their heads over the queue, and go away. But with Christmas not far off shops will restock. I stopped for coffee at the Szwajcaria. I sometimes see Roger Boyes there. The gypsy musicians had just come in and they usually wink and smile at me for I know them well. The cello player has a dirty plaster strip across his chin. A direct hit by a woman's shoe?

I fight for a place on a tram to take me back to Plac Zbawiciela and I am squashed against the door by men with small angry eyes and heavy bodies. I get off at the church in the square with its two pointed spires, which I use as a landmark. The church seems to be poor. There is not much gold paint, the pews are not polished, the nave is draughty and full of gritty air from the street. On this occasion there were only five worshippers: three bald men and two women, one half asleep. In the vestibule photographs of gravestones remind people to commemorate All Saints' Day (which had passed some time ago), to respect the dead and honour their burial places.

REMNANTS

Ostatni (Remnants), an exhibition of Jewish photographs, has just been opened in a gallery in the Old City. The pictures are of survivors of the Jewish community in Poland. Almost all of them are old people, spinning out lonely lives in small single rooms with a few sticks of furniture, pots and pans and mementoes. There are very few young Jews in Poland and it is rare for children to be born here. Some of the old people are helped by neighbours. They live in Warsaw, Cracow and Lodz or in small provincial places. Despite the temptations to emigrate with most of the remaining Jews after the wave of anti-Semitism that swept Poland in 1968, they say they have decided to stay because of their love and attachment to the country. The only "horror" picture in the exhibition is of a pile of dead victims' shoes in Oswiecim; and there is a sad picture of a mongrel sniffing at some bones in an old Jewish graveyard. Some photographs show Jewish celebrations and religious services. There are over 430 Jewish cemeteries in the country.

One's impression is of a tiny, dying community that will leave no successors in Poland. There is not a single rabbi. A kosher butcher visits Poland only once a month. It seems that world Jewry is not interested in this pathetic remnant. Jews have been forced to swallow such bitter medicine in the past that one can scarcely blame them for losing hope and trust in a future in Poland.

Beautiful recordings of Jewish music were being played in the exhibition rooms, emotional and melodious music that one associates with Russian and Balkan pathos. The visitors I saw were mostly elderly Jews or Americans. In the visitors' book I read these remarks: "Fascinating. Should be made into a book." "There is nothing more to say." "Let us never forget."

ASTLES

Bob Astles, who became a close advisor of Idi Amin during the "village tyrant's" last maniacal years, has been released from a Kampala gaol and has been flown to England. I knew him in Uganda and his ghost has now appeared on Emma's doorstep. Stoneman has had a message from the *Mail on Sunday*, which wants to interview me about Astles. I told Stoneman that I don't want to say anything about the Astles affair and he has promised not to give the newspaper Emma's telephone number. However, today the *Mail* has rung.

"Astles is skint and trying to sell his story to the press," said an editorial voice from London. "We would like you to speak with him. It should be an interesting piece." I said no. "A confrontation between you and Astles would be a first-class story." "No." The voice then changed its approach. "I hear you're writing a book about Poland." "Oh?" "I was in Warsaw two years ago, staying with some Solidarity people, very good fellows." "Oh?" "What are you doing in Warsaw?" I said I was semi-retired, comfortable and no longer interested in the Astles affair. "Why is that?" "For me it is dead and forgotten." The voice rang off.

This sort of rash telephone talk with a journalist is the very thing to get me into trouble. Foreign calls are tapped; and I am not curious to know whether the *Mail on Sunday* newspaper man finds his Solidarity acquaintances good fellows or not. I am glad of course that Astles has been released from the Uganda gaol in Luzira. In an interview in *The Times* (10 Dec. 85) which has been sent to me Astles glosses over his relationship with Idi Amin. "I was caught up in events," he says. "Besides, I genuinely felt that by being there I could moderate Amin's excesses."

More trouble. A letter from the Polish Consulate in Köln dated 5 Nov. 85 has been sent on to me from Brunswick. It has taken over a month to reach me but the delay can be blamed on the Polish mail service. It is a blunt refusal of my original written application (dated 16 July 1985) for re-entry to Poland. "You are informed that your visa request submitted to the Ministry has been refused (*zostalo zalatwione odmownie*)."

According to this letter I have no right to be in Poland; and the Polish consulate in Köln, by issuing me with a valid visa on

18 Sep. 85, was wrong. It looks like a bureaucratic muddle, with headquarters lagging behind its branch office. As I am the beneficiary I have no reason to complain. But if the Ministry's letter has by now caught some diligent official's eye I may be in for further complications. Lard-face had not mentioned the existence of such a letter. When I visit the visa department just before Christmas I may learn more.

However I have just had some welcome news. The university *Anglistyka* department has invited me to take over the English literature course after Christmas, and I have agreed. Instead of being a drone I shall be able to support myself in work that I like. The syllabus is familiar to me. Surely the visa department will look more kindly on me now that I have been enrolled by the teaching establishment.

15
SHOAH

The Lenin Museum has opened a new exhibition entitled "The Polish-Russian connection in revolutionary times". There are records of Lenin's stay at Cracow university and of Polish collaboration with the Bolsheviks. Two photographs show Stalin as a young man – Oriental looking, dark, with a mass of strong black hair and shifty eyes. The Polish contribution to academic and scientific life in Tsarist Russia is illustrated by early pictures of joint expeditions to the Tsar's Asiatic provinces. They show Mongols – prehistoric-looking creatures wrapped in furs with faces like wrinkled lumps of cheese, Taziks, Circassians and Khirgiz, bearded and colourful. In the Asiatic historical section there is a photograph of Mount Ararat taken from the Russian side. When I told the attendant that the Armenians claimed Ararat to be their own and not a Russian or Turkish mountain, and that I had climbed it (three times!), she was not interested in my silly boasting. The five women in attendance at the museum (three in the cloakroom) told me I was the only visitor that morning. They were heavily wrapped up against the cold. As soon as I left they put out the lights.

I walked back to Emma's over frozen pavements. It was windy and cold – four degrees below zero. I met Rod, who had been shopping. He was wearing a new fur cap. "I had a job finding it," he said, "as I've a very large head – one of the largest, I think, in Warsaw!" I noticed that his shoes were in poor shape – English-made of black leather. "I'm now searching for shoes – I look at people's feet." My own plastic boots have developed cracks which are impossible to repair, but I use two pairs of socks.

ROGER

I have dined with Roger Boyes and his wife in their flat. It has fine large rooms and an interesting past. It was a Gestapo HQ during the war. Later Gomulka lived there. It stands on al. I Armii Wojska Polskiego, which in Gestapo days was the notorious Szucha street, and faces the Foreign Ministry. Roger tells me that Polish Jews who had been trained and rehearsed in Russia to take over political posts in post-war Poland lived in the block. After the anti-Jewish scare of 1968 the Jews left and many went to Israel. The flat is elegant but filled with ghosts. As a western journalist Roger is, of course, closely watched. This doesn't seem to worry him. He says the East German security organisation is reputed to be the best.

Two students from the Polytechnic have told me how sick they are of the words "Polish Honour". "Honour for whom? We feel no loyalty towards the Warsaw Pact and we don't want to fight NATO." One of them said jokingly, "If it came to war I would desert. But where? To the Germans?"

Winter is the time for cinema going and I have seen two British films, *The Shooting Party* with James Mason, shown by the British Council, and *The Dogs of War. The Shooting Party* had been advertised as an authentic piece of British culture and the Council hall was packed (some eighty people).

When the head beater, a likeable rogue with a flair for poaching, is accidentally shot by one of the country house guests and lies dying in the bracken, his last words are "God save the British Empire". This sounded absurdly corny (I thought) and in the presence of a Polish audience I felt embarrassed. The Poles liked the film. It confirmed their old-fashioned picture of England as the home of gentlemen with shot guns, tweeds and deer stalker hats, mad on country sports and bullied by plain, elegant women.

Forsyth's toughs have been doing the round of Warsaw cinemas for months. Here the dogs of war are blasting their way to bloody victory over an African tyrant. Oddly, despite the smoke, ruins and corpses I remember seeing only one casualty among the white raiders. The cinema usher grinned when I asked him what he thought of the film. "It's not like that at all in a real battle – anyway not in *our* wars."

SHOAH

Critics have called Lanzmann's film *Shoah* (Annihilation) a
masterpiece. I have spent nine hours this week seeing it at a
cinema in Dzerzhinsky square. The film was shown in three
separate parts to audiences of about fifty. They were mostly
middle-class Poles, not young, with a sprinkling of Jews. When
the film was first seen in France it provoked angry protests from
the Polish government and press for stressing the involvement of Poles in the execution of the Nazi final solution. With
General Jaruzelski's approval it is now being shown for a week
in Warsaw.

Shoah is not a film about miraculous survival in the camps. It
has no pictures of grisly horrors. Not a single corpse is seen.
It is a film in memory of death, in a vision obsessed by Lanzmann's need for detail. Lanzmann touches, inspects, measures
what is still left of the paraphernalia of murder – the broken
bricks of a dismantled gas chamber, grass where tiny splinters
of bone are embedded, a weed-covered offloading ramp. He
introduces a few Jewish survivors (they were hard to find),
some ageing Germans who were involved in the extermination
machine, peasants who lived near the camps, using a shrewd
interrogation technique, trickery and a gift of persuasion to get
them to talk. We see the abandoned camps in their seasonal
landscapes: under snow, oozing mud, cooled by summer woodland, at sunset and in autumn mist. Throughout the film old
rolling stock (provided by the Polish government) clanks to
the rustic station of Treblinka and through the archway into
Auschwitz reminding one that the death trains never ceased to
run right up to the last days of German resistance. Lanzmann's
probings are witness to his own relentless antipathy to the Poles
in whose midst, alas, these millions of Jews were murdered, as a
result of which many are still widely accused of complicity.

One of the camp's survivors is a Jewish barber from Treblinka,
posed for Lanzmann's camera in a rented barber's shop in Tel
Aviv. At Treblinka he cut off women's hair minutes before they
were pushed screaming into the gas chamber. "I was doing my
job," he explained. "These were their last moments on earth.
They didn't know they were about to be killed. I tried to
reassure them. I didn't want to upset them or cause panic." The

barber was a tanned, healthy-looking man. While he was talking
he broke down and when he resumed his face continued to
twitch.

A corpse handler at Auschwitz was another survivor, a good-
looking man with expressive brown eyes, a powerful body and
an unlined, sun-burnt skin. He said he had survived various
camp Kommandos because he was strong. He described the
stink and dirt of the gassed bodies from which the fluids, nose
slime, menstrual blood and excrement had escaped through the
orifices. This man also broke down but quickly controlled himself. "There was a terrible screaming," he said, "when the
victims realised they were going to die. Sometimes I had a crazy
urge to step into the gas chamber with them."

It seems a paradox to me that both men, who had lived
through such experiences and assisted at mass butchery, should
forty years later look so hale and well.

In a notable scene Lanzmann interviews some Polish villagers in front of the Catholic church at Chelmno where the
Nazis herded the Jewish victims overnight ("Some of them
called out to Jesus for help!") before driving them into the
forest in gas lorries – they were slowly suffocated during the
journey by carbon monoxide engine fumes and their bodies,
which fell out when the doors were opened, were thrown on to
pyres. The congregation is seen leaving with the priest and
holy relics after mass. While Lanzmann is talking with them
through his interpreter (he doesn't know Polish) the organist
suddenly takes charge and spoils everything. "The Jews,"
he said, "murdered Christ. So they had to suffer for it. Now
that they have gone we live here in peace and quiet." This
was a macabre moment: the villagers grinning and making
jokes, the spirit of the litany turned into a message of hate and
vindictiveness.

Other unpleasant moments follow. Lanzmann's probing
questions trap a group of village women into damaging con-
fessions and complaints – "Good riddance to the Jews. We're
better off without them. They were not Poles," – which, if they
had not been egging each other on, they might not have said
openly. One horrid fat babushka is seen staring like a bad-
tempered watchdog through the window of a former Jewish
house. The men – bony-faced peasants with lined faces, great

being ordered out of bed. In the workshop he had hung a huge bath tub with about thirty carp swimming in it – "I caught them in the forest – my hobby" he said (it was plainly a black market enterprise). He stripped the dynamo ("*kaputt*"), checked the wiring and after two hours of fiddling and cursing the engine fired and I was off. The frontier was twenty miles away.

It was 4.30 a.m. when I got out at the two small frontier sheds into the cold white world. The night was dead, powdery snow was sliding off the trees, the stars had gone. This time my luck was in. Instead of the regular police and customs officials two young men were on duty and it was too cold and late for them to budge from their cabins. They gave me a sleepy look, stamped my passport, asked me no questions about what currency or goods I was carrying, and I was through. The East Germans were equally perfunctory. I had a clear passage now as far as Brunswick. It was a pity I had left my travel notes behind. There was no knowing when I should see them again.[1]

At Frankfurt-an-der-Oder there was a petrol station and an all-night garage. The battery was beyond repair. The mechanic said, "Don't stall the engine, keep moving," and wished me luck. It was 180 miles to Brunswick.

Late that afternoon in Brunswick I found my old parking place at the edge of a small wood under a beech tree and switched off the engine. It had done well. But I had no current (and of course no heating) and I faced a doleful Christmas cooped up in my cold tin box. I listened to the church clock chiming a few yards away. Tomorrow was Christmas Eve and Brunswick was making plans for feasting and singing. I wrapped myself in everything I had – after the theft in Cracow I hadn't much left – and lit the candle. Poland was not my lucky country. For the third time in my life I had been forced to leave in disarray.

BRUNSWICK

I arrived in Brunswick at the worst possible time. The garage cannot repair my van until after the New Year; and Ingrid is

[1] The travel notes for my "less than complimentary book about the communist regime", which I had left behind in Poland, were delivered to me some weeks later.

away. So I face a fortnight of discomfort in frost and snow. The
van is like an ice-box. On Christmas Eve the streets were
inhospitable and empty. The brilliant lights of the shopping
centre shone on deserted pavements as though the population
had fled. I came across a few Turks looking despondently for
a bar but everything was closed. Behind suburban windows
Christmas trees glittered with little coloured bulbs. At nine the
church clock next to my van ceased to chime (the chimes are
stopped at nine in order not to disturb the burghers' sleep) and
I went to bed feeling angry with Lard-face for casting me out
into the cold at Christmas.

There are daily falls of snow and a hard frost at night, and
when I flounder from my van in the morning I look wretched
and absurd. To keep warm I have been spending much time in
Café Haertel and the Vier Linden *Gasthaus*. In this I am
cultivating two extremes: at Haertel I sit among the *Spiessbürger*
– rosy faced, well-fed men with polished pates and growling
voices who put their overcoats on hangers and read *Die Welt*
while their ladies eat chocolate cake; at the *Gasthaus* I drink
beer with the drop-outs, *die Grünen* ("Greens") – bearded,
untidy young people, misfits and nonconformers who cheer me
with their humour and their contempt for money and possessions. One of them has painted "Fuck the Army" on the
tank of his motorcycle. They share digs and from time to time
are thrown out with their old chairs, tables and bedding,
which are left on the pavement till they can find someone to
remove them.

New Year's Eve was a night of noise and explosions with family
fireworks let off in the street – the apartment blocks have no
communal gardens, and no policeman was in sight. At last, on 5
January, the garage overhauled my van and I was ready to start.
I had a brand-new French battery, the dynamo was working,
the horn sounded like a klaxon and the lights and windscreen wipers were functioning, and I had mended the curtains.
I could do nothing about the damp, fungus-like smell that clung
to the inside of the van. But with a surge of hope I turned south
on the road through Basle. I have an old friend who lives in
Alicante. He has a farm house, wine skins and a beret. He has
promised to find me a temporary sanctuary where I can start

writing in the sunshine. It was warmth more than anything that
I needed. I was in flight from the cold.

It was a clear morning when I set off for Basle. At midday it
began to snow and then, near Heidelberg, my lights failed, the
windscreen wipers stopped working, and I had to creep along
the *autobahn* through a flurry of snow like a blind man. This
was maddening and dangerous. Lard-face's evil eye was still on
me. I pulled into a village and in the morning found a garage.
The diagnosis was simple but disastrous. The mechanic in
Brunswick, unused to a British vehicle, had fitted my new
battery the wrong way round and the leads had been wrongly
adjusted. The dynamo was finished and the electrical system
had gone. It was time, I decided, to beat a retreat. I had been
resisting the thought for days. But it would have to be England
now: digs in a windy street and a bottle of milk on the doorstep.

I still had some way to go. I drove back to Aachen (more
repairs), was towed on to the ferry at Ostend, towed off at
Dover (it was night) and without lights chugged up a steep hill
leading from the harbour to a gap off the road where I could get
a running start in the morning. A horrible wind was blowing off
the sea. Some time after midnight I was roused by two policemen in a patrol car. "You can't stop here, sir. Some bloody
great lorry will drive straight up your arse." They were helpful
and gave me a push-start down the hill. In my rear mirror I saw
that one of them had lost his hat in the wind and was chasing
after it. I found a space on the sea front where a gale was
thundering over the breakers.

The following day I recharged my battery and had got as far
as Newbury when there was an explosion and the engine died.
Luckily David Winfield, my old friend from Trebizond, was at
home in Oxford. He came with his Land Rover and a rope and
towed me to his fireside. By the following day, with a new
dynamo, I was back at my brother's in Dorridge.

So my dismal return journey from Warsaw was over. I felt
very angry with Lard-face – and with the BBC and its informant – for trying me with this adventure. Still, I had been lucky.
On the very day I had started to pack for my journey to Poland,
eleven months earlier, the door had fallen off; it was rusted
through and a village handyman welded it into place near
Broadway. A few hours later part of the roof had flown over a

hedge somewhere near Bedford. The van had left a trail of rust in many lonely camping places. It had been admired by gypsies, coveted by Polish boys and jeered at by Germans. But it had carried me home and I was grateful.

PETERBOROUGH

The mystery behind the BBC report that had led to my expulsion was quickly cleared up. A friend sent me a copy of the following news item that had appeared in Peterborough's *Daily Telegraph* column on 15 June 1985:

> Battling on
>
> Totalitarianism it seems holds no fear these days for Denis Hills, the British lecturer and wartime intelligence officer once sentenced to death by Idi Amin whom he had described as a "village tyrant". Reports reach me that Hills, now in his 80s, is living in Poland where he is writing a less than complimentary book about the communist regime.
>
> Visitors to his rusting caravan, ironically sited between a Red Army cemetery and Warsaw airport, are proudly shown a cutting from the Soviet newspaper Pravda which describes him as a "notorious fascist agent" – a reference to his efforts after the 1939–45 War to save Russian refugees from forcible repatriation and the wrath of the Soviet secret police.

No wonder the Poles, seeing me with this warning light tied round my neck like a bellwether, had found me an undesirable guest. Evidently the *Telegraph* columnist thought he had unearthed an amusing piece of gossip: something that fitted into the journalist's conception of a *provocateur*, an itinerant trouble-maker deliberately sticking his neck out behind the Iron Curtain. Worse, the BBC itself – "the voice of England" – had given this piece of mischief the stamp of authority. Amusing. But amusing for whom? Not for the Poles, and not for me.

Intelligence work or subversive writing are not joked about in a Communist country. You mention them at your peril; the prison door awaits you. "You are a spy. Your own country says so." That was Lard–face's summing up of me: and if he had been less icily polite he might well have added (what was surely in his mind), "Now, get into your van and drive through the snow and eat your Christmas pudding under a hedge."

I don't mind being described as a dashing octogenarian. But to be accused of "proudly showing off" a Soviet newspaper cutting (I have no cutting) that calls me a "notorious fascist agent" makes me into an idiot. As for my "ironic" choice of camping site (between a Red Army cemetery and Warsaw airport) – surely this is Philby (he must be short of breath by now) waiting for a courier in some bug-ridden Dogubayazit dosshouse under the shadow of Ararat! Alas, the report has finished me with Poland and the Poles.

EPILOGUE

CHANGES

Three things have been to my advantage in putting together this book. My pre-war years in Poland have helped with the perspective. I know the Polish language – and it is language that unlocks hearts and is the key to understanding people. And I have seen the Poles at their best – as front-line soldiers and in the moment of death in war time: everything else by comparison with those memories seems slightly ignoble, trivial and self-centred.

During my return visit I have noted the many changes. As a result of war damage much of the past has had to be reconstructed. Warsaw's historic buildings and monuments have been painstakingly rebuilt from the ashes, put together again like bits of broken eggshell, copied, reforged, like the old patrician houses of Stary Rynek, the domed churches refashioned from splintered stones and smashed altars, the re-roofed palaces, and the Chopin monument in the Lazienki Gardens. It is not the originals that we see. The fallen walls and figures have been restored with fresh mortar and cement by modern artisans, and in this sense they are a sham: a brave and obstinate gesture to show her enemies that Poland was not and never will be destroyed.

There is something alien, too, about her post-war building fashions. The Soviet-type war memorials, for instance, where the rifleman or *strzelec* with his automatic weapon, silhouetted as a massive gladiator against the skyline, succours a wounded *towarzysz* over the boastful inscription "Death to Fascists!" A Muscovite monstrosity, Stalin's Palace of Culture, 234 metres high with over 3,000 rooms, menaces the heart of Warsaw.

Socialist tower blocks and tenement buildings, badly plastered,
jerry-built, uniform, looking down over ruts and scruffy grass,
have replaced the old slum dwellings where families used to live
their private lives among grubby little yards and gutters strewn
with empty vodka bottles.

One could fill a book with the changes: motorways that
enable a driver to cross Poland in a day: television aerials
hanging from windows like coat hangers; supermarkets, pack-
aged goods, modern kitchen appliances and plastics; loudspeakers in churches, jeans, Nike footwear, young women in
trousers; cheap socialist transport, the disappearance of the
dorozka (cab). Still these are trifles. The fundamentals haven't
changed. There is the same black earth turning after rain or
thaw into glutinous mud; the same bright green farmland
spotted with woods, small herds of cows, tumbledown cottages and sheds; fruit blossom and wild flowers, spires and
wayside shrines, mushrooms hiding by forest paths, sour
gherkins, carp and pork; rough drinking dens where unwashed
men smoke and quarrel and eat potato soup. The peasant
(though he may be literate and drive a tractor) is true to his
ancient prototype, his small sharp eyes stuck in a solid fleshy
face, his wife thick and powerful, wearing a faded head cloth.
There are the rosy-cheeked children wrapped up against the
cold, the same pale office clerks and overworked shop girls,
funeral flowers, country carts pulled by steaming brown horses.
Maple leaves spatter the autumn grass like flattened yellow
butterflies. Birch trees turn scabby and leprous with the length-
ening nights. In winter the population in its fur hats and
padded coats looks like a nation of lumberjacks or Finns. Un-
altered are the wooden street kiosks that sell newspapers, strong
tobacco, cheap combs, shoe laces and stationery.

TRENDS

The great changes, though, are not in fashions or temporary life
styles but in the long-term trends or pattern of events. The
shifting of Poland's frontiers westward has altered the very
shape of the country. The result has been to extend the Soviet
empire in the east, weaken the Germans by depriving them of
land and resources, and leave a bone of contention over their
lost territories that may never be satisfactorily resolved.

Massive industrialisation and the growth of cities have led to their proletarisation and the birth of a new artisan and middle class. There are new ideologies – not merely the demand for cheap meat, but Solidarity itself in which Polish Christians and democratic socialists, students and old-age pensioners, have sunk their differences and joined ranks in defence of fundamental human and civilian rights. The *szlachta* and the cavalry tradition (*kon, koniak, kobieta* – horses, cognac, women) are out. The new heroes are a Danzig shipyard worker and two priests, one murdered and cast into a dam, the other the Pope.

Unloved by her neighbours, half in the east and half in west, with one foot beyond the Vistula and one along the Oder-Neisse, her Roman church exposed to Marxist and atheist pressures, Poland remains, as of old, the odd man out, the wayfarer among Great Power brigands. And she has lost her Jews – three million of them in circumstances that have brought obloquy to the unhappy generation of Poles that were made to stand by and see the tragedy happen in their midst. Many Poles, it is true, welcome their disappearance. Immigrants and a new generation have replaced Poland's own enormous losses. But the Jews have gone for ever. Without them, Poland has fewer frictions but is immeasureably poorer in culture, resources and brains.

The partitioning of Germany, the loss of the DDR and of Germany's eastern territories, are another unhealed wound that festers behind the Iron Curtain. East Germany looks and feels like an enemy occupied country. The Red Army is thick on the ground. The people, by contrast with the West Germans, are spiritless and cowed. The lessons of defeat may have been good for them. They are humbler. But I cannot conceive that the division into two Germanies can last. It is against nature. The Saxons, Silesians, Pomeranians and Prussians are equally Germans. The Harz mountains in the border zone, where the Red Army keeps its garrisons, were the home of Luther, Bach and Goethe. A glance at the list of great and notable men from generals to philosophers and scientists who originated from the lost territories of Silesia, Saxony, Pomerania and East and West Prussia shows a dazzling record of achievement.[1]

---

[1] Here are a few of them: Catherine the Great, Eichendorff, Fahrenheit, Gustav Freytag, Günter Grass, General Guderian, Gerhardt Hauptmann,

THE FUTURE

What of the future? One has to assume that with the passing years the nature of Russian society will gradually change and that its government, within limits, will become more liberal even towards Poles. There are some who hope for a dramatic reshuffle in the present pattern of Super-Power relations, with the "Yellow Peril" coming to Poland's rescue (when the Russian finds himself in real trouble with his Far Eastern neighbours he will point to his skin and say to the Westerner, "Look, I'm white too – the same as you!"). But for the time being Moscow, with its obsessive fear of aggression from the West, is unlikely to loosen its stranglehold over Poland. Poland, however, will be allowed to use the church as a safety-valve and to continue privatising the economy.

One may count on further upheavals in Poland herself, part of the chain of spasmodic uprisings already witnessed in 1956, 1968, 1970 and 1980. The Solidarity movement may be quiescent at the moment. But its ideas and political programme have come to stay. They have been enshrined in Polish mythology and will surely break out again.

Poland remains one of Europe's chief trouble spots. The Poles are not an easy people to satisfy. They make much of their grievances and regard patriotism as the key to their survival. Poland would not welcome a unified Germany.[2] With Russia, her relations have been set in a mould that has not changed for well over two hundred years ever since the Tsar's government assumed its fateful protectorate over Poland in the eighteenth century.

Looking back over my years with the Poles, two or three

Herder, Field-Marshal Hindenburg, E.T.A. Hoffmann, Kant, Lessing, Lassalle, Field-Marshal Moltke, Richthofen (the "Red Baron" flying ace), Schopenhauer, Admiral Tirpitz, Arnold Zweig. See Norman Davies, *God's Playground*, 1981.

[2] Czeslaw Milosz, in his *Native Realm*, said he "couldn't bear Polish nationalism". He declined to join the Home Army, considered the Warsaw uprising of 1944 "a blameworthy, lightheaded enterprise", and felt in his despair, as he surveyed the ruins of war in a small Polish town, that "a curse hangs over this particular piece of Europe and nothing can be done about it. Had I been given the chance, perhaps I would have blown the country to bits ..."

memories come immediately to mind. One is the oil painting that hung over the porcelain stove in my room in Pani Petrovna's apartment. It showed the Tsar's Cossack horsemen charging a crowd of Polish civilians. They – flashing their sabres in the dusty room – were the enemy. Another memory is of the bugle sounding 'Réveille' in a Polish desert camp and the noise of hundreds of tough, sunburnt men spitting and hawking as they rinsed their throats and faces in mess-tins of water. Later, there was the fighting: my batman George, who had been detailed as stretcher-bearer, carrying back the dead wrapped in blankets from Phantom Ridge.

My last memory is of that icy night on the Oder where, instead of preparing for a Christmas dinner of goose with my friends, I had been sent off by the *apparatchiks* of Okrzei Street into a dead white world of snow.

Oxford – Twickenham
May 1987

APPENDIX 1 (A)

BEGIN AND IRGUN

Begin took full advantage of his release from "the white nights" of Soviet imprisonment. He was the terrorist commander at the time of the Irgun-LEHI (Stern Group) massacre of 250 defenceless Arabs (over 100 of them women and children) in the village of Deir Yassin outside Jerusalem in May 1948. Noam Chomsky, whose book *The Fateful Triangle* (London 1983) is a severe indictment of Zionist policies in Palestine and Israel, quotes an internal message of congratulations sent by the Irgun command to the Deir Yassin killers on their "wonderful operation of conquest". The message ran "As in Deir Yassin, so everywhere . . . Oh Lord, Oh Lord, you have chosen us for conquest." The Holocaust may help to explain why Zionists turned themselves into armed men with a Messianic mission. But how far does it justify their atrocities or vindicate the blowing up of the King David Hotel or the bombing in the Lebanon? For an account of Begin's prison experiences in Russia see Appendix 1 (B).

APPENDIX 1(B)

BEGIN'S WHITE NIGHTS

Menachem Begin's autobiographical odyssey *White Nights* (Jerusalem 1957) includes a fascinating account of his wartime imprisonment and interrogation in the USSR. For a time he shared a cell with Poles. "Of the ten degrees of pride that came down to the world," he says, "the Poles took nine." But a sort of comradeship developed between them. As a Zionist leader in Poland (Begin was head of the BETAR) he was regarded by the NKVD as an enemy of the revolution and after severe interrogation was sentenced to eight years in a correction camp. "Zionists want to go to Palestine," his interrogator told him. "Zionists are diverting forces that should overthrow the bourgeoisie and are sending them to a non-existent state. That is sabotage. That is why you are in gaol; as a leader of Zionism."

Begin confirms the despair and hopelessness of a prisoner

under interrogation. "There is no platform . . . No one will hear what he says, no one will learn of his stand – the thread between him and the ideal is severed. For who will know? Who will come in my place? What point is there in my suffering? There is no point. When the prisoner realises this he is doomed."

As a disciple of Jabotinsky, Begin was dedicated to putting an end to British rule in Palestine, and when thousands of Poles who had been interned in Russia after the September 1939 war were authorised under Sikorski's agreement with Stalin to raise an army under Anders, he was released ("But he's a Zhid not a Pollak!" one of the camp convicts shouted) and managed to get himself accepted as a soldier despite Polish objections to re-cruiting Jews (Sikorski said Jews were speculators, Anders called them potential deserters and Stalin said "they are poor fighters"). Through this stroke of fortune Begin found himself in the Promised Land and in a position to achieve his dream of organising underground war against the British colonial power.

Begin makes the apposite comment that whereas Himmler's camps aimed at immediate extermination, Beria's were on the whole "slow-death camps". "It might seem that brief torture is preferable to death after years of torture. But that is not the case. The chance of being saved is the thing that counts. If six million Jews had been sent to Archangel, Vorkuta, Kolima or the Urals perhaps a quarter, a third or a half would never have returned. But our people would have numbered today not eleven million but fourteen to sixteen million."